ON THE NEW FRONTIERS
OF GENETICS AND RELIGION

On the New Frontiers of Genetics and Religion

J. Robert Nelson

WILLIAM B. EERDMANS PUBLISHING COMPANY
GRAND RAPIDS, MICHIGAN

Copyright © 1994 by Wm. B. Eerdmans Publishing Co.
255 Jefferson Ave. S.E., Grand Rapids, Michigan 49503
All rights reserved

Printed in the United States of America

00 99 98 97 96 95 94   7 6 5 4 3 2 1

Library of Congress Cataloging-in-Publication Data

Nelson, J. Robert (John Robert), 1920-
On the new frontiers of genetics and religion / J. Robert Nelson.
p.   cm.
Includes bibliographical references and index.
ISBN 0-8028-0741-0 (pbk.)
1. Human genetics — Religious aspects. 2. Human Genome Project.
3. Genetics — Research — Moral and ethical aspects. I. Title.
QH431.N43 1994
241'.649574 — dc20   94-19012
                                        CIP

Contents

CHAPTER THREE

CHAPTER FOUR

CHAPTER FIVE

Contents

Foreword

VERACITY and accuracy are the ideals of good science and good medicine. Public statements should be made with caution, predictions with reserve, until supporting evidence is presented. Professional papers are published only after strict peer review. So we must take very seriously the assertion of highly respected medical scientists when they say that no current project in science and medicine is of greater importance to humanity than the Human Genome Project. This is the considered judgment of my colleagues, James D. Watson and Francis S. Collins, prior and current Directors of the National Center for Human Genome Research. I agree with them. Of the marvelous innovations of the past half-century (such as antibiotics, atomic energy, computers, space travel) none exceeds the delineation of the knowledge content of the DNA molecule. This is not just a speculation. The evidence is being found at a pace of increasing rapidity, and the scope of research on the genetic basis of heritable diseases increases.

The emerging field of molecular medicine is a direct consequence of this research program. While the humanitarian character and ethical principles of medical practice remain, the discoveries in molecular genetics alter the scientific base from which medicine operates and offers it new intervention strategies. Genetic discoveries are revolutionizing the diagnosis, prevention, and therapy of many common diseases (heritable, autoimmune, and cancerous). Medical students now become proficient in genetics; and established physicians study to "retrofit" their knowledge base.

Citizens in many nonmedical fields also need genetic knowledge retrofitting. In particular, I identify leaders such as health care providers, employers, insurers, lawmakers, and theologians. Many of the medical and ethical decisions we face today and increasingly in the future will deal with quality and existence of life, i.e., reproduction and limits of disease intervention attempts. Our present technology is powerful, but it will pale in comparison to that of the future. Expanding genetic knowledge and derivative medical options impose new obligations upon clergy, religious scholars, counselors, teachers, patients, and physicians. Those who are skeptical about the value of religious truth may feel the need to listen to the new dialogue between genetic scientists and theologians. They may be surprised to hear a scientist of Francis S. Collins's stature say "there is no conflict between being an absolutely rigorous scientist and being a person of faith."

This meeting for interaction of specialists in genetics, medicine, theology, and ethics was supported under the ELSI (Ethical, Legal, and Social Implications) Program of the Human Genome Project. Baylor College of Medicine and The Institute of Religion within the Texas Medical Center (Houston) co-sponsored the meeting. I am grateful to all who contributed to the meeting by spoken thoughts, written concepts, and active debate. This book offers the opportunity to review thoughts of leading theologians on the coming era of Molecular Medicine. Should we or shouldn't we utilize the knowledge? Does the adage, "The truth will make you free," hold for our personal genetic traits? Give the issues consideration. This book will stimulate your thinking.

C. THOMAS CASKEY, M.D.

A Prefatory Note

LESS THAN two years after a pair of young scientists at Cambridge University verified the helical structure of a DNA molecule, the Oxford University Press published in 1955 a revision of its magisterial dictionary. In brief, sparse sentences it defined "gene" as one of the factors in heredity, "genetics" as a part of biology concerned with heredity, and "helix" as anything of a coiled or spiral form, like a screw or a snail. No more than that. Even as the dictionary was being printed, however, the implications and connotations of those words were being rapidly amplified like cells in a culture. Today they are the basic vocabulary of a new order of scientific research, technology, and medicine. They are also, surprisingly for many, terms of growing importance for religion, theology, and ethics.

My personal interests, which embrace both scientific and religious concerns, have in recent years grown incrementally in four specific areas of study and activity. These are ecumenical relations, systematic theology, biomedical ethics, and the Human Genome Project. These interrelated interests have had a cumulative character. The knowledge gained, however inadequately, in the first three has come to a defined focus on the fourth.

Like that of countless people today, my work could be chronicled as a succession of conferences. A drawer full of name badges and a file of workbooks and reports testify to hundreds of days spent in hotels and conference centers. These gatherings of common-minded professionals and special interest devotees have many things in common besides name tags. One unfortunate characteristic seems evident: namely, their formal reports go unread by most who attended, and assuredly by those who did not. I hope that the present book, which grew out of two national conferences on "Genetics, Religion and Ethics," will be able to convey the content and import of papers and issues discussed there and thus to stimulate further conversation.

The two conferences in question were held at the Texas Medical Center, Houston, in 1990 and 1992. Representing eight countries and many states, the two hundred sixty participants from various Christian denominations as well as Judaism, Hinduism, and Islam, included persons of differing professional and occupational fields: clinical medicine, molecular research, theology, ethics, and public policy. Thirty-two prepared addresses and responses were given on questions of human nature, the limitations of genetic knowledge and technology, the particular concerns of women about genetic science, the theology of creation, and current research cases in genetic medicine. Selected portions of these papers are included in this book, with due thanks to the writers.

The preparatory studies, the conferences themselves, and this book have constituted a four-year project of the Institute of Religion and Baylor College of Medicine. Funding was provided mainly by the United States Department of Energy and the National Center for Human Genome Research of the National Institutes of Health (DOE Grant No. DEFG05-91ER61181). I wish to thank Daniel W. Drell and Michael S. Yesley of the Department of Energy and Eric T. Juengst of the National Institutes of Health for their official support and personal involvement in this project. Additional funding came from the Trustees of the Institute of Religion, the M. D. Anderson Foundation, the Episcopal Church Foundation, the Linbeck Foundation, the Park Ridge Center, and several donors.

Under the federal grant, the principal investigator was the distinguished geneticist, C. Thomas Caskey, professor and director of the Institute for Molecular Genetics of Baylor College of Medicine and president of the international Human Genome Organization (HUGO). My work as program director was most helpfully assisted by Hessel Bouma III, professor of biology at Calvin College, Grand Rapids, Michigan. Indispensable word processing was done by Pia Grove. Belinda J. F. Rossiter and Joy B. Redman of the Baylor staff screened the typescript for distortions or errors of fact.

By the time this book has been published, more important discoveries will have been made in gene mapping and applied clinical genetics. Every book on this subject has what might be called a heritable disease, which we call obsolescence. Any changes in religious and ethical thought will come much more slowly, but come they will.

Houston, Texas   J.R.N.
June 1993

CHAPTER ONE

The Two Frontiers Converge

An EXPANDING knowledge and understanding of human life is the primary purpose of both genetic science and religious thought. Some people who are expert in one of these fields of knowledge may be ignorant of the other field and treat it with disdain. Occasionally their attitude toward their counterparts may be defensive and polemical. Even a mood of conflict and hostility, however, cannot obscure the fact that both are contending about the nature of human life.

The geneticist and theologian both have high stakes in this search for knowledge. But the bodies of knowledge they represent are of radically distinct character. One is ancient and perennial; the other is modern and just emerging. One is based upon alleged revelation and established tradition. The other rests upon empirical observation, experimentation, measurement, tentative hypotheses, imagination, and reasoning. Religion in general advocates obedience to moral imperatives and principles of value such as compassion, justice, faith, and responsibility to neighbor and God. Science is typically understood to be value-free, eschewing such judgments. Moreover, those with expertise in religion and genetics tend to inhabit distinct communities with little or no natural opportunity for dialogue. Yet there are increasing numbers of persons who belong to, or at least converse with, both sides simultaneously. Their experience of the encounter of scientific method with beliefs and convictions of a religious nature provides a valuable means of exploring how the subject matter of both fields of inquiry is related, and indeed how in some ways it interpenetrates.[1]

If by using a territorial analogy we can describe the fields of genetic research and religious inquiry as having a common boundary, we may add that their frontiers are open from both directions. Passports and visas in the form of professional credentials may be required, but the frontiers are not impassable — a fact to which this book will testify.

A. The Frontier of Genetics

1. From Mendel to Eugenics

High school students today are learning the basic scientific information and laboratory techniques of "the new genetics." They are conversant with knowledge and research methods which were known only to advanced experts of their parents' generation and utterly unavailable to their grandparents. The older, classical genetics prevailed until 1953. It was mainly a matter of statistics: the predicting and recording of inherited traits. Yet there was an incipient courtship between biology and chemistry, which led to their marriage as biochemistry and molecular genetics.

Well known in our educational culture is the story of the Austrian monk, Johann Gregor Mendel. Patiently experimenting in the breeding of diverse kinds of pea plants, he demonstrated how their visible characteristics could be foreseen according to simple mathematical probabilities as they were passed on from one generation to the next. He noted how certain traits of shape and flower color were expressed as "dominant" types, while others were suppressed as "recessive." He speculated that a "germ of inheritance" accounted for the process. Mendel's epoch-making statistics and hypothesis were published obscurely in 1866 and then remained virtually unknown until 1900.[2]

1. An excellent explanation of various ways of relating science and religion is in the Gifford Lecture by Ian Barbour, *Religion in an Age of Science,* vol. 1 (San Francisco: Harper & Row, 1990), ch. 1, 3-30.
2. See *The Human Genome Project* by Thomas F. Lee (New York: Plenum

An English biologist, William Bateson, rediscovered Mendel's now famous law, and it was he who coined the word "genetics." About the same time, three botanists — Dutch, German, and Austrian — were also verifying Mendel's earlier findings.

Meanwhile Johann Friedrich Meischer, a Swiss chemist, had discovered almost accidentally in 1869 the material of deoxyribonucleic acid; this DNA was not proved to be the substance of genes, however, until 1943, by Sewell Wright and colleagues. In 1888, the "color bodies" seen in cells by means of improved microscopes were stained and called "chromosomes." August Weismann concluded that chromosomes constituted the hereditary substance which he called "germ plasm." During the first decades of the twentieth century, a succession of ingenious, patient, persistent scientists endeavored to prove the chemical processes which account for physical inheritance. They worked with simple organisms such as viruses, bacteria, and fruit flies to learn how cells grow and reproduce. Among the leaders of research were T. H. Morgan, Herman J. Muller, Sewell Wright, Walter Beale, Max Delbruck, Salvador Luria, and Barbara McClintock. Many others, both the remembered and forgotten, constituted the corps of pioneers.[3] And all the while, researchers were amassing data from social studies of families in which diseases of mental retardation or physical illness were prevalent.

Prior to 1953, the study of genetics by statistical analysis of inherited diseases was distorted to a large extent by popular bias in favor of eugenics.[4] The more people learned about heredity, the more inclined were many to seek the improvement of a given population. Improvement was conceived to be approximation to a normal, or even idealized, kind of person. This implied, in broadest terms, the selective breeding of ostensibly superior human beings, or the elimination —

Press, 1990), 33-38. Dr. Lee's book is among the best for elucidating the basic science and the first year of the Human Genome Project. Its sequel is *Gene Future* (New York: Plenum Press, 1993).

3. Lee, *Human Genome Project,* 53-72. Another concise history of modern genetics is Horace Freeland Judson's essay in *The Code of Codes,* ed. Daniel J. Kevles and Leroy Hood (Cambridge: Harvard University Press, 1992), 37-80.

4. Daniel J. Kevles's chapter in *The Code of Codes,* "Out of Eugenics: The Historical Politics of the Human Genome Project," 3-36. Also, Kevles's definitive history, *In the Name of Eugenics* (Berkeley: University of California Press, 1985).

somehow! — of inferior ones, or both together. The eugenic ideology fed upon the ignorance and prejudices of many Americans as betrayed by colloquial vocabulary. Infants, children, or adults who inherited physical malformations were called "monsters." If they also manifested mental deficiencies, however mild or extreme, they were known as "imbeciles," "idiots," "lunatics," "tetched in the head," "feeble-minded," or "mongoloids." Society in general was inhospitable to them. As Alexander Pope observed, "a little learning is a dangerous thing"; in this instance rudimentary knowledge of genetics gave impetus to discriminatory prejudice.

An American prophet of eugenics, H. H. Goddard, seized upon the Binet I.Q. test to prove that people he dubbed "morons" were, in effect, weeds in the garden of humanity. He convinced many that there is one gene which determines intelligence, just as every human trait or behavior is caused by only one particular gene. He invented a fictitious family named Kallikak as a model of the effect of both good and bad genes (the good, from Greek *kalos,* the bad from *kakos*). School pupils of the twenties and thirties learned about genetics from this deliberately biased illustration.[5] Of course, both latent and unconcealed racism intensified genetic myths. Men and women of (obvious!) high quality were urged to procreate more fruitfully. Those who were manifestly and incurably inferior in mental and social status, or afflicted with congenital diseases, were either urged or legally mandated to be sterilized.[6]

Such thinking has been, and remains, endemic in most cultures. In theory, at least, the democratic egalitarianism of the United States should have mitigated the attitude. However, the trafficking in African slaves, the century of aftermath to slavery, recurrent oppression of Mexicans, Asians, and indigenous Indians, and acts of cruelty toward the disabled have contradicted Constitutional assertions of the equality of all persons.

It took the horrifying brutalities of the era of National Socialism

5. Stephen Jay Gould, *The Mismeasurement of Man* (New York: W. W. Norton & Co., 1982), 158-74.

6. Philip R. Reilly, "Eugenic Sterilization in the United States," *Genetics and the Law, III,* ed. George J. Annas and Aubrey Milunsky (New York: Plenum Press, 1985), 227-41.

in Hitler's Germany to reveal to many Americans the ultimate destination of programmed eugenics. Yet, the question remains open as to whether the new techniques of assisted procreation, prenatal diagnosis, and genetic manipulation will encourage eugenic planning in new ways.

2. Watson and Crick to Manipulating DNA

The year 1953 is to genetic science what 1492 is to geography. Prior to the mid-twentieth century, pioneers had indeed explored living cells. But no scientists had unlocked the secret of genetic inheritance before the team at Cambridge University turned their ingenious key. The four scientists who discovered the structure of the DNA molecule and perceived how it creates proteins of myriad kinds were not equally yoked in quest. Neither did they receive equal acclaim for the discovery. Rosalind Franklin and Maurice Wilkins used X-ray crystallography to detect the morphology of the molecule. Francis Crick and James D. Watson capitalized on the data, and with bright imagination constructed the metal model of the now familiar "double helix." Crick and Watson published the brief article which announced in modest style the long-sought solution to the puzzle of genes: "We wish to suggest a structure for the salt of deoxyribonucleic acid." Their suggestion was the correct one. The era of molecular genetics in the field of biochemistry was thus begun, confirmed, and soon acknowledged universally. The three men were awarded Nobel Prizes in 1962; Rosalind Franklin had died of cancer four years earlier.[7]

The structure of DNA as they correctly conceived it consists of the estimated three billion pairs of nucleotides, called base pairs, fitted like steps of a twisting ladder at regular intervals, held together by sugar molecules and phosphates. The analogy of a zipper is also useful. The two strands of the helix are joined by the zipper's teeth, which are the pairs of bases. These nucleotides are marvels of simplicity. Only four of them are

7. The story of discovering the structure of DNA has become a modern, dramatic saga. Lee tells it briefly (*Human Genome Project*, 73-86). The autobiographical account is James D. Watson, *The Double Helix* (New York: Athenaeum Publishers, 1968). The standard history is *The Eighth Day of Creation* by Horace Freeland Judson (New York: Simon & Schuster, 1979).

needed: adenine (A), thymine (T), guanine (G), and cytosine (C). In the pairings, which occur three billion times, A and T form one link and G and C the other. All along the helical ladder these same pairs occur in endless variation, or sequence. They are marked off by clusters of some thousands or even millions of base pairs, which constitute the genes. Each gene serves a specific purpose in determining protein production by the cell's cytoplasm. Scientists estimate the number of genes in human cells at a maximum of one hundred thousand. Their accepted challenge is now to identify, locate, or "map" all the genes, one by one, and discover each one's specific function. Having rightly discovered the structure of the DNA molecule, Doctors Watson and Crick and their thousands of colleagues in research have been enabled to investigate its function.

The discovery of DNA structure confirmed the theory that nucleic acids rather than proteins constitute the matter which determines and enables organic growth. Having settled that question, scientists confronted literally hundreds of questions about the chemical powers within cells and the manner by which they cause growth and development. The rapidity of research activity and sheer quantity of important findings have been compared to the output of a Texas oil gusher. The analogy aptly suggests not only the magnitude and anticipated benefits of such research but also its potentially hazardous consequences.

First in importance after 1953 was the explanation of how messages of instruction for protein synthesis are conveyed. The messages are the genetic code. The messengers are RNA or ribonucleic acid units, which are sent on a one-way only track from particular genes on DNA fragments in the pairs of twenty-three chromosomes plus X or Y sex chromosomes. Francis Crick had perceived this mechanism even before it was demonstrated in 1960 by the work of two French geneticists, Jacques Monod and Edmund Jacob, and by a young American, Marshall Nirenberg. Indian-born Har Govind Khorana was able to apply this knowledge to the actual synthesizing of a gene in 1970.

Indispensable to genetic science and wider biological research has been the remarkable surge of inventions of mechanical and optical instrumentation. The word "microscopic" has taken on a new meaning as the measurements of "nano"-lengths called micrometers and angstroms narrowed invisibly to millionths and billionths. The dimensions of the DNA molecule strain the mind's conceptual ability. While occupying so little space that it can be seen only by the most powerful electron-scanning

6

microscope, the molecule's two strands, if extended, measure 2.02 meters. The DNA is so tightly packed in the chromosomes during metaphase that the packing ratio of bulk to length is 15,000:1. As one scientist explained, if the width of a DNA molecule were like angel hair pasta, its length would be twelve kilometers. Robert Pollack describes the length of a DNA molecule as "a hundred million times as long as it is wide."[8]

It seems almost providential that such technological wonders as laser beams and super-computers have been developed just when needed for new, unprecedented methods of doing molecular genetics. The machines for synthesizing genes and sequencing nucleotides have taken over much of the familiar, tedious laboratory work done by hand. One distinguished geneticist, David Galas, even predicts that laboratory glassware will soon become redundant and obsolete.[9] The sequencing machine invented by Leroy Hood uses fluorescent dyes to color the four DNA bases, enabling a person operating a computer to do what was formerly a year's work of sequencing in less than a day.

The year 1973 marked a major new technique which gave currency to the expressions "genetic engineering" and "manipulation." It had been found that large numbers of enzymes are generated in each cell; and each enzyme is chemically specific for a definite fragment of DNA. Its purpose is to cut the helix at a certain location. Researchers reasoned that knowledge of particular enzymes and their precise cutting function would enable the "engineers" to insert genetic material taken from other species into the DNA, where it would grow as a new transgenic form of organic life. If this could be done with bacterial genes, it could also be done with any organisms, plant or animal, including humans.

This theory became a reality in the laboratories of three Californians: Stanley Cohen, Paul Berg, and Herbert Boyer. They had done in biology what medieval alchemists had unsuccessfully attempted in metallurgy. Or, according to some, they were the Drs. Frankenstein who could create new forms of life. The discovery and its limitless possibilities stimulated in many minds the mixed feelings of triumph, apprehension, and greed. Triumph because of the prodigious break-

8. Robert Pollack, *Signs of Life* (Boston: Houghton Mifflin, 1994), 19.
9. David Galas in *Los Alamos Science,* vol. 20 (1992), 150. For the DNA packing ratio, molecular length, and the analogy of angel hair pasta, see pp. 39, 50, and 169.

through to hitherto unknown knowledge. Apprehension because of fears of unknown dangers to health and environment. And greed because of many imagined commercial applications in what has come to be known as the world of biotechnology. The triumph was indeed rewarded by Nobel prizes and lasting fame. Profitable commercial uses of recombinant DNA (rtDNA) became feasible and multiplied after 1980, when the U.S. Supreme Court decided in favor of patenting genetically modified bacteria (*Diamond* v. *Chakravarty*, 1980).

Fears and anxieties have since been largely, but not entirely, allayed both because of prudence and caution on the part of scientists and inhibiting regulations of research applied by governmental agencies. These fears arise from three kinds of concern: laboratory safety, environmental damage, and the possibility of as yet unknown genetic mutations. The first of these was resolved by the leading scientists themselves between 1973 and 1975. Their self-imposed moratorium on rtDNA research was an almost unprecedented event in the history of modern science. Perhaps the refusal of some German physicists to work on nuclear weapons may be considered a precedent. It is usual for researchers to grumble or become defensive about government restrictions on their freedom of inquiry. In this case, however, they pre-empted such restraints by agreeing to meet at Asilomar, California, and deciding to suspend research until the safety of laboratories from dangerous modified microbes could be guaranteed. Fortunately, the moratorium did not need to last very long and research was soon resumed. However, the nation's leading source of scientific funding, the National Institutes of Health, set up a Recombinant DNA Advisory Committee (RAC) for screening and overviewing all projects suspected of being dangerous. That committee continues to judge proposals and protocols.

Fears about some damaging effect of genetic engineering upon the natural environment and ecosystems of plants, insects, and animals have aroused both vigorous debate and cautionary policies of public and private control. These concerns have abated somewhat, but not altogether. Testing of modified plants in open environment has been shown to be harmless when carefully monitored.

More difficult to assess are the possible dangers, especially to humans, of unintended, inadvertent mutations which may be caused by genetic therapy in germ-line cells. Experimentation with gamete cells of mice, cattle, and other animals led to early successes in producing

8

variations within species, or mixing genes of differing species to create strange transgenic animals. Why not, some asked, use the same techniques with humans? Not for frivolous purposes, of course, but to eliminate genetic diseases or congenital disabilities is what they proposed. The method of *in vitro* fertilization (IVF) of a woman in England enabled her to bear a healthy baby girl in 1979; and hundreds of so-called "test tube" babies have since been born. In the same way, fertilized eggs at eight-cell stage could be altered by the exquisite methods of micro-injection and micro-surgery. Disease-causing genes could be removed or replaced by others at will.

While possibly feasible and theoretically desirable, tampering with the human germ-line has not been done at this time of writing. A major obstacle is the length of the human life cycle from one generation to the next. In trying to eliminate from sex cells a deleterious gene, it is argued, a would-be gene doctor could cause unfortunate mutations which would remain irrevocably in the germ cells of all future progeny. The risk is great. In addition, there are widely held moral objections to opening the door to experimentation with human embryos.

In spite of these and other causes of concern the march of progress in the 1970s became a quickstep in the 1980s. From dozens of laboratories come papers in professional journals, describing newly found data about genes of bacteria, plants, worms, flies, mice, larger animals, primates, and humans. As expected, public interest has been aroused most keenly by stories affecting human disease and health. Of this kind of information waiting to be discovered and interpreted there appears to be no end.

3. The Human Genome Project

Not all scientists in the field of biology and molecular genetics are philosophers and prophets, but many of the leaders have visionary qualities. A few are also good politicians and entrepreneurs. Some of these with broadest vision and ambition conceived the plan for a "Human Genome Initiative." It would mobilize manpower and public financial resources ultimately to identify and analyze all the genes of the DNA molecule which make up the chromosomes in each cell. That goal may be stated simply, but its implications are exceedingly complex and far-reaching. It is essentially defined in a government publication by two words: sequencing and mapping."Sequencing is the process of determining the order of the nucleotides, or base pairs, in a DNA molecule." It is in the grouping and sequence of the three billion nucleotides that the coding for innumerable proteins occurs. Describing all the variable combinations in the double helical molecule is the long-term goal of the HGP, estimated to require fifteen years.

According to the same publication, "Mapping is the process of determining the position and spacing of genes, or other genetic landmarks, on the chromosomes relative to one another."[10] Two kinds of maps are being constructed: the physical map and the genetic linkage map. On the physical map, large genes of ten million base pairs can be located microscopically, but smaller ones cannot. Small, invisible regions of DNA are detected by using flourescence, radiation, or gel electrophoresis to identify the unique properties of sites where restriction enzymes cut the chain of nucleotides. As determined by invariable chemical reaction, the fragments of DNA form contiguous, overlapping patterns. Their physical distances one from another are measured in base pairs. Researchers have adopted a system of uniform measurement of distances between "sequence tagged sites" (STS) so they can refer to the exact location of genes and the configurations called markers. As these are being discovered by many researchers, they are stored in a common computer database for general access.

Genetic linkage mapping depends upon the tracing of inheritance in family lineage of distinct traits. The variable forms (polymorphisms) of genetic markers or genes for two traits or diseases may be inherited together, indicating that they are linked on the same chromosome. The more frequently two or more genetic traits or diseases are inherited together in a family the closer they are on the chromosome. This information enables scientists to determine the relative positions of the markers or genes.

The HGP has set proximate goals for work on these maps and development of cost-efficient technology by 1995. However, the whole project will continue until the year 2005. It is predicted that "The information generated by the human genome project . . . [will] be the source book for biomedical science in the 21st century."[11]

10. *Understanding Our Genetic Inheritance,* U.S. Department of Health and Human Services and Department of Energy (Washington: NIH Publication No. 90-1590, 1990), 9.
11. *Ibid.*

The rapidity with which the HGP moved from a "What if?" concept in 1986 to a "Let's go!" program in late 1988 is truly astonishing. It reflects the unprecedented volatility of genetic science itself as waves of new discoveries and application of new data come tumbling upon the shore of previous knowledge. Despite the usually slow processes of drafting and implementing federal legislation, Congress was able to authorize generous funding in 1990 for two departments. The Department of Energy (DOE) and the Department of Health and Human Services (DHHS), after some dissension about priority, launched the program jointly. It was obvious why DHHS should assume responsibility through its vast National Institutes of Health (NIH), since it is the source of most funding for biological research. But why the DOE?, people asked. What does human genetics have to do with energy? The answer is mutations. From the time it introduced nuclear fission and atomic energy, the DOE has had to study genetic mutations caused by radiation; therefore, its laboratories and funding policies were ready to collaborate with the NIH. The man chosen to direct the entire HGP in its first years was both a scientist of high public reputation as master of the field and a persuasive advocate of the program before Congress and government officials, James D. Watson. As initiator of the HGP he served until 1992, to be succeeded by a rising star in molecular genetics and medicine, Francis S. Collins of the University of Michigan. Collins achieved recognition for being one of the discoverers of the genes causing cystic fibrosis in 1989, neurofibromatosis in 1990, and Huntington's disease in 1993.

Many of the nation's most prominent molecular geneticists and biochemists have been mobilized to lead hundreds of others in research projects. Nine centers in universities and medical schools have been assigned specific tasks and given ample funding. More may be designated. The estimated cost of the HGP over a period of fifteen years is three billion dollars — or a dollar for each nucleotide! West European nations and Japan have joined significantly in the international project.

The project has not lacked critics, of course, as Chapter Three, below, makes clear. Some of these criticisms have been economic, some strictly scientific, some essentially "political." The extraordinary and far-reaching nature of the HGP has also, however, aroused significant concerns of a legal, social, ethical, and even religious nature.

The organizers of the Human Genome Project did not dismiss

these concerns as being outside the sphere of "hard science." On the contrary, they perceived that the genetic revolution was already raising momentously significant questions about law, morals, social justice, medical practice, and human nature itself. Consideration of these issues is actually provided for within the terms of reference of the project as a whole, under the acronym ELSI (Ethical, Legal, and Social Implications). Just as the Asilomar conference on recombinant DNA experiments demonstrated an unprecedented show of restraint, so the ELSI component of the Human Genome Project models a concern for accountability which is virtually unique in government-funded "big science." Philosophers, ethicists, theologians, physicians, anthropologists, sociologists, lawyers, and educators have been invited to collaborate with the molecular biologists in studying and discussing the numerous implications of the project.

Four areas of concern have been given top priority for the funding of research projects, educational programs, conferences, and public discussion. These are: fairness, privacy, medical care, and education. In general terms, fairness calls for nondiscrimination and justice in employment and insurance; privacy means control over one's genetic information; medical care embraces genetic counseling, diagnosis, therapy, and health care policy; and education refers to dissemination of information and discussion of a host of scientific, moral, social, and legal issues.

It is remarkable that a space has been opened in the HGP for consideration of some profound questions of religious faith and theology. The decision may not be popular with civil libertarians who insist that the Constitution's First Amendment excludes any payment with public funds for study of religious matters, or for atheists who reject religion. But the evidence is more than sufficient to show that exploring the DNA molecule opens questions about human nature, identity, behavior, and destiny for which religious answers are most appropriate.

The history of modern genetics, which began in the garden of a cloistered monk, has been accompanied by a persistent and increasing interest in correlating emerging knowledge of genes with beliefs and insights of a religious or theological nature.

B. The Frontier of Religion

1. Early Responses to Genetic Science

The religious interpreters of human life and ethics in relation to the discoveries of molecular biologists were slow to respond to the decoding of DNA and its putative meaning for human experimentation and medicine. The discipline of bioethics did not exist until the late 1960s. Even in medical ethics there was little writing on human experimentation except for revulsion toward reports of cruel and wanton mistreatment by fascist powers.

In 1966, the relevant basic principles of traditional Judaism were tersely defined by Immanuel Jakobovitz. Those desiring and seeking answers to moral questions have "recourse to the absolute standards of the moral law which, in the case of Judaism, has its authentic source in the Divine revelation of the Holy Writ and its duly qualified interpreters."[12] The categorical imperative of this religious basis is the almost absolute value of human life; i.e., a single human life at any moment of existence and in any physical condition. Life is "almost" of absolute value because three violations of moral law can weigh against its preservation. These are idolatry, murder, and adultery or incest.

This doctrine clearly implies that infants born with severe genetic defects must receive all necessary care to maintain life. And for many Jews it also means prohibition of abortion for any cause. This strict reading of the Torah and Halakhah surely inhibits the purposes of prenatal diagnosis of genetic diseases which in a general view indicates abortion. The disorder most prevalent and dreaded among Jews from Eastern Europe (Ashkenazic) and causing most concern is known as Tay-Sachs disease. Control of the spread of the disease by screening carriers of the gene mutation is acceptable, whereas terminating pregnancies is not.[13] On the other hand, if it should become technically possible to modify the nucleus of a woman's egg cell by microsurgery before fertilization this would be licit, declared Azriel Rosenfeld in

12. Immanuel Jakobovitz, "Medical Experimentation on Humans in Jewish Law" (1966), reprinted in *Jewish Bioethics,* ed. Fred Rosner and David Bleich (New York: Hebrew Publishing Company, 1979), 379.

13. Fred Rosner, "Tay-Sachs Disease: To Screen or Not to Screen" (1976), reprinted in *Jewish Bioethics,* 181.

1972.[14] In such a case, it is only the potential life, not a developing one, which is put at risk.

Within Jewish theology and ethics, as in Christianity, there are differing hermeneutics and a diversity of opinion. But the conservative statements of Jakobovitz — chief rabbi, recently raised to the House of Lords in Britain — carry much influence.

Three early (pre-1970) responses by Christian authorities defined diverse understandings of the new genetic challenge. They were by a Protestant, a Roman Catholic, and a member of the Eastern Orthodox faith. Paul Ramsey, a Methodist pioneer in the then nascent field of bioethics, published a provocative essay in 1965. While thoroughly informed of the scientific and medical developments, he did not hesitate to advance assertively his understanding of a Christian critique of eugenic ideology, materialistic humanism, and mechanistic modes of genetically altering procreation.[15] With dialectical and even polemical vigor he refuted the eugenic recommendations of Herman J. Muller — genetic control, sperm banks, artificial insemination — by defending the traditional Christian teaching of procreation within monogamous covenant and loving bonds. If and when genetic surgery should become practicable, thus removing defects from progeny, cautionary risk-taking would be warranted, but only for purposes of health. Ramsey's conservative opinions were posited on a concept of divinely ordained natural law not very distant from Roman Catholic doctrine. While remarkably conversant with scientific and medical discourse, he felt no need to dilute or modify his Christological belief in life and its purpose. "Christian ethics," he wrote, "is not found among the contents of any natural science, nor can it be disproved by any of the facts that such sciences know."[16] This he stated, not as a matter of defiance of genetics, but of fact. He adhered to his deontological line of argument for twenty more years, challenging other Protestants who have felt justified in applying more flexible and permissive styles of theology and ethics. He was appalled to see Aldous

---

14. Azriel Rosenfeld, "Judaism and Gene Design" (1972), in *Jewish Bioethics*, 402.

15. Paul Ramsey, "Moral and Religious Implications of Genetic Control," first published in 1965, and again in *Fabricated Man* (New Haven: Yale University Press, 1970), 1-59.

16. *Ibid.,* 47.

Huxley's prediction of procreative technology coming to practice in *in vitro* fertilization and selective infanticide for genetic defects.

A more liberal position was taken by the German theologian, Karl Rahner, S.J., one of the most influential thinkers of the century, who readily perceived some of the opportunities and problems engendered by genetic science. His seminal essay on "The Problem of Genetic Manipulation" (1967) has remained a standard challenge to traditional Catholic thought.[17] It constitutes a decisive break from the long tradition of reacting negatively to findings of modern biological sciences. In a time when the ambiguous phrase "playing God" came into currency, Rahner expressed a new openness to possibilities of improving the physiological condition of humans. Natural law theology does not require a static, non-evolutionary view of human nature. To resist human self-manipulation, he argued, would be "symptomatic of a cowardly and comfortable conservatism hiding behind misunderstood Christian ideals." The appropriate attitude for Christians should be "cool-headedness" when addressing genetic manipulation. This is a mark of human courage which God has made possible by granting responsible freedom to seek the ultimate goals of life as humans are able to conceive them.

Rahner recognized the fact that the human race has always modified the natural environment, using intelligence and skill effectively if not always wisely. Whether intentionally or not, and most likely not, people have also wrought changes in genetic characteristics and status of health through diet, medicine, environment, and voluntary selective breeding. Now it has been made possible to exercise God-given freedom of choice to affect the course of humanity's evolution. Rahner's knowledge of genetic manipulation could not include gene splicing, of course, because this was hardly anticipated in 1966. Even a successful "engineered" procreation by *in vitro* fertilization was more than a decade in the future. Nevertheless, Rahner had enough foresight to imagine that great changes in human life sciences were soon to take place. He deplored the limitations of the Church's experience and ability to pro-

17. Karl Rahner's 1967 publication appeared in English as "The Problem of Genetic Manipulation," in *Theological Investigations* (New York: Herder and Herder, 1972), vol. 9. A sympathetic exposition of Rahner's ideas is given by the Catholic moral theologian Bernard Haering in *Ethics of Manipulation* (New York: Seabury Press, 1975).

vide counsel on this "adventure into the unforeseeable." Christians should consider "what sacrifices could be expected of humanity today on behalf of humanity's tomorrows . . . without being too quick to speak of immoral cruelty, as the violation and exploitation of the dignity of man today for the benefit of man's tomorrow."[18] Theologians must admit their incapability of passing judgments on scientific matters about which their knowledge is far from adequate.

Does Rahner's commendation of freedom and openness toward the future mean unconditional license for genetics? No, because he draws back from giving approval without reserve. His position on the subject becomes somewhat ambivalent. He first says Yes and then No to genetic manipulation. Indeed, like a traffic light he flashes green at first, then amber, and finally red. How can this be? Because his thinking distinguishes two levels of human existence: the biological and the spiritual. As Ronald Cole-Turner interprets these essays: ". . . while his theology affirms the necessity of self-transcendence, this self-transcendence occurs at a spiritual level rather than at the level of evolutionary biology."[19] The two planes are distinct but related. Led by research scientists, humanity will undoubtedly bring about changes in man's physical nature, and because such changes will probably be irreversible they must be approached with caution. "At all events," he concludes, "if the new humanity of the future is to survive, it must cultivate a sober and critical resistance to the fascination of novel possibilities."[20] The main question is not whether to use techniques of genetic science but how to discriminate between applications which are in consonance with human nature and thus beneficial and those which are detrimental.

Theodosius Dobzhansky was an eminent American biologist with a strong attachment to his roots in the Russian Orthodox religious tradition. What he perceived in the recent stage of research was not an array of threats to human integrity but rather a vista of coming developments in the history of human evolution.[21] God's purpose for

18. "Problem of Genetic Manipulation."

19. Ronald Cole-Turner, *The New Genesis* (Louisville: Westminster/John Knox Press, 1993), 65.

20. "Problem of Genetic Manipulation," 250.

21. Theodosius Dobzhansky, *The Biology of Ultimate Concern* (New York: New American Library, 1967).

humanity is a salvation from carnality and mortality. This is expressed in the Greek word *theosis,* or becoming divine. Such optimism is not unambiguous since sin and evil are realities, not illusions. Yet present investigation into the workings of genes in organisms, especially in humans, is in harmony with God's saving action for humanity. The physical and spiritual evolution of the race is the purpose of divine and human synergism. Evolutionary teleology is perceived by faith and known in the experience of persons transformed by grace in a sacramental community with others. That is its personal meaning. But there is a cosmic meaning as well for humanity as a whole. The Orthodox liturgy keeps pointing to this eventuality as an object of hope.

The implications of genetic research for the human race were seen very differently by Ramsey, Rahner, and Dobzhansky. New reports and predictions of human genetic engineering, such as cloning, were regarded with suspicion and resistance by Ramsey. His theology made him well aware of the morally flawed motivations and judgments of human beings. The tragic irony that some who intend good do evil, as well as the attested fact that some actually intend evil, could not be dismissed from consideration of human progress. Any hope for the realization of a healthier and happier human stock, in this perspective, is not a historical expectation but an eschatological one. Genetic diseases of children keep us struggling with the perennial problem of theodicy. Does our loving Creator allow such evil?

During the decade of the 1960s there was a widespread interest in the mystical, evolutionary theology of Rahner's fellow Jesuit, the paleontologist Pierre Teilhard de Chardin. Christians of various communions were attracted to his distinctive ideas of humankind's physical and spiritual evolution. This was not the same as the neo-Darwinian idea of progressive, social evolutionary destiny. Rather than foreseeing the goal of human history as a political and social utopia wherein secular ideals are realized, Teilhard prophesied the ultimate transformation of human physical existence, intellect, and spirit. In this "omega point" of evolution, humanity was to conform to its perfect paradigm, which is the figure of Christ.[22]

In a somewhat related way, there was a developing and spreading

22. Pierre Teilhard de Chardin, *The Phenomenon of Man* (New York: Harper and Row, 1959).

new "process philosophy," derived from the seminal thought of Alfred North Whitehead. This included more than humanity within its evolutionary scope, but also animal and plant life, cells, molecules, and even seemingly inert matter. Therefore, not only the biochemistry and morphology of organisms in slow process of evolutionary change but also physical sources of atomic and molecular energy became subjects of theological consideration. As Ian Barbour explains, "The influence of biology and physics is evident in the process view of reality as a dynamic web of interconnected events. Nature is characterized by change, chance, and novelty as well as order. It is incomplete and still coming into being."[23] The relevance to genetics is obvious.

Such speculative thinking may seem very remote from the practical realities of highly sophisticated molecular biology laboratories and clinics of genetic medicine. However, to religious minds the connection to theologies of human nature and history have been, if not always lucid, quite important.

Another theologian who began early to respond to the challenge of the new genetics was James M. Gustafson. In a 1969 lecture in Boston, he called for the reconception of a normative concept of a normative humanity. This would have to be an alternative to the deeply etched idea of human nature as conventionally taught and believed by many people in the West: namely, the non-evolutionary, fixed, unchanging, and essentially dualistic concept of humans as split bodies and souls. Like some others, he advocated an emergent theological anthropology adequate to conserve the ancient biblical and philosophical insights and still appreciate new scientific knowledge. In terms of making ethical judgments about human genetic experimentation, he said, "the weight is on human initiative, human freedom (if you choose) to explore, develop, expand, alter, initiate, intervene in the course of life in the world, including his own life."[24] But not without prudence and caution.

In a conference address delivered in Houston twenty-three years later, 1992, Gustafson showed how the question of normative human

23. *Religion in an Age of Science,* 28.
24. James M. Gustafson, "Genetic Engineering and Normative Humanity," in *Ethical Issues in Biology and Medicine,* ed. Preston N. Williams (Cambridge, Mass.: Schenkman, 1973), 57.

nature persisted; but it has been amplified and intensified by genetic discoveries during those years.[25]

"Where do, or could, the work of theologians and geneticists meet? At what points in human thinking and action does, or can, their work intersect? What role do inchoate, or explicit, appeals to 'nature' play at the points of intersection? These are the three principal questions that this paper attempts to address. . . . The hypothesis that generally governs the paper is this: at the points of intersection some notion of what is 'natural' functions in making choices.

"Two points of intersection can be distinguished. One is the most frequently and visibly shared concern for the morality of certain forms of genetic research and therapy. At this, the *ethical* intersection, very familiar questions are asked. Given the experiments and technology that make possible increasing knowledge of genetics, are there procedures that are morally questionable? Given present and future knowledge what interventions ought to be done? What ought not to be done? Which seem to be morally ambiguous? What criteria are invoked to guide both restraints and interventions into biological processes that are genetically based, if not determined? What ends are worthy of pursuit? What risks are tolerable in the light of the probability of certain beneficial and harmful outcomes? What means are judged morally permissible, and why? Other familiar questions could be added to this list. My point is simply that both geneticists and theologians, particularly moral theologians, have expressed opinions and made arguments about appropriate answers as we know from at least twenty-five years of literature about ethics and genetics. At this intersection theologians, geneticists, and moral philosophers all function as practical moralists, applying principles to particular cases or classes of cases, or adopting other procedures of practical moral reasoning to defend their judgments. Where they often differ, and this is a point of interest in this paper, is in the beliefs which predispose them to make the particular judgments they do, or adopt the particular procedures of argumentation that they use.

"The second point of intersection is the significance and use of genetic knowledge for interpreting the 'nature' of human life, its mean-

25. James M. Gustafson, "Theologians and Geneticists," Conference on "Genetics, Religion and Ethics," Houston, March 14, 1992.

ing and its value. At this, the *scientific-theological intersection,* very different questions come to attention. What do those geneticists and other biologists who expand beyond the strict scientific entailments of their work say about the meaning and value of human life? What premises do they include to justify their moral and 'religious' thinking? What seem to be elided premises? Mary Midgley's *Evolution as a Religion: Strange Hopes and Stranger Fears* sets a good example of how this intersection has been crossed by persons from the biological sciences. How do theologians address genetics and other biological knowledge, if they do? If it is taken into account in their theological interpretations of the human (theological anthropologies, to the initiated), how does it function? If it is judged to be insignificant for the theological and ethical interpretation of the human, how is this case made? Do theologians take genetics and other biological knowledge into account in their theological interpretations of nature, of creation? If so, does it involve a specification of how God or the Divine is ordering or governing life in the world. Or, for various theological reasons, is genetic and biological knowledge bracketed out of serious consideration? Some geneticists do not cross this scientific-theological intersection, recognizing that to do so is to go beyond strict science; but biologists who do cross it to speculate about the meaning of the human in the universe come to very different conclusions. Many theologians do not cross the intersection, and for different reasons. Those that do have different ways of relating theology to the knowledge of science."

2. Ecumenical Deliberations

The questions raised by Gustafson about the two intersections of genetics and religion have constituted the agenda of several study commissions of churches for a quarter of a century (see below, Chapter Six). The earliest study was initiated by the World Council of Churches in 1971, and a conference was held in Zurich in 1973. Contrary to popular stereotypes of church inquiries into scientific and medical subjects, only one-sixth of the participants were theologians or religious professionals. The large majority were experts in biology and medicine. Probably for this reason they focused attention mainly on practical problems of genetic counseling, prenatal diagnosis, abortion, and artificial aids to conception. (R. G. Edwards of Cambridge University, a vocal member of the conference, was the first researcher to "produce" a baby by *in vitro* fertilization six years later.) The information and pragmatic advice offered by the summary statement was reasonable and useful; but it betrayed little interest in, or need for, illumination from theology. Only a noted ethicist, Roger L. Shinn, suggested the relevance of biblical and theological insights on human nature and the value of persons in God's creative purpose. The chairman of the project, an Australian biologist, Charles Birch, did not introduce his own well-known commitments to process theology.

The Whiteheadian influence was more explicitly evident in Birch's address six years later at the World Council of Churches conference on "Faith, Science and the Future." This unprecedented and as yet unrepeated event took place at a citadel of the sciences, Massachusetts Institute of Technology (M.I.T.), in 1979. Again, of the more than nine hundred official participants from many countries, churches, religions, and occupations, the religious professionals were a minority. The main concerns of conferees were equitable participation opportunities in new technologies for all people; protection of global environment; political and economic self-determination for developing (i.e., poor) and formerly colonial nations; and suppression of nuclear weapons. Delegates were also anxious to formulate a relevant theological understanding of humanity's uses of divinely created nature. The conference report vigorously supported an Eastern Orthodox theology of humanity and nature as distinct from the Western Catholic and Protestant embracing of subject-object dualism. It noted that Western theologians in modern times have not resisted, and thus have tacitly accepted, the subjection of nonhuman nature to human exploitation. It charged that "science and technology, by reducing non-human nature to the status of a mere object, have denied the intrinsic value that inheres in every creature because it comes from the hand of God."[26] Eastern theology has emphasized instead "union-participation" not only between God and humanity in Christ but also between humanity and nature. The "image of God" in humanity should be understood to indicate "both human-

---

26. *Faith and Science in an Unjust World*, vol. 2, Report of the World Council of Churches' Conference on Faith, Science and the Future (Philadephia: Fortress Press, 1980).

ity's relation to God and also the relation of humanity to non-human creation."[27] Thus, human society and the earth's ecosystems are inseparable, and "humans share as partners in its (nature's) life and accept responsibility for the sustainability of the total system."[28]

How this mode of thinking applies to genetics has become clearer today than in 1979. Recognition that all organic life shares much of the same DNA substance and that humans and chimpanzees come within two percent of having the same DNA is an empirical evidence of its interrelatedness. However, this fact is not of itself a warrant for the scientific materialistic reductionism which implies that human life, like all life, is *merely* in our genes.

One of the ten conference sessions at M.I.T. dealt with "Ethical Issues in the Biological Manipulation of Life."[29] It made a strong statement against allowing persons to be socially stigmatized because of genetic disabilities. It rejected cost-benefit calculations in determining indications for abortion. Somatic cell gene therapy, whenever it might be feasible, was accepted in principle, but germ-line gene alteration was rejected because of unknowable risks to progeny.

The M.I.T. conference gave impetus to other religious bodies to take a critical look at the fast-moving developments of genetic technology and medicine. Attitudes varied between affirmation and apprehension of catastrophic perils. The National Council of Churches undertook a study which led to generally positive conclusions.[30] Indeed, the 1986 report was entitled "Genetic Science for Human Benefit," even though it pointed out the dangers of human *hubris* ("playing God") and of allowing canons of nondiscrimination and equitable access to genetic health benefits to be breached. Concern about possible abuse or reckless applications of engineering prompted leaders of the nation's Christian and Jewish communities to ask President Carter to commission a thorough review. This was done very responsibly by the already constituted President's Commission for the Study of Ethical

27. *Ibid.*, 30.
28. *Ibid.*, 33.
29. *Ibid.*, 49.
30. Frank Herron, ed., *Genetic Engineering*, National Council of Churches (New York: Pilgrim Press, 1984); "Genetic Science for Human Benefit," National Council of Churches brochure (New York, 1986).

Problems in Medicine and Biomedical and Behavioral Research. Under the direction of Alexander M. Capron, the resulting book, *Splicing Life,* offered reassurance that there were no inherently dangerous, wrong, or irreligious outcomes to be feared.[31] As subsequent position statements by several churches demonstrated, however, the Commission's assurance was not entirely convincing.

An articulation of dominant views of American religious communities was heard in 1982 by (then) Representative Albert Gore's House Committee on Science and Technology. Professor Roger L. Shinn made four points:

(a) Though risks in experimentation are inevitable, a strong bias toward the sacredness of human life requires highest regard for the patient or subject.
(b) Programs of positive eugenics are dubious and dangerous, even though elimination of genetic diseases is a laudable effort.
(c) The allocation of human, economic, and scientific resources is a matter of continuous ethical concern to those with a religious commitment to equity and justice.
(d) While "reverence for life" in the context of Christian faith may be exaggerated and raise mistaken fears about modifying humans, "some sense of human inviolability" remains rooted deeply in our national and religious traditions.[32]

The testimony of this Protestant spokesman was supported in substance by Father Richard A. McCormick, S.J., and Rabbi Seymour Siegel. Both of them added, however, a stronger concern about the integrity of human life at fetal stage and thus about whether there are acceptable conditions for abortion. Inasmuch as Father McCormick is not an absolutist on unconditional protection of embryonic and fetal

31. *Splicing Life* (Washington, D.C.: Government Printing Office, 1982), 77.

32. J. Robert Nelson, "The Role of Religions in the Analysis of the Ethical Issues of Human Gene Therapy," in *Human Gene Therapy* 1.1 (1990.) The full discussion is in *Hearings before the Subcommittee on Investigation and Oversight of the Committee on Science and Technology,* November 16-18, 1982 (Washington, D.C.: Government Printing Office, 1983), 299-341.

life, his testimony was less rigorous than the Vatican's official pronouncement of 1987 against *in vitro* fertilization or any procedure which is not directed to the subject's good health.[33]

Several Protestant denominations within the last decade have adopted official statements of policy regarding issues of procreation and genetic procedures. Unlike official Catholic declarations, however, these formulations of theological, ethical, and social views are not considered binding on the thinking or even the consciences of the members. They are carefully prepared by representative members of study commissions; and they serve useful purposes of educating members as well as serving as points of reference in the wider ecumenical and public debates. As is often remarked, the authority of the statements inheres in their power to command assent, not in the fact that they are approved by the church's governing bodies. If their validity is attested by reference to such accepted criteria as the Bible, Church tradition, and reasonable assessment of scientific and sociological evidence, these statements are more likely to command support. Yet, disputes arise as to the ways these sources are to be interpreted. This diversity of thinking and persuasion within and among religious communities is a major cause for what has been termed "asymmetrical" dialogue between the genetic scientists and religious ethicists. Even so, this need not discourage the dialogue. In fact, as they will be discussed in Chapter Six, there have been issued within the past decade several substantial policy statements by the National and World Councils of Churches, the United Church of Christ, the Episcopal Church, the United Methodist Church, and the Church of the Brethren. Their common agreements testify to an emerging, limited consensus, but their differences are also worthy of analysis and serious consideration will be given them below.

33. *Instruction on Respect for Human Life in Its Origin and on the Dignity of Procreation* (Vatican City, 1987). In his 1993 encyclical letter *Veritatis Splendor,* Pope John Paul II vigorously rejects the teachings of certain Catholic moralists (unnamed but recognizable) who differ from what they deem "the excessively categorical position adopted by the Church's Magisterium on many moral questions" (Rome: Vatican Press, 1993), 87, 112-16.

3. *The Houston Conferences on "Genetics, Religion and Ethics"*

ELSI is the acronym for Ethical, Legal and Social Implications of the Human Genome Project. Could it be changed to ERLSI, with the "R" for Religious? Officially, no, since it is generally assumed that a federally funded program excludes research or conferences on religious matters. This assumption is based upon a popular but dubious interpretation of the Constitutional separation of Church and State — popular because of the promotion of secularism in realms of education, journalism, and government; dubious because it equates widely held religious views with particular organized communities of believers. Additionally, many scientists also believe firmly that the gulf between science and religion is so wide and deep that there can be no reasonable relationship between them.

Neither the political nor the ideological exclusion of religion has prevailed in the HGP. In 1990, funds from both the NIH and DOE were granted to two projects concerning the explicit religious implications of the genome initiative. The first is the Conference on "Genetics, Religion and Ethics" (GRE) at the Texas Medical Center in Houston, a project of Baylor College of Medicine and the Center's Institute of Religion. The second is in Berkeley, California, at the Center for Theology and the Natural Sciences of the Graduate Theological Union, a consortium of divinity schools. The present book is a product of the first of these.

The GRE project grew out of the ecumenical studies on genetics fostered by the World Council of Churches and the National Council of Churches. Having made their inquiries and promulgated reports, neither council after 1989 had the resources to continue work in the field. This termination was very regrettable to many persons, in view of the advances of the HGP and related research. Moreover, wider discussion of the reports and recommendations of the two councils had not been adequately implemented in the United States and Canada. A few denominational positions were being defined, but none to represent a broad spectrum of churches, synagogues, and other communities. Which independent agency could fill the gap and meet the need?

The Institute of Religion was seen to be admirably suited. First, it is officially independent of any Christian denomination or other faith and its leadership well informed by long, global, ecumenical experience. Second, since 1955 it has been an integral member institution of the renowned Texas Medical Center. Consisting of forty-one medical institutions, it is the largest medical complex in the world by a factor of two. Third, it cooperates with one of the HGP's chosen research centers: the Institute for Molecular Genetics of Baylor College of Medicine, directed by C. Thomas Caskey, M.D. Literally hundreds of researchers, physicians, and counselors in the Medical Center are actively working in laboratories and clinics on gene mapping, diagnosis, and therapy. In addition, the Center for Ethics, Medicine, and Public Issues provides internationally recognized consultation and publications.

Letters and telephone calls to key persons of various religious communions elicited positive support for the conference. In some instances the participation was endorsed by official agencies; in others by individuals who are respected for their knowledge of theology, ethics, science, medicine, and public policy. Official endorsement and some financial support were given by the Greek Orthodox, Episcopalians, Methodists, Lutherans, and officers of the United Church of Christ. Endorsements came also from the National and World Councils of Churches. Roman Catholics, other Protestants, Jews, Muslims, and Hindus took part as representative individuals. The American Medical Association gave its counsel and endorsement, as did the American Scientific Affiliation and the Institute for Molecular Genetics of Baylor College of Medicine. The Park Ridge Center, publisher of *Second Opinion,* gave support.

The plan was to convene two conferences in Houston by invitation only. The intent of invitation was not exclusionary but purposeful: namely, to have proportionate representation of the diverse religious, professional, ethnic, and gender categories. Due in large part to which persons were designated by their communities and how individuals responded to the invitations, this intent was not fully realized. Funding for the first conference held from March 30 to April 1, 1990, was supplied mainly by the trustees of the Institute of Religion and two foundations. Costs of the second one, on March 13-15, 1992, were covered by the HGP grants from the DOE and NIH. In all, some two hundred sixty people took part, representing eight countries. In numbers and diversity it fell far short of the 1979 ecumenical conference; but in that event genetics and biological manipulation constituted only one section among ten.

The schema for the project involved four platform addresses with three respondents to each, informational presentations, discussions in small groups, and plenary sessions. Francis S. Collins opened the first conference with an exposition of the current state of human genetic research, and also explained the bearing of his personal Christian faith upon scientific understanding of life. The problem of general ignorance of science and the need for education was addressed by William B. Hendee of the American Medical Association. John C. Fletcher, bioethicist of the University of Virginia, interpreted the findings of his research (with Dorothy C. Wertz) on attitudes of physicians toward privacy and confidentiality with respect to their patients' genome information. The relation of new genetic science to traditional theology of human nature and identity was discussed by J. Robert Nelson. Overviews of Eastern Orthodox and Roman Catholic positions were given by Stanley S. Harakas and Albert S. Moraczewski, O.P. Coming from Germany, Hartwig von Schubert of Heidelberg gave an exposition of ecumenical European thinking on genetic manipulation.[34] Non-Christian perspectives were provided by Maimon M. Cohen for Judaism and Hassan M. Hathout for Islam. Two leaders of the HGP, Robert M. Cook-Deegan and C. Thomas Caskey, gave up-to-date information on its progress.

At the closing session, participants agreed on nominating four groups to study and clarify these issues during the next two years in preparation for the second conference. These groups were established by participants in Chicago, Boston, Washington, D.C., and Houston. Their reports became grist for the mill of discussion in 1992. Platform addresses and statements by respondents pressed further the issues of how genetics and religion are related or interrelated. Ruth E. Bulger, from the Institute of Medicine, focused on the particular interest of women. Some exciting new advances in gene therapy as well as certain morally perplexing techniques of reproductive intervention were described by three geneticists whose successful research had recently received public recognition and acclaim. Dr. W. French Anderson, a researcher at the NIH, explained his satisfying results in the first clinical trials ever attempted for human gene therapy. Dr. Caskey told of opening windows on the genetic causes of five diseases by researchers in his laboratory: Duchenne muscular dystrophy, Lesch-Nyhan disease, fragile X syndrome, adult polycystic kidney disease, and myotonic dystrophy; in addition, he explained the new technique of individual

34. Hartwig von Schubert has written in German the most comprehensive of analyses of writings of English-speaking theologians and ethicists in *Biotechnologie und evangelische Ethik* (Frankfurt and New York: Campus Verlag, 1992).

identification by "DNA fingerprinting." Then his colleague at Baylor, Dr. Mark Hughes, explained the radically new method of diagnosing cystic fibrosis in human embryos prior to implantation in the womb, and then correcting it by microsurgery. All of these were breakthroughs receiving attention in scientific and medical journals, but considered from a religious and ethical perspective, they highlight some of the inherent ambiguities of such research: the promises of diagnosis and therapy as well as problems of manipulating embryonic cells, diagnosing diseases as yet untreatable, and also deciding the fate of untreatable newborn infants. By what standard are these procedures to be measured? That remains the primary theological question.

The Archbishop of York, John S. Habgood, came from England to present his insights on the science in which he took his doctoral degree, biology. He tackled the frequently posed question of how far we should keep looking for knowledge of natural data and inventing ways to apply them to technology. Is there not a "peril of trying to know too much?" "The accumulation of massive amounts of information is not knowledge," he said, "though it may provide a basis for knowledge. Knowledge is more than an abstract pattern in the mind or in the computer. It is an understanding of what to do with such patterns, how to use them." The inseparability of knowledge, reflection, and praxis prompted a less cautionary approach by bioethicist Paul D. Simmons, who asserted: "We can only will genetic health by intervening in the process as God gives us to know the details of the process itself. In doing so we are exercising uniquely human prerogatives in response to God's challenge to have dominion and not be merely passive victims of inexorable forces."

The inter-faith character of these two GRE conferences excluded the possibility of theological consensus. Nevertheless, any manifestation of broad agreement among well-informed and critically reflective representatives of the differing religious communities will have important bearing upon the shaping of public understanding and will influence the makers of public policies and laws. This perception prompted participants to write a Summary Reflection Statement. It shows significant points of agreement while recognizing divergences of opinion. While the statement expresses a near consensus, it has not been endorsed in all particulars by all participants. The text has been published in Japan, France, Britain, and the United States, and copies have been widely disseminated. The text, which follows, indicates how much of the religious frontier participants hold in common and where further continuing conversation is needed.

C. "Summary Reflection Statement" of the Houston Delegates

1. Religious Concern and the Human Genome Project

Faith and Theology as a Basis for Ethics   Today, as in the past, religious traditions are a rich source of knowledge and practical wisdom concerning human life. The unique origin, value, and purpose of human life continue to be enduring themes in much religious literature and life. Discussion of questions of right and wrong, good and evil are inherent features of religious discourse. It is therefore reasonable to expect religious perspectives to continue to contribute to the discussion of the ethical, legal, and social implications of the Human Genome Project, the international effort to map and sequence the human genome.

The task is formidable. The major religious communities of the entire world are being dispersed among the continents and nations. Religious pluralism is a new factor in many societies. Generalized statements about religion are decreasingly valid or applicable. And yet, within the global complex of religions, the distinctive integrity of each remains. Where the biblical traditions of Judaism and Christianity prevail, God is believed to be the omnipotent Creator who is revealed through canons of Scripture, nature, and history as just, loving, and merciful. From these traditions proceeds an ethic which limits autonomy, values neighbor as self (not just avoiding harm but actively promoting good), and tempers justice with love and mercy. The religion of Islam shares a belief in one God, but with differing interpretations. Hinduism and Buddhism look to their distinctive deities, sacred writings, and moral tenets. Within these and other religions many diversities of moral opinion occur.

Religious voices should be heard and respected in discussion of delicate and difficult moral issues associated with genetic research and counseling. Likewise, specifically religious perspectives should be tested in relation to other points of view. The beliefs and insights of all religious groups have a legitimate role to play in the shaping of public

29

attitudes and in the formation of public policy. Diverse doctrines and commitments have rightful claim to be respected, heard, evaluated, and applied in policy-making.

2. Six Specific Issues

Human Diversity   A religiously based consensus on the full and equal dignity of all human persons is often contradicted in practice by discriminatory prejudice of one group against another. Ethnic and racial diversities among human beings are due in large part to genetic factors which must never be interpreted as indices of personal or social worth. Neither should the presence of physical or mental disabilities, whether or not they are due to genetic inheritance, detract from one's personal or social value. Due attention should be given to needs, ideas, and opinions of people in all lands, lest the values of genetic research, medicine, and technology be enjoyed only by the most developed nations.

Many of the social and ethical implications of the Human Genome Project have a distinct and significant impact upon women. The insights and experiences of women are often overlooked, despite the fact that they typically carry a heavier role in decision making about reproduction and childcare and spend more time with children who suffer from genetic diseases. Women's perspectives must be fully appreciated in dealing with genetic issues. It should also be noted that diseases (including genetic diseases) which uniquely affect women are not receiving the attention due them, and individual women researchers do not receive as much support as their male colleagues. These are matters of justice which religious groups should address.

Genetic Engineering   Genetic engineering techniques can be used to prevent certain diseases and provide treatment for therapy. They may also be used to modify physical and mental traits of the human person. Various religious viewpoints exhibit different degrees of openness to genetic manipulation. Religions which teach the divine creation of the world include varying interpretations of two dissimilar categories which construe human beings to be responsible either as stewards or as co-creators of most things, whether living or nonliving. According to the first, members of the human community are destined to be caretakers or stewards of God's creation, including human life itself. Some believe that such interventions as genetic manipulation are permissible for improving health and preserving life, but that we must guard against sinful abuses — e.g., manipulation of power, justice, economic gain, or perpetuation of ignorance. (In a stricter version of stewardship, all such interventions are ruled out.) The second category elevates the human role as co-creator with God above that of stewardship. Powers of genetic engineering for physical or therapeutic purpose consummate all previously known means of exercising co-creation. In short, this variety of theological perspectives illumines some of the promises and possible implications of the Human Genome Project as well as the complex problems presented by it.

Because the Jewish and Christian religious worldview is grounded in the equality and dignity of individual persons, genetic diversity is respected. Any move to eliminate or reduce human diversity in the interest of eugenics or creating a "super strain" of human being will meet with resistance. These issues compel us to continue to struggle with our understanding of such fundamental concepts as life, death, humanness, health, and disease. While many religious thinkers or groups are open to genetic manipulation of somatic cells to prevent, treat, or cure disease in a particular individual, they object to attempts proposed simply to enhance a person's looks, stature, or intelligence. There are also serious doubts and disputes over manipulating the germline to prevent the transfer of genetic disease from one generation to the next. Most have serious reservations concerning genetic manipulation that is designed solely to enhance the physical traits or intellectual endowment of future generations.

Counseling and Education   Religious groups should advocate access to reliable genetic information and counseling services, and appropriate training for genetic counselors. It is essential not only that genetic testing be accurate with an absolute minimum of error, but also that genetic counseling recognize and accurately convey the variability or diversity of phenotypes associated with any particular genetic condition. Moreover, genetic counselors must be aware of and inform counselees about the gap in time between the time of genetic testing and the possibility of improved treatment and potential cure, if such be possible.

The nature of genetic counseling requires appropriate respect for the values and beliefs of both the counselee and the counselor without imposing the counselor's own commitments.

The unique contribution of pastoral care and spiritual counseling should be affirmed and developed in relation to medically oriented genetic counseling. Utilizing interdisciplinary teams of clinical and pastoral professionals would probably enhance patient and family care.

It is important that counseling techniques be sensitive to the needs of the patient and the patient's family and interpersonal relationships, as well as to significant cultural and religious variation. Informative dialogue and mutual education should be maintained among genetic counselors, pastoral care-givers, and counselors, with the help of members of national, voluntary organizations for genetic disorders. Such cooperation will allow the unique language of each to be "translated" into that of the other. Effective education in biology (particularly genetics and development), risk evaluation, decision making, and religious ethics is needed in the public domain.

Genetic Screening   Religious values mandate the defense of personal privacy, integrity of the family, and good social relations. Therefore, they support policies and methods of securing consent to have access to genetic information obtained through screening. Moreover, the use of confidential information must be carefully circumscribed to avoid embarrassment, social stigmatization, disruption of marital and familial relations, and economic discrimination. Care should be taken to avoid or prevent the unjust uses of an individual's genetic data in respect to his or her securing and holding employment, insurance, and health care.

It is important to take account of how the various cultural and religious values influence understandings of privacy, family dynamics, and community. Sensitivity to diverse cultures and their prevailing values should thus characterize both the development of screening programs and the communication of screening results.

Pregnancy Termination   In society in general as well as within religious groups pregnancy termination is a serious and divisive moral issue. Through the Human Genome Project the development of more and better genetic diagnostic tests on pre-implantation embryos ("pre-

32

embryos"), embryos, and fetuses may increase the frequency of selectively implanting embryos or opting for pregnancy termination after implantation because of genetic conditions. The same tests may enable childbearing for couples who otherwise would remain childless because of concerns they have about genetic risks. Religious groups and the public at large should be encouraged to engage in discourse about defining what constitutes acceptable, serious, or severe genetic conditions as indications for embryo selection or pregnancy termination, and to identify alternative appropriate responses to these choices. These groups should also address the question of whether and under what conditions fetal tissue should be available for research and transplantation. Whether pregnancy termination is accepted or rejected, religious groups and society are morally obligated to continue seeking means of supporting and caring for affected persons and their families.

Public Policy and Legislation   Religious groups should work to promote systems of health care wherein access to genetic counseling and all medical care is equitable and just. Religious groups should help to identify and resist premature legislation which could jeopardize an informed, deliberative public debate on bioethical issues, as well as support legislation which protects the value and dignity of individual humans. They should actively promote education of their members and the public, encouraging broader understanding of issues arising from the Human Genome Project. Endorsing oversight and review of public research or experimentation before they proceed may be appropriate and desirable.

3. Religious Bodies: Responsibilities and Opportunities

Religious bodies of denominational, ecumenical, and interfaith nature should continue to establish study groups to consider formally the new genetics, including the Human Genome Project and its implications for the churches and society at large. They should re-examine both traditional doctrinal formulations in light of scientific advances and these advances in the light of their doctrines. Their beliefs and insights can be translated into pastoral care, ethical education, and social justice advocacy. Where moral decisions and actions for human good are needed, the wisdom and fervor expressed by people of faith are most compelling. Religious groups share the responsibility to educate their own members and the general public about the issues raised by the Human Genome Project. Each religious group is encouraged to implement special education programs as well as to adopt policy statements which express the values of its own traditions. Reticence due to ignorance, modesty, or a failure of nerve in the face of the current biotechnological challenge will diminish chances of improving health and well-being in the lives of many persons of this and future generations. Now is the opportunity to meet the challenge.

CHAPTER TWO

Genetic Advances in Medicine

MILITARY metaphors have been the most popular in literature and journalism to describe the advances of medical research and practice. The so-called "microbe hunters" have carried out a "search and destroy" campaign against the causes of infectious diseases. Vaccinations and the antibiotic medicines have been combined with public health programs as the doctors' "armamentarium" in the battles. Smallpox was totally defeated, disarmed, and eradicated in unconditional surrender. The forces of poliomyelitis are under medical siege and may suffer the same annihilation. Meanwhile, the "war against cancer" has broken out in a different theater, and new, smarter tactics are employed. The infiltrated tobacco agents are first identified and immobilized. It is now found that the "enemy" is not only "in our midst" but within our cells. A new strategy is developed which relies less on direct confrontation with disease — pills and syringes — and more on accurate intelligence reports concerning the enemy's sources of strength. This is a radical change, going to the roots of disease in the invisible world of intracellular chromosomes and strings of DNA genes. Not only some fifty varieties of cancer but four thousand other genetic diseases are being driven from concealment so they can be confronted openly and neutralized. In terms of the rapidly developing skills of medical genetics, then, the Human Genome Project can be likened to a vigorous program of counter-intelligence.

Molecular genetics has many applications, of which the prediction, prevention, diagnosis, and treatment of heritable diseases are most prominent and hopeful.

A. Basic Strategies in Resisting Disorders

For most people of the world, no doubt, the process of procreation is rightly described as a lottery. Babies are procreated "in the natural way" and their individual genotypes are matters of chance or unknown cause. Contraceptive methods are largely unknown or denounced for religious and cultural reasons, or else disregarded because of carelessness and sexual impetuosity. As a result of indiscriminate reproductive activity, ironically combined with improved care of infants and extended longevity of the elderly, the warning signals of imminent population catastrophe are becoming more insistent and credible. But we do not look to the Genome Project to solve this problem. Its concern, instead, is to decrease the incidence of congenital diseases and to enhance the health of those who inherit them. This double goal will be approached in four ways.

1. Prevention by avoiding conception. This calls for extending public education on the nature and etiology of numerous genetic diseases and metabolic disorders. It means encouraging prospective parents to seek counsel and be tested for possibly being carriers of suspected defects, and securing information on genetic histories of families.

2. Prenatal diagnosis. Pregnant women can rely upon increasingly available, accurate, and less costly testing for some two hundred common or rare diseases. Occurrences of disorders within families indicate the need for testing, which in ninety-eight percent of cases proves fortunately to be negative.

3. Prenatal therapy. Still in experimental stage, the treatment of some fetal afflictions by surgical or biochemical methods may become feasible and effective.

4. Neonatal testing, screening, and therapy. Some diseases cannot be identified before birth. It is now common practice to screen all newborns for phenylketonuria (PKU) and galactosemia, both of which can be treated almost immediately by dietary regimens. Individual testing by DNA analysis is required for other diseases. Dietary, medicinal, and surgical means are used for viable infants, for those born prematurely, and those suffering from disabilities caused by alcohol, drugs, or viral infection *in utero*.

B. Diagnosis before Birth

1. How It Is Done

As is evident in various areas of genome research, the story of inventions of methods and instruments of analysis is almost as fascinating as the molecular phenomena they explore. In reference to prenatal diagnosis, the development of methods seems to be synchronized by destiny with the particular needs of researchers. Improvements are measured in terms of accuracy, early use, safety, economic cost, and comfort for the woman. Recent experience shows that innovations score high in respect to all these criteria as they become more routinized in hospitals and clinics.

(a) Being able to see the fetus *in utero* was once unimaginable, but in the past forty years it has been made quite possible by two methods. These are ultrasonography and fetoscopy, which are often used together. Just as a ship's or airport's radar transmits radio beams which encounter solid substance and "bounce" back to form a visible image, so the high frequency sound waves directed through a woman's abdomen are translated by the sonograph to the screen of a monitor. Accurate measurements of the body and delineations of malformed limbs and head can be made, and other anomalies may be detected as characteristic of certain diseases. Sonography is not invasive and thus can cause no harm to the fetus or the woman.

Fetoscopy enables the obstetrician to have a direct view of sections of the fetus. It employs a fiber-optic device, inserted by hollow needle into the uterus. An ultrasonograph guides the needle in its exploration. In cases where fetal blood is in need of analysis it may be withdrawn in this process. Though the woman is locally anesthetized and not harmed, there is a recognized risk of harming the fetus by this method or even, in rare cases, of inducing premature delivery.

(b) Amniocentesis is also invasive, as the hollow needle enters the abdomen; it penetrates the uterine wall and the amniotic sac, from which fluid is extracted for chromosomal, biochemical, and DNA analysis. Although a well-established procedure with very slight risk of injury, standard amniocentesis has two disadvantages. It cannot normally be used before the sixteenth week of gestation; and then it requires two weeks or more to allow the cells to multiply to the point where chromosomes can be analyzed.

(c) The time factor makes the newer method of chorionic villus sampling (CVS) the most expeditious, allowing the earliest diagnosis at only ten weeks of pregnancy. Membrane tissue next to the fetus is extracted by aspiration transcervically or transabdominally, without incision or penetration. Laboratory analysis for signs of disease can then be completed in only a week or two. As compared to amniocentesis, however, the favorable timing of CVS is purchased at the price of somewhat greater risk of infection or miscarriage.

The testing procedures for viewing the fetus and examining its cells, as described above, are now considered conventional weapons in the conquest of genetic aberrations. But the science never stands still. It moves so fast that textbooks in medical genetics are to some degree obsolescent even before they can be printed. One book explains: "The number of disorders that can be diagnosed and the precision and efficiency of analysis are increasing *weekly* as new mutations are characterized and as additional diseases are mapped by genetic linkage studies."[1]

(d) It is possible, or even likely, that diagnosing by CVS or amniocentesis will be largely replaced in the future by analysis of maternal blood cells. The method is already being tested for possible commercial use.

2. Who Is Helped?

A large majority of Americans who, with their families, enjoy good health may feel no inclination to celebrate the latest advances in genetic research and medicine. The numerous, bewildering names of inherited diseases have no existential meaning when neither family member nor friend suffers from one. Indeed, some have criticized the government's funding of the HGP because, they say, it will help relatively few people.

---

1. Margaret W. Thompson, et al., *Genetics in Medicine,* 5th edn. (Philadelphia: W. B. Saunders Co., 1991), 420. This text provides admirably informative and lucid explanations for the reader who has limited knowledge. Equally valuable and more accessible to persons who are beginners in genetics is Aubrey Milunsky's *Heredity and Your Family's Health* (Baltimore: Johns Hopkins University Press, 1992). This is the revised edition of *Choices Not Chances* (Boston: Little Brown and Co., 1989). I am indebted to these books for information and data.

But population and morbidity statistics belie that attitude. In fact, about twenty-five million Americans — one in ten — suffer from congenital conditions. The technical names of dozens of diseases are heard in the daily conversations of pediatricians, but only overheard, so to speak, by most people. Let us remind ourselves of the afflictions which these names indicate. Diseases are not all of the same severity, of course. They range from those which are certainly lethal at early age to those which do not prevent one from enjoying, despite disabilities, what is often called a "useful and productive life," or (in less utilitarian terms) a happy, meaningful one. How can the diseases be arranged on a scale from extreme severity to a tolerable acceptability? The question was put to Dr. Aubrey Milunsky at the meeting of the American Association for the Advancement of Science in 1993. He responded by giving examples of nine levels.

(*a*) Anencephaly is the worst of the neural tube defects, which also include spina bifida. The babies lack a cerebral cortex, which means they are literally brainless and doomed to die in days or weeks. When detected by prenatal diagnosis, they are considered by many to be prime candidates for abortion. Even persons who are generally opposed to abortion often conclude this. But some parents, knowing the prospects, have chosen to bring the babies to birth for the express reason of supplying infant organs for lifesaving transplantation. This remains an issue of ethical debate.

(*b*) Trisomy 13 is caused when an extra chromosome 13 is added to the normal pair. It happens also on chromosome 18 with similar manifestations of extreme retardation of mental and motile capabilities, small head, heart defects, and physical deformities.

(*c*) Infantile spinal muscular atrophy prevents development of physical motility and leads to death after six months. It is similar to the notorious Tay-Sachs disease, which afflicts mainly Jewish families of Eastern European (Ashkenazic) descent.

(*d*) Down syndrome, or trisomy 21, is recognized at birth by facial and physical characteristics when no prenatal diagnosis has been made. Before people became sensitive to racist language, the name "mongoloid" was applied to Down children. The frequent occurrence of a blocked esophagus (atresia), which can be surgically corrected soon after birth, has been the occasion of "Baby Doe" debates and, for a time, federal rules requiring lifesaving procedures. There are degrees of severity among Down cases. Some children are so retarded that they are helpless; others attain a level of intelligence that enables them to live quite happily in families or communities.

(e) Spina bifida is a neural tube defect of varying severity. Hydrocephaly at birth, which is common, can be corrected by shunting fluids from the brain to the thorax. Paralysis of the legs and concomitant incontinence are usual. Mental capacity is usually not affected, however. Prenatal testing can also be done routinely, using a method which measures the amount of maternal serum alpha fetoprotein in her blood.

(f) Huntington disease falls into the late-onset category: its crippling symptoms do not appear until about the fortieth year. Then the brain and nervous system begin an irreversible degeneration with devastating effect until death, usually ten to twenty years after appearance of symptoms.

(g) Cystic fibrosis causes chronically blocked breathing due to the mucous accumulations and infections. It also prevents normal digestion of food. Persons affected require constant care, and they usually die in their mid-twenties. This disease is most prevalent among white persons.

(h) Phenylketonuria (PKU) is a serious, mentally retarding disease if not treated, but a constantly supervised diet permits normal activity.

(i) The fragile X syndrome usually affects only male offspring because females make an additional chromosome that masks the effect of the defective gene. Its effects are enlarged head, soft skin, certain facial features, and mental retardation.

Such are the gradations of severity according to one notable expert. Others might quarrel with his ordering or prefer to include other diseases. This is not a light matter, of course, because of the issue which overarches the whole discussion: namely, justification for terminating pregnancies following diagnosis. Those who categorically reject any abortion can recognize the variations of severity, of course, but are not dissuaded by them. Others make judgments according to prognostications of persistent discomfort of the subject person, brevity of life, burden upon the family, or an unacceptable "quality of life" (however that may be defined).

For professional geneticists, the question of degrees of severity is apparently overridden by the freedom and right of a woman to choose the future of her fetus. The American Society of Human Genetics in 1991 voted by a ninety-nine percent majority to support her choice on two conditions: first, that her fetus "has not reached the point of viability," and second, by professional diagnosis, that it "is likely to have a serious genetic or congenital disorder."[2] Does "serious" mean a condition milder than "severe?" Or are matters of definition also irrelevant? Another recognized authority in the field of prenatal counseling, John C. Fletcher, proposed a usable definition: "By 'serious genetic disease' I mean a disease in which the child struggles for all or the majority of its life simply to survive the disease without adequate therapy, and that the child's chances for human growth and communication would be completely or to a great degree submerged or overwhelmed by the disease."[3] The designation "severe" could then be applied to a disease which certainly causes early death.

The issue of abortion is as inescapable in this discussion of genetics as it is insoluble to everyone's satisfaction. Even within some of the largest religious communities, those having formal doctrines and policy positions based upon theological and ethical perceptions, the issue continues to be divisive and controversial.

The uncontroversial point to make is that the revelation of new data under the aegis of the HGP has a positive value for thousands of families. With information and counseling on the risks or likelihoods of defects, men and women may avoid procreating, or employ methods of assisted reproduction that increase the probability of a healthy baby. Additionally, we can note early progress in procedures of therapy for children with certain diseases.

The fact that some four thousand single-gene diseases are known, but only two hundred can be prenatally diagnosed, suggests the wide field of opportunity for research. These diseases may be classified in three ways: first, diseases for which the gene has been identified and testing is practicable; second, those for which the gene is known, but no testing is yet feasible; third, those for which the gene's location is suspected but not yet confirmed.

This parade of the more familiar genetic diseases passes by with freshly reported successes in identifying and mapping the causes on specific lengths of DNA. When we keep in mind the structure of the

2. *American Journal of Human Genetics* 48 (1991), 1011.

3. John C. Fletcher, *Coping with Genetic Diseases* (San Francisco: Harper & Row, 1982), 131.

molecule, we can understand when researchers delineate stretches of thousands, or even a million, base pairs of nucleotides as the loci for markers of the gene's proximity. Better still, they locate the gene's exact position on the chromosome, thus opening the way to develop testing procedures.

In addition to genetic diseases already mentioned and character-ized, several more have recently been pinpointed. Adult polycystic kidney disease is the cause of thousands of cases of renal failure. It can be diagnosed years before the symptoms appear, but treatment in ad-vance of the onset is not yet perfected. The person's eventual options at present are: either a surgical transplantation of a kidney donated by a compatible family member or a regular regimen of machine-driven dialysis, paid for by a unique and costly program of governmental support. However, the beginnings of therapy by diet and medicine are underway.[4]

Of particular interest to participants in the Houston Conference were the diseases attributed to the X chromosome. A co-sponsor of the conference was the Institute for Molecular Genetics of Baylor College of Medicine, where a dozen or more genes have been mapped. Its leading researchers (C. Thomas Caskey, Arthur L. Beaudet, David Nel-son, Edward R. B. McCabe) specialize in this sex chromosome, on which genes, mutations, and deletions abound and cause as many as two hundred-fifty diseases.

One disease, though very rare, has been much publicized: SCID is short for severe combined immune deficiency. The dramatic story of "David the Bubble Boy" gave identity to the disease, just as Lou Gehrig's name attached to ALS (amyotrophic lateral sclerosis) and Arlo Guthrie's to Huntington disease. David lived all twelve years of his lifetime in a sterile tent, a remarkable if controversial treatment. Ten years later, in 1993, cells grown from his preserved tissue were used in mapping the gene.

Duchenne muscular dystrophy (DMD) causes degeneration of

4. General statements on these diseases, stripped of technicalities, are based on material by C. Thomas Caskey, a presentation to the Houston Conference, and also on his essay "DNA-Based Medicine — Prevention and Therapy," in *The Code of Codes*, ed. Daniel J. Kevles and Leroy Hood (Cambridge: Harvard University Press, 1992), 112-35.

skeletal muscles from deficiency of the protein dystrophin, crippling the person until premature death due to respiratory or cardiac malfunction. It affects one in 3,500 newborn males.

The fragile X syndrome affects one in up to 1,500 males, second only to Down syndrome as the cause for mental retardation. It may also be related to the mental disability known as autism and associated with behavioral difficulties.

Hemophilia A is the dreaded disease of non-clotting blood. It is generally known as the X-linked disease carried by women of royal families, but more recently is feared in the epidemic of HIV-AIDS. The same kind of research which has identified this large gene has led to genetic engineering of the indispensable factor VIII, which inhibits the flow of blood by clotting it.

With an incidence of one in 4,000 male infants, retinitis pigmentosa (RP) is a leading cause of blindness. The retina degenerates and capacity for vision keeps on diminishing until blindness darkens all. This may be delayed but not prevented by vitamin E, as shown in current research.

The most bizarre and unsettling manifestations of an X-linked disease are those of the rare Lesch-Nyhan syndrome. Severe mental retardation is a distressing but not unusual consequence. Most extraordinary, though, is the child's irresistible habit of biting his own flesh to the point of mutilation. He may need to have his hands tied and teeth pulled in order to restrain the biting impulse. The disease may not lead to early death in childhood, so daily care must be extended for up to twenty years.

The better-known X-related diseases are complemented by many caused by genes on other chromosomes. Since it is not intended here to do more than indicate the variety, only some others may be named: myotonic dystrophy, retinoblastoma, neurofibromatosis, thalassemia, Marfan syndrome, Waardenburg syndrome, etc. The list goes on and on. It illustrates the virtuosity of nature in loading the DNA molecule with so numerous and complex a variety of single gene diseases, not to mention those of multi-factorial causes.

The long catalogue also emphasizes the need for comprehensive knowledge on the part of genetic physicians and other counselors, specialists in obstetrics and gynecology, pediatricians, neurologists, primary care clinicians and, very importantly, patients and their families.

The task of learning is immense for specialists, intimidating for non-specialists in health care, and seemingly impossible for patients and the public except in respect to the particular disease which affects them personally.

3. Access and Cost

Given the large and growing body of knowledge which genetics specialists must acquire, there is no doubt that their professional compulsions will drive them to it. Much less certain is the prospect for generalists and family practitioners, especially those of middle age or older, keeping abreast of genetic research. Will they become adept enough to recognize symptoms and know how to treat or to whom to refer? Before long, a doctor lacking knowledge of genetic medicine will be like one in 1945 who had failed to learn about antibiotics.

Access to testing and genetic counseling becomes more urgent as skills in medical genetics rapidly improve. The benefits are most easily available to people living near large urban hospitals and medical schools where expert services are available. A large academic health center with medical faculty, laboratory technicians, and appropriate hospital facilities offers DNA diagnostic and cytogenetic services for various diseases. Networks of clinics in small cities and centers of rural population are also being developed across the nation with the help of state departments of public health. Contrary to what the newspaper and television reports convey, genetic diagnosis is by no means limited to research laboratories.

Improving availability and access to genetic medicine make welcome news; but they are made less gratifying to people of limited means when costs rise too high. The cost of DNA analysis of one sample in a laboratory is about two hundred fifty to three hundred fifty dollars. In some cases the test must be repeated two or three times. Other charges for physician's, counselor's, and clinical services, including the securing of family information, may increase the cost to two thousand dollars. Since not all medical insurances cover prenatal diagnosis, the burden for some parents is beyond their means to pay. This is one more difficult economic matter to be resolved as Americans struggle to achieve an equitable national policy.

While diagnostic and clinical services become more numerous and accessible, there are other kinds of assistance that are not sufficiently well known as yet. These are specialized organizations of national scope that provide information and support services concerning particular heritable diseases. The sheer number of them is comparable to the catalogue of known genetic defects for which affected persons are treatable. There are two hundred twenty-five such organizations included in the 1992 *Directory of National Genetic Voluntary Organizations*.[5] These range in size from a one-person office with a scattered group of supporters to large organizations with huge budgets and dozens of chapters nationwide. It is the frequency of occurrence of the disease that usually determines the size of the organization. All of them disseminate newsletters or publish other appropriate literature. Some raise funds for research. Most offer help in organizing peer support groups for patients and families. A considerable number, about seventy-five, are concerned with general categories of persons (children, mothers, disabled) rather than specific conditions. Considered all together, they constitute a praiseworthy body of uncounted numbers of persons devoted to prevention of disease and care for those affected.

There is another source of personal support for couples anticipating parenthood, whether or not they have familial genetic knowledge which could cause anxiety. It is a potential but as yet untapped resource of vast dimensions: namely, the organized religious communions and churches. No human experience involves more cause for religious interest than the bringing into viable existence of a new child of God and member of the family, the nation, and the human race. It may be the occasion for pondering the mystery of personhood, the wonders of gestation and birth, and the creative power of God; or, to the contrary, it may be fraught with disappointment and tragedy. In either case, birthing is a matter of intense pertinence to religious belief and practice. The new possibilities and opportunities of prenatal genetic testing should arouse the clergy, counselors, and caregivers to a recognition of the importance of the procedures which can assure healthy babies or mitigate the sorrow of disappointment due to unfortunate pregnancies. The next section on counseling will show that only belated beginnings

5. *Directory of National Genetic Voluntary Organizations* (Chevy Chase, Maryland: Alliance of Genetic Support Groups, 1992).

have been made to include genetic concerns within the domain of pastoral counseling and religious ministry. Christian congregations can profitably learn from Jews how education and organized counsel and support have reduced the incidence of the deadly Tay-Sachs disease. Somewhat less dramatic has been the success in America of Greek Orthodox communions in dealing with thalassemia, or of mainly black American churches with sickle-cell anemia.[6] However, ethnic identity and loyalty need not be the only reasons for sensitive religious people to recognize the growing need for including genetics among the regular concerns of religious ministry.

C. Counseling

Counseling has become a prominent profession in modern society. The city telephone directory lists many kinds of counseling services: those which advise on careers, family relations, finance, religion, and other issues — but not genetics. Not yet! People have always, of course, needed information, advice, and comfort from others. As never before, however, in our mobile, frenetic, science-based technological society, they turn to counselors for specific guidance. In the new, high technology world of medical practice — with its jungle of pharmaceuticals with esoteric names and therapeutic procedures of dazzling ingenuity — people often feel lost and confused. Among the most baffling yet promising displays of medical science and art is genetics. And the main access to genetic information and advice is through qualified genetic counseling.

In contrast to its usual connotation of bringing benign comfort and practical help, the phrase "genetic counseling" is often a threatening one, however, for many who need assistance. There is a popular, cheerful scenario in which the wise and sympathetic counselor offers a warm hand, a patient ear, and a quantity of essential information to the comprehending and grateful pair of clients. Like a Norman Rockwell drawing of the visit of the family doctor, however, this contradicts the usual scene. The mood of the meeting is often one of uncertainty. As

6. See Milunsky, *Heredity and Your Family's Health,* 118-24, for discussion of ethnically specific diseases.

one survey showed: "A study of some 900 counseling sessions found that in almost half the encounters, neither client nor counselor was aware of what the other most wanted to discuss."[7] Of course, the experienced counselor learns how to put a client at ease in order to facilitate conversation.

Contrary to another popular notion, very few people seek genetic counseling on their own initiative. Most are referred by obstetricians when there is some reason to suspect an imminent difficulty in a woman's pregnancy. She may be of the age of thirty-five with a higher risk of the fetus's being affected by Down syndrome. She may have already experienced the birth of an affected baby, or elected to terminate a precarious pregnancy. She and her husband may know they are carriers of a disease that has never been expressed by symptoms; or they may know of near relatives who carry or manifest the condition. The reasons for referral are many. Very rationally, some couples seek consultation prior to marriage or, if married, before planning conception. In the new era of unconventional, uninhibited sexual union of teenagers and unmarried couples the purposes of consultation have a somewhat different character. In brief, genetic counseling is a serious, important experience which ought not to be romanticized. It is most often satisfying when discussions are hopeful and the outcomes of tests are favorable.

1. Theory of Counseling

Genetic counselors are of several kinds. Given the rapidly expanding scope of the field, proportionately few physicians qualify to be called experts. These are the ones constantly engaged in both research and clinical practice at medical schools, research centers, and teaching hospitals. The typical counselor has earned a Master of Science degree in Human Genetics (often from Sarah Lawrence College, New York).

Counseling involves a two-way communication of information. One-way teaching by the counselor is indispensable, but it is insufficient without the self-disclosure of the patients' health, personal history, understanding of genetics, emotional disposition, and, in many cases,

7. "The Telltale Gene," *Consumer Reports* (July 1990), 488.

religious and moral commitments. As an expert with long experience writes: "I recommend and practice the total-communication approach. I believe that everyone has a right to know and a freedom of choice. All available information should be given out freely, the whole subject explored, and all matters of consequence discussed. The flow of information should not depend solely upon the questions asked by those who are seeking advice. How could they, after all, anticipate the eventualities?"[8]

In discussing the technique of counseling, people often discredit directive counseling and applaud the nondirective approach. They make it seem as if there must be a clear choice between the two. It is an abstract distinction, far from reality. Everyone in the field recognizes the preeminence of nondirective counseling, as commended and popularized by the psychiatrist, Carl Rogers. No one favors crassly telling the clients what to think, decide, and do. It is common, however, for patients confronted by difficult choices of therapy to ask the physician, "What would *you* do, doctor?" In states of perplexity and anxiety, they are willing to forfeit their much vaunted patient autonomy. Good physicians know the peril of this temptation, and will try to give advice and suggestions in a noncoercive, nonpaternalistic way. The accepted rule in the ethics of doctor-patient relationship is that the patients be given every encouragement to make their own informed choices. Absolute obedience to that rule is difficult to maintain in practice, however.

Counselors normally endeavor to "stick to the facts." They describe the disease and how it is genetically activated; define the options and comparative risks; tell how others have reacted to the same anomaly; give all the information which is pertinent. They then let the patient(s) decide.

The only hindrance to abiding by this standard of strict objectivity is that the counselors are human beings. When doing an experiment in biochemistry, using measurable quantities of cells, chemicals, and electrical charges under controlled temperature and time, a researcher attains maximum objectivity. Even here, however, the situation is modified by subjective thinking and behavior. When dealing with specific problems of acting individuals under variable circumstances it is virtually impossible for a counselor to prevent the intrusion and expression

8. Milunsky, *Heredity and Your Family's Health*, 225.

of his or her personal beliefs, feelings, and biases. Even when there is a determined intention to be impersonal and objective, the pull of a subjective gravity is almost irresistible. This is dangerous but not altogether deplorable. Some degree of subjectivity is inevitable when counselor and patients together, as human persons, are involved.

Clinical case studies always are confined to descriptions of the patients and their conditions. Perhaps each case study ought also to include something about the person who is physician or counselor, who should know how to draw a line between involvement and detachment. From his own long experience John C. Fletcher states: "The consultant in a moral dilemma cannot simply 'step aside' from the recommendation. Of course, clergy and other counselors can avoid getting into this dilemma by not making any recommendation at all. I wonder if the real function of non-directive counseling and moral guidance is to help the counselor never get into the dilemma of 'What ought I to do if the proposed resolution is morally unacceptable?' If you never make any recommendations, then you never have to face the question, except in your own conscience."[9]

2. When Counseling Goes Wrong

How are these theoretical ideas about genetic counseling realized in practice? The Houston preparatory group for the GRE conference sought the answer in extended personal interviews with men and women who had participated in counseling sessions. These persons had been counseled on a variety of cases involving themselves, their children, and such diseases as cystic fibrosis, Klinefelter syndrome, Hurler disease, and Down syndrome, among others. The cases were selected for their variety only. Counselees were not known beforehand to the interviewers, who did not expect to hear such negative reports.

Interviewers had to resist the inclination to generalize about counseling as widely practiced. One couple with Hurler syndrome described their experience as "horrible." "The father reported that he was 'forcibly removed' from the room while genetic counselors spoke to his wife alone, and that upon their return home, having made the decision to

9. Fletcher, *Coping with Genetic Disease*, 114.

49

carry the affected fetus to term, counselors continued to call long distance, urging them to 'terminate the pregnancy.' Both husband and wife described their initial counseling experience in thoroughly negative terms, and recounted that several members of the medical team exhibited extreme insensitivity to the couple's own values and beliefs."[10]

Another couple reported on a Down syndrome case. The counseling physician chose to talk separately with the man and woman. He first told the husband of the suspected diagnosis. Two days later he told the wife. "This physician's unwillingness to deal with the couple as a team created an unfortunate situation where the husband was asked to bear an unnecessary burden of silence."[11]

This carelessness about the manner of informing parents is a dangerous step on the way to inadvertent breach of confidence. As in most medical practice, as well as in various kinds of counseling and confessions to priests, it is axiomatic that strict confidentiality must be maintained, except in rare situations where other persons may be imperiled. A government commission declared: "It might seem that a genetic counselor ought never to disclose information against the wishes of a client, because the counselor's professional obligation is to the client, not to others. Both the law and morality recognize, however, that a professional's primary obligation is in some circumstances subsumed by the need to prevent harm to others."[12]

In a case occasioned by trisomy 18, a very serious disorder, the couple was under strong pressure to terminate the pregnancy. "Although she described herself as being 'in shock,' and she and her husband both reported 'being numb,' they recalled the sense of being hurried by the professionals to make the decision to abort the affected fetus. In the visit immediately following the sonogram, which revealed the anomalies, they said, 'The doctor tried to get us to abort right then.' He gave the wife vaginal suppositories and instructed her to take them that evening."[13]

10. B. Andrew Lustig, "Genetics, Religion and Ethics: The Clinical Connection" (Houston: Institute of Religion, 1992). Photocopied.

11. *Ibid.*

12. *Screening and Counseling for Genetic Conditions,* President's Commission for the Study of Ethical Problems in Medicine and Biomedical and Behavioral Research (Washington, D.C.: U.S. Government Printing Office, 1983), 44.

13. Lustig, "Clinical Connection."

Another interview was concerned not with prenatal diagnosis but with the condition of Klinefelter syndrome in a mature male. This disorder brings on a number of physical and mental abnormalities, chief of which is a confusion of gender. Certain female characteristics, such as breast development, cause obvious problems of identity and social acceptance. This patient, to say the least, found both the doctor who counseled him and the therapist who worked with him to be lacking in understanding of his illness and insensitive toward his feelings of being a social misfit.

The Houston interviewers were dismayed to find that none of the persons with whom they talked had had satisfactory counseling. They knew, of course, that no generalizations could be made about genetic counselors on the basis of so small a sampling. However, they came to agree on one observation: the physicians involved in all these cases were specialists in genetic diagnosis and treatment rather than the art of counseling. The group hypothesized that "patients often express considerable dissatisfaction with quality of genetic counseling by physicians, whether generalists or specialists. Only when further or follow-up genetic counseling was done by trained genetic counselors to whom patients were referred did patient and family satisfaction with quality of counseling rise dramatically."[14]

3. The Religious Factor

One subject about which professional counselors are expected to be reticent is religion. This is somewhat understandable, because it is too much to expect them to be knowledgeable about the numerous, complex, and often contradictory implications of religious belief and practice. It is also ironical, because religious concerns permeate much of the thinking and feeling people manifest with respect to procreation and genetic problems. The issues are settled in advance for those people who are faithful to the teachings of their chosen branches of Judaism, Christianity, or Islam. When they absolutely refuse to accept such alternatives to normal procreation as artificial insemination, *in vitro* fertilization, surrogacy, abortion, or sterilization, their need of counsel-

14. *Ibid.*

ing is mainly for empathy, comfort, spiritual encouragement, and practical arrangements. For others, the guidance offered by their religious communities is of limited or equivocal help. This limitation may be due either to high respect for individual moral autonomy or else because of failure to come to consensus on the problems. In either case, whether authoritarian or relativistic, there should be a place in the counseling process for a pastor, priest, rabbi, or chaplain.

If genetic counselors typically avoid religious matters, and yet if the moral teachings and spiritual direction of various religions are inherent in some genetic problems, the conclusion may be drawn that some pastoral counselors should have an important role in association with genetic clinics. Reasonable as this equation may appear to be, it has scarcely been put into effect as yet. The large, standard *Dictionary of Pastoral Care and Counseling* (Nashville: Abingdon Press, 1990) gives barely seventy words to genetics! This deficiency may be overcome when a large number of clergy can be persuaded to appreciate the rapidly advancing importance of genetics in the maintenance of health and life.

Clergy are often just like millions of citizens in one respect — namely, their ignorance of genetic science, diagnostics, and medicine. They have not been stimulated or had opportunity to learn the basics. To be sure, even the basics are difficult to learn. But so is the operation of a home computer. People can learn if they have good reason to try. At the least, as Fletcher urged more than a decade ago, ministers can learn enough of genetics to counsel couples before they are married and to know when to refer them to genetic experts for the more technical discussion.[15]

Clergy are generally well prepared to learn to be helpful to individuals, couples, and families confronted by problems of living with genetically disordered children. For more than two decades, most accredited theological seminaries have required students to take courses in clinical pastoral education, augmenting them with field experience in hospitals and special institutions. Some graduates then become hospital chaplains or licensed family counselors and psychotherapists. It is obvious that such people are superbly prepared to collaborate with genetic counselors, not only on strictly religious matters but on a range of personal and psychosocial issues which usually arise.

15. Fletcher, *Coping with Genetic Disease,* 50-74.

Most clergy, moreover, are the shepherds of congregations. Chaplains have their hospital populations and professional religious counselors have their clients. But each pastor of a congregation ministers to a "fellowship" of many members, wherein may be found not only those in need of genetic counseling but those who can assist in ministering to them. In many churches, more and more emphasis is being given to the concept of "caring community," in which members assist one another. Hence the marked increase of specialized mutual support groups of the unemployed, the divorced, the bereaved, the disabled, and the addicted. These are hopeful developments which can readily embrace those with genetic problems. Some of the Houston interviewees told of such congregational support when making a hard decision about abortion.

There are times when a pastor's counsel regarding theological questions is more important than advice regarding a specific decision. The two most frequently and earnestly posed questions are: "Why suffering?" and "Why does God allow so many tragedies?" The fact that these are ageless, familiar cries of humanity does not neutralize their poignancy and mystery. No believing mother, looking at the malformed or sickly infant in her arms, can avoid thinking the question of how the God she trusts as infinite goodness and power can allow this genetic catastrophe to occur. Is she being punished for her sins, as some religions teach? Is her fidelity to God being tested, as Job's was, so that she might become a better person through adversity? Are there dualistic supernatural powers of good and evil at work, to the evil one of which she has fallen victim? Is she simply being victimized by the biological fact that all organisms are subject to random chance in an earthly environment which is ruled by chemical processes, has no purpose, is dangerous to all and utterly indifferent to human desires? In that case, the problem of theodicy, as it is called (literally "the justifying of God"), is denuded of meaning because in fact there is no God. But what if the virtue of love is a cosmic reality, and the Creator suffers along with the mother and her deformed, retarded child for reasons which "God only knows?"

This is an enigma for which none of the traditional answers is emotionally satisfying or rationally coherent. And yet, people in distress cannot avoid it. They look to the spiritual advisers, chaplains, pastors, and theologians to say the right words of consolation and encouragement. If such counselors are to rise to their new challenge and opportunity, they have the "obligation to reflect upon, and to formulate, however haltingly, their own theological understandings of the mystery of suffering," so as to avoid "the twin evils of numbness or glibness in the face of tragedy."[16]

The idea of bringing together in cooperation the genetic and pastoral counselors is not a novelty. Some have offered training seminars for clergy and prepared helpful literature.[17] But the need is overwhelming for such initiatives.

D. Prevention and Treatment

1. An Ounce of Prevention . . .

Prevention of illness is the highest ideal of medicine, followed by treatment and therapy, followed by care and comfort. To revert to the military metaphor, there would be no war on a certain genetic disease if the disease itself were eliminated. This scale of priorities seems obvious enough, until one considers how prevention is to be effected. The rational answer to that question is to eliminate as nearly as possible the breeding of genetically affected infants by people who, as it is said, "pollute the gene pool." If all who are known carriers would desist from procreating, and if their gestating offspring that test positive for diseases were terminated, so much cleaner the human pool. Such is the cold logic of eugenicists, of course: a logic so thoroughgoing and consistent that it is widely repudiated as horrendously inhuman. In the background of declarations of eugenic policy one hears of martial condemnations of the *Lebensunwertigenleben* — the life unworthy of living.

It is a conventional exaggeration, of course, to imply that all the advocates of eugenics would agree with the Nazi solution to genetic problems. That is the ideological hard line. But there is a nonideological soft line which is distantly related to it and which commends itself to

16. Lustig, "Clinical Connection."
17. Pioneering educational programs for clergy have been conducted at Georgetown University Medical Center by Frank D. Seydel and Robert C. Baumiller, S.J.

many quite decent people. It is the presumption that it would be best for everyone if most of the unborn which are, say, on Dr. Milunsky's scale of severity were not allowed to be born. This may be the implicit, if not explicit, idea which informs many counseling sessions. A British medical geneticist challenges his colleagues to face squarely the question of the primary aim of counseling: "If the primary aim of medical geneticists includes the welfare of all those with genetic disorders, but not the secondary prevention of genetic disease by termination of pregnancy, how do we judge the ethical issues that surround prenatal diagnosis? Are we not obligated to give precedence to the welfare of existing affected individuals rather than to the 'prevention' of their successors?"[18] Or do some admit that the primary aim is indeed prevention for reasons of relieving families and society of the burdens and costs of caring for the ill and disabled?

The most effective efforts to reduce the incidence of a certain disease have been those within populations which meet three qualifications: a relatively small, homogeneous population, a fairly high standard of living, and a high literacy rate. Under such conditions, there can be developed a common motivation to prevent the transmission of a certain disease which is prevalent within that society. Frequently cited as an example is the community of Jews having ancestral roots in Eastern Europe. Their particular affliction is Tay-Sachs disease. An equally gratifying and impressive story of prevention comes from Cyprus. The disease specific to Cypriots and Greeks and other Mediterranean people is named for "sea" and "blood": thalassemia. The Greek population of Cyprus meets the three criteria. The government and the Orthodox Church have led a program of public education, counseling, and clinical service. The church made testing mandatory before accepting couples for marriage, and also provided health facilities. Within one generation, the incidence fell from one per thousand births to zero in 1986. As of 1992 there had been no more reported cases.[19]

---

18. Angus Clarke, "Is non-directive genetic counseling possible?" *Lancet* 338 (October 19, 1991), 991.

19. Frasso Parrisiadou, "Public education, population screening, genetic counseling, and antenatal diagnosis, the four independent aspects of Cyprus programme for the prevention of thalassemia," *The Quality of Life in the Mediterranean Countries* (Palermo: Istituto Siciliano Bioetica, 1993), 127-35.

A window of encouragement is also opened whenever a new way is found to prevent a heritable disease from taking effect *in utero,* or to mitigate and even correct its symptoms after birth. Very few instances of such successes are so far reported, but there is no lack of research. An example of the first sort is the treatment of women who are at higher risk for having a child with a neutral tube defect, notably spina bifida. Following treatment, both before conception and after, with folic acid and vitamin supplementation, the incidence of the serious disease can be significantly reduced in offspring.[20]

More dramatic is the bold new method of preventing a deleterious gene from expressing itself in an embryo. This has been done by the remarkable technique of testing zygotes. The initial procedure involved three couples in London who had previously produced children with cystic fibrosis and had a one-in-four chance to do so again. They were willing to be subjects in an experimental effort to bear infants free of the disease. Ova were removed from the women and fertilized in Petri dishes *(in vitro)* by their husbands' sperm. On the third day the embryonic cells were in clusters of four to eight. Only six hours remained for them to split and double in number again.

An ingenious method of infinite delicacy employed a hollow glass needle only one-fifth as wide as a human hair. One cell of each embryo was removed for biopsy and DNA testing. The rapidity of the testing by using the so-called polymerase chain reaction (PCR) made this possible within those few hours. By analysis, the researchers found and discarded the cells containing two copies of the nucleotide deletion of the gene causing cystic fibrosis. An embryo of just one of the three couples was thus found to be free of harmful gene mutation and the embryo was transferred to the woman's womb. Implantation took place normally; she became pregnant, and at term delivered an infant girl with no sign of cystic fibrosis. This was the first such achievement of preventing CF prenatally by blastomere surgery.[21] The same procedure

20. Andrew E. Czeizel and Istvan Dudas, "Prevention of the first occurrence of neural tube defects by periconceptional vitamin supplementation," *The New England Journal of Medicine* 327:26 (December 24, 1992), 1832-35.

21. Alan H. Handyside, Mark R. Hughes, et al., "Birth of a normal girl after in vitro fertilization and pre-implantation diagnostic testing for cystic fibrosis," *The New England Journal of Medicine* 327:13 (September 24, 1992), 905-9.

enabled an infant to be born free of Tay-Sachs disease in January 1994. Lesch-Nyhan syndrome, hemophilia, Duchenne muscular dystrophy, and fragile X syndrome may also be overcome in this way.

The obvious virtue of this method is that it artificially prevents a heritable disease from affecting the child. To those who object to abortion the genetic engineers who succeeded in this experiment can say that this is actually a way to avoid consideration of terminating pregnancy. To those who object to violating an embryonic "person" the answer is given that no cell in the zygote of four or eight cells, nor the zygote as such, is an individualized human entity. Twins can and do develop. The uncertainty remains until nidation, or implantation, of the embryo in the woman's uterine wall on the fourteenth day.

In presenting his experiment to the Houston Conference, Mark R. Hughes said those who do research in genetics, reproductive medicine, and embryology are well aware of the moral, religious, and legal questions their work gives rise to. Of course, one's first concern must be is for the couple who will beget and conceive the child. Their formal consent must be genuinely, not nominally, informed by knowledge and understanding of relevant data; and it must be given freely, without coercion or deception. The procedure itself must be recognized as both feasible and free from risk to the human subjects. Professional codes of ethics, institutional review boards, and federal regulatory agencies are to provide the controls against imperfect procedures.

Experts are not infallible, however, and space is open for public debate. A recognized authority on legal aspects of genetic medicine, John A. Robertson, wrote eight years before the pre-implantation diagnosis had been done: "If the embryo has been identified as having a gene defect, which will lead to its being discarded or born damaged if carried to term without treatment, then gene alteration of the embryo with the intent of transferring it to a uterus and bringing it to term is therapeutic and beneficial in intent."[22] But critics ask whether that worthy intent is not outweighed on the ethical scale by the risks that

---

22. John A. Robertson, "Genetic Alteration of Embryos," in *Genetics and the Law III,* ed. George J. Annas and Aubrey Milunsky (New York: Plenum Press, 1985), 119. For an enlightening symposium by eight persons on the social and medical implications of pre-implantation diagnosis see *Hastings Center Report* 22:4 (July-August 1992), S.1–S.20.

the experiment entails. One risk is that further procedures will not have the happy outcome of a good birth. And what is to prevent successful researchers from moving on toward more prodigious and ethically debatable experiments, using similar laboratory methods to modify the DNA of sperm, ova, and embryonic zygotes? The usual objections to *in vitro* fertilization are intensified here by questions of superovulation, wasting embryos, freezing them or using them for nontherapeutic experimentation. It is evident to some that the dark warnings against "tinkering" with the biological components of procreation are more than justified; the slope is indeed slippery, they say, and the ice is thin.

Robertson remains unimpressed by the fear of a slippery slope that allows unethical abuses of preimplantation selection of blastomeres. In a 1992 essay he admitted the possibility that embryonic "de-selection" could be practiced for less serious reasons than avoiding disease and that it opens the way for germ-line therapy, which most oppose. Even so, he maintains that preimplantation analysis and "nontransfer of embryos" is ethically permissible "because embryos are so rudimentary in development they are not generally viewed as having interests or rights."[23]

Hughes himself called for urgent debate on the issues raised by this new procedure, observing that "science is being pushed by technology and is pushing society and cultures and established religions to think on all these areas. What was true for Copernicus is true for the Human Genome Project." His challenge was accepted by a religious bioethicist, Paul D. Simmons, who is a Baptist. He disputed a common idea that there is "a radical distinction between the artificial and the human," and then argued, further, that "the moral grounds for believing that whatever is 'natural' is 'good or godly' and whatever is 'artificial' is 'ungodly' are extremely shaky. The biblical notion of stewardship seems to bring technology and humanness together. People recognize God as the source of all wisdom, including that which makes it possible to enhance human well-being and serve human need. People are not 'creators' but stewards; they work with the givens of God's creation. There is no manufacture of anything *ex nihilo* in the manipulation of genetic material. Technical skills are wed to nature's processes." He then gave reason to endorse the

23. John A. Robertson, "The Human Genome Project and Protective Liberty," in *Gene Mapping*, ed. George Annas and Sherman Elias (New York: Oxford University Press, 1992), 222.

preimplantation diagnosis, including the necessity of discarding the adversely affected zygotes. "The embryo is treated with regard and concern because it is being deliberately planned. It is accepted and anticipated as a child to be. It becomes a patient as a venture between woman, or couple, and physician. Together they seek the well-being and health of this child." If things go amiss, however, Simmons sees no theological objection to discarding an embryo. This is what happens when nearly half of all pregnancies end in miscarriages. "A genetically flawed embryo viewed under a microscope is not different intrinsically from such an embryo discarded with a monthly menses. . . . If we can be prayerfully grateful that nature discards the fatally flawed, we should be morally responsible enough to do it knowingly and willingly."

Finally, Simmons expressed a liberal religious perspective on the status of the fetus, making no appeal to belief in the sanctity of its life. "God has given us the grand opportunity to discover how to prevent, not just try to treat or cure, the illnesses that plague humankind. The embryo will thus be treated with due regard without our lapsing into a posture of respect or reverence. Learning to prevent genetic illness is as moral as Jenner's learning to prevent smallpox. The bacteria that bring illness and death are not unlike the deleterious genes of DNA. As long as these afflict the body of humanity and threaten the genetic future, science has a moral mandate to pursue knowledge through research that will include embryos obtained through IVF. We cannot choose either passivity or ignorance toward affliction and claim to be moral."[24]

Whatever other theological and ethical considerations may follow the announced success of the preimplantation experiment, one ought not to assume that this procedure will soon become routine. Eventually it may follow the lead of IVF, which has enabled hundreds of infertile couples to have children. Like IVF, however, this procedure's path may be strewn with many huge bills for unsuccessful efforts, with accompanying broken hearts and disillusionments. But this cautionary note does not lessen the import of the experiment for progress toward both prevention and therapy.

24. For explication of the theological basis of his views see Paul D. Simmons, *Birth and Death: Bioethical Decision Making* (Philadelphia: Westminster Press, 1983).

2. . . . Worth a Half-Pound of Cure

People who predict the future of genetic medicine engage in a kind of high wire act. To maintain their stance they must avoid falling two ways. On one side is the peril of being too credulous about imminent achievements; on the other, the peril of being too hesitant. Mass media journalists tend to fall the first way; science writers are more inclined to fall the other way.

A fine book on gene therapy was commissioned by the National Academy of Sciences and the Institute of Medicine. It described the procedure by which a child born with the very rare lethal adenosine deaminase (ADA) deficiency could be treated by gene replacement in bone marrow. The predicted year of this first experiment on a human was 2007. The book was published in 1988.[25] The actual experiment took place in 1990. After more than three years of carefully reviewing the protocol, the Recombinant DNA Advisory Committee of NIH, chaired by LeRoy Walters, granted permission to W. French Anderson and R. M. Blaese to proceed with clinical trials. In September 1990, Anderson began treating a four-year-old girl named Asanthi DeSilva, who would otherwise have died from infection against which she had no immunity. This required a transfer into her body of infusions of modified white blood cells and retroviruses conveying the disease-resistant gene. Another girl was treated in January 1991. The good effects were observed very soon. In March 1992, Anderson was pleased to tell the Houston Conference that both girls, with periodic attention, were enjoying excellent health. In fact, when members of the family of the younger girl all came down with flu, she alone did not.

The barrier to human gene therapy had thus been broken, opening the way for treating patients with other blood diseases, cystic fibrosis, diseases of the liver and the central nervous system, cancers, and AIDS. The list will be extended as more and more experiments succeed. The prophesied era of genetic medicine has truly begun.

Such notable scientific victories do not just happen. Anderson's personal preparation of tireless research extended over more than thirty years. Who can say what really will be done in this field by the year

25. Eva K. Nichols, *Human Gene Therapy* (Cambridge: Harvard University Press, 1988), 1.

2000? The mapping of genes under the HGP and international associates is ahead of projected timetables. Some forms of treatment, as for cystic fibrosis, are being tried much sooner than the geneticists expected. The number of protocols approved by the Recombinant DNA Advisory Committees of NIH for human therapy rose to twenty-four by February 1993, with twelve more pending final decisions. Four more had begun in other countries.[26] Cancer in its various forms commands the research in thirty-four of these protocols. Five of them focus on cystic fibrosis. The others are devoted to seeking therapy for ADA deficiency, HIV, liver failure, hypercholesterolemia, and hemophilia B.

Gene therapy is not all of one kind. Single gene diseases that cause deficiencies in the body's immune system or dysfunctioning abnormalities of the blood are one kind. Therapy consists of removing the marrow of the patient's bone — a delicate and painful process — and then exchanging the diseased marrow cells for cells that have been genetically altered to function properly.

Attacking cancers by means of genetically engineered agents is a different kind of gene therapy. Steven A. Rosenberg of the National Cancer Institute, a colleague of Anderson's, undertook human clinical trials in 1991. The patients were a young woman and middle-aged man, both of whom suffered from advanced, metastasized melanoma, or skin cancer. They were each infused with a hundred million white blood cells which conveyed copies of an anti-cancer-producing enzyme, called tumor necrosis factor.

Scientists at the M. D. Anderson Cancer Center in Houston were granted permission to proceed with two protocols. The first is intended to counteract the spread of lung cancer, caused by smoking tobacco, which activates the oncogene named K-ras to manufacture tumors. A neutral virus injected in the lungs serves as a vector to deliver the arresting gene. Potentially this therapeutic treatment could benefit tens of thousands of patients suffering from deadly lung cancer. The second procedure is designed to make it possible for leukemia patients to profit by chemotherapy without the painful side effects which it usually

26. *Human Gene Therapy* 4:3 (June 1993), 391-98. By October 1993, as the field expanded, the number of approved protocols had risen to fifty-two. Manal A. Morsy et al., "Progress toward Human Gene Therapy," *Journal of the American Medical Association* 270:19 (November 17, 1993), 2344.

imposes. This will also involve bone marrow transplant and irradiation, as in other cancer treatments, but will introduce a modified gene to block tumorous growth.

Another indirect application of genetic technology to cancer treatment is the use of interleukins produced by engineering recombinant DNA. These are effective deterrents to the spread of melanoma and lymphoma.

The gap of time between the mapping and cloning of a particular disease gene and the perfecting of practical therapy may be years. Persons who suffer from the disorder, along with their families, are at first often elevated by hopefulness of a new treatment and then deflated and depressed by the delays. That is why a pioneering researcher like Francis S. Collins advises people not to be too expectant and impatient. Some say it is better not to be tested for a late-onset disease, such as Huntington disease, until an effective treatment is made available. Soon after he and his colleagues located the famous gene for cystic fibrosis in 1989, Collins indicated that treatment for CF might be years in the future. In fact, however, only three years were to pass before the NIH gave permission to three teams to commence clinical trials. Since the physical distress of CF is caused by secretions that block the lungs, it seemed natural to attack the disease by the simple method of spraying through the nose. The spray contained a common cold virus which had been genetically altered to convey a healthy gene. Next, it was administered by dripping down the windpipe to the clogged lungs. The congestion was relieved in just hours. The Genentech Corporation intends to market the spray.

These therapeutic treatments, here described so briefly, are not yet cures. They may be life-extending and allow a good state of health, but will require continuing medical attention to sustain that state. An ounce of prevention is still to be preferred to a pound of therapy and even half a pound of cure. There is validity, then, in the advice of geneticist Arthur L. Beaudet, who wrote of CF: "The prospects for somatic gene therapy are a legitimate cause for optimism for patients and families, but not so definite that families should be encouraged to undertake the birth of additional affected children based on the assumption that a 'cure' will be available."[27]

27. Arthur L. Beaudet, "Genetic Testing for Cystic Fibrosis," *Pediatric Clinics of North America* 39:2 (April 1992), 225.

Stories of clinical trials on human patients necessarily omit information that affected persons and families are eager to know. When will the therapy be generally available? Will it be accessible? How much will it cost? What side effects might there be? Are there any serious ethical questions about the procedures? Only the last question can now be answered with relative certainty. No. Except perhaps for Jehovah's Witnesses, no ethical or religious problems inhere in various kinds of gene therapy involving the body (somatic) cells. The developing appropriation of them will be recognized as good medical practice.

As French Anderson has observed, however, ethical problems *will* arise in the employment of the same method for nontherapeutic purposes. "It is fine to talk about therapy and curing kids," he remarked, "but what we are really doing is manipulating the genetic information of our bodies." And that is a matter with which our exploration of the uses of genetics continues to be concerned.

CHAPTER THREE

Genome and Some Social Issues

A. Is the Human Genome Project beyond Criticism?

THE POPULARITY of science fiction is not due mainly to its unreal fantasy, but rather to its tantalizing suggestion of real possibility. Whether in the form of sophisticated literature, comic book cartoons, movies or vulgar tabloids, predictions of technological wonders to come cannot all be dismissed as fantasy. Today's imagination becomes tomorrow's invention and next week's technological reality. The fault with some of the writers of science fiction is not that their predictions are too fantastic to be taken seriously but rather that their imaginings are often too modest and uninspiring. Even such writers as Aldous Huxley failed to foresee nuclear submarines, space travel, microchip computers, or dozens of electronic devices to which we are already accustomed. The cartoon hero, Buck Rogers, was a figure predicted for the twenty-fifth century; but already before the end of the twentieth some of his tools and feats appear to be commonplace.

One consequence of the astonishing explosion of composite technology is that we are scarcely astonished by the newest inventions. We have come to take them so much for granted that we casually expect still more from researchers, inventors, and engineers. There seem to be no limits or boundaries which will inhibit human achievement. Credulous popular attitudes toward the achievements of technology engender technophilia, which inspires technolatry and willing submission to technocracy.

Such uncritical credulity and expectation appear especially to accompany the new biotechnology and genetic medicine. Public approbation of the Human Genome Project may not be unanimous, but it has largely triumphed over skepticism and opposition. Even so, the arguments which have been raised against the project since its inception are still pressed by its critics. The points they emphasize are principally of three kinds: scientific, economic, and moral. All three are of concern to people who give high place to religious standards of special concern for the weak and poor, of distributive justice, health, and social well-being.

"The project to map and sequence the human genome," wrote ethicist William F. May, "threatens eventually not only to alter the human germ line and therefore human destiny, but also more immediately to alter the nature of the organized scientific community and therefore the nature of scientific inquiry."[1] The main alteration would be — or is — the change of the discipline of molecular biology from conventional science to "big science." Just as the needs of the nation for electrical energy and military armaments transmuted atomic research into a massive scientific enterprise, so on a smaller scale the Genome Project has mobilized hundreds of researchers, both the famous and the inconspicuous, in a concerted effort.

Defenders of the project do not take pride in its large scale as such, but rather in the practical matter of getting the job done more effectively, efficiently, and sooner than uncoordinated research could achieve. So claim Nobel laureates James D. Watson and Walter Gilbert. Genome leaders Victor A. McKusick, Francis S. Collins, Leroy Hood, and others point to the project's early record of achievement: the accelerated pace of mapping and sequencing, the building of successive discoveries upon their predecessors, the computerized banking of research data, and easy access to it. Their optimistic assessments are not shared by some other prominent geneticists, however. Leading opponents such as Nobel laureate David Baltimore of M.I.T. and Rockefeller University, the late Bernard D. Davis of Harvard Medical School, and Martin Rechsteiner of the University of Utah have complained of this tectonic shift. They hold that independent research by small teams

---

1. William F. May, "Genome Research: Power, Organization and Money." Unpublished.

of researchers, guided by individual motivations and insights, can accomplish the decoding of DNA with less cost to taxpayers and results equivalent to those of the HGP. They deplore the exclusion of younger researchers from the opportunities of securing federal grants of modest but indispensable amounts. Thousands of aspiring Ph.D.s and postdocs are now, and will be, discouraged from pursuing careers in molecular biology, it is claimed.

A more cogent scientific complaint is that the stated goal of mapping *all* genes and sequencing *all* base pairs cannot justify the expenditure of so many available human resources, even apart from the public money. This is because the proportion of DNA in a molecule which actually determines necessary protein synthesis is extremely small: less than five percent of the whole. The other more than ninety-five percent is now generally called "junk" DNA and presumed to be useless. Why, then, use up the time of scientists whose work could be more profitably employed? The accusation may seem to be unanswerable by defenders of the project who have to admit ignorance of the function of the DNA in question. But in the spirit of scientific adventure they can still say, who knows? Perhaps continuing research will reveal the function and value of all parts of the molecule.

The scientific concerns also have economic implications. The two categories cannot be separated. That is why the commercialization of genetic research is both disturbing and inevitable. A clean line of separation cannot be drawn between the public and private sectors of gene research and application. If that were possible, one could say that all the findings of projects funded by the government (NIH and DOE) are public property. No funded scientist could own equity in commercial ventures which were made possible by government grants. But such is not the nature of much scientific research in America. Numerous companies which manufacture and market instrumentation, genetic testing equipment, genetically engineered medicines, agricultural and animal products are staffed by persons who have been enabled by government assistance to learn their profession and to pursue it.

The economic factor is seen to be still more complex when the question of ownership is encountered. Who owns a gene? Who is entitled to secure a patent on a gene? A commonsense answer might be: nobody. Because genes belong to organic nature as a whole, they are discovered, not invented or manufactured. So it may seem to those who assert, often on theological grounds of divine creation, "you can't patent life." But the issue is of such a commercial magnitude that a three-way struggle is engaging the NIH, commercial corporations, and advocates of common, public ownership. The financial rewards are potentially immense for those who can gain exclusionary patents on genes of particular importance. Expert analysts predict with confidence that genetic technology, which is already big business, will soon rival or exceed such fields as heavy industry, electronics, and computers.

The patenting of genetically modified "life forms" first became a reality in 1980, when the Supreme Court found in favor of scientist Chakravarty's claim to own an original strain of "oil eating" bacteria. Seven years later, a mouse was born in the laboratory of Philip Leder and patented because it had been genetically altered to be uniquely useful in cancer research. Since then, numerous patents have been awarded. The judicial barrier having been removed, the issue has become, not whether to patent, but who should be entitled. The NIH made a policy decision and took steps in 1991 to implement the policy by applying for patents on all genes identified by its researchers. Critics were given a defensive explanation that could be called either patriotic or nationalistic. The policy was intended to protect American possession of genetic secrets against competition from countries such as Great Britain and Japan. However, the Clinton administration negated the plan.

Such protectionism is disputed by scientists who want to avoid allowing commercial interests to disrupt international cooperation. In 1990, James D. Watson and Robert M. Cook-Deegan wrote: "The human genome project is inherently international. It necessitates a coordinated world-wide effort to share resources, to spread the burden of funding research, and to take advantage of unique genetic resources that can be found anywhere in the world."[2] Watson's disagreement over restrictive patenting was in part the reason for his resigning the position of director of the project in 1992. The troublesome episode gives aid but not comfort to critics who had warned against allowing commercial interests and the political bureaucracies of "big science" to fragment, hamper, and confuse the effort.

2. James D. Watson and Robert M. Cook-Deegan, "The Human Genome Project and International Health," *Journal of the American Medical Association* 263.24 (June 27, 1990), 3324.

In ways which have been described above, the Genome Project has been faulted for reasons of scientific methodology and for complicity with American economic interest. Whether or not these are valid objections remains debatable. But no huge-scale scientific enterprise, dependent upon public funding, can be impervious to such criticisms.

But questions of another kind are also raised, questions about moral and social values relating to the health of all the people. The problem of allocation of scientific, medical, financial, and human resources pertains to genetic research and medicine just as much as to other health-related actions. Religious convictions about egalitarian care for all persons undergird the call for fairness and justice. If the Genome Project should succeed in reaching its stated goals by the year 2005, will the success have been purchased at the expense of more urgent public health needs? Does it contribute to a kind of elitism which will benefit a small portion of the population while leaving a majority unserved? Does the much-publicized project convey to the people an exaggerated idea of genetic medicine as a panacea for most human disease, giving the impression that effective therapy follows very soon after the isolating and cloning of a particular gene?

The current critical talk of genetic discrimination and stigmatization is justified and necessary, but includes two dimensions, not one. The more prominent social problem is obviously the widespread bias against persons of all kinds of impairments due to congenital causation. Fortunately, people are becoming better educated, sensitized, and responsible with regard to the genetically disadvantaged who constitute a large segment of the population. Society has come a long way from the time when such persons were customarily closeted or institutionalized or, earlier, treated as burdens, freaks, and monsters. More humanitarian progress is yet needed and may now be expected.

The second cause for concern is less well recognized. It is the disposition of some persons who support the HGP to think that radical improvements in the diagnosis and treatment of genetic defects and illnesses will by themselves bring about a healthier condition for all. It is an attitude expressed in the field of genetics which is already prevalent in our technological society — namely, that scientifically achieved medicines, devices, and procedures can eventually resolve most problems of poor health. It ignores the reality and effect of adverse environmental and societal conditions wherein the root causes of dysfunction and illness are located.

How should the priorities of human gene therapy be weighed in the balance with broader public health needs such as sanitation, immunization, drug and tobacco control? What meaning does high-technology genetic medicine have for people living in relative or abject poverty? These kinds of questions were posed at the Houston Conference in responses to the address by W. French Anderson on his first clinical trial of gene-replacement therapy for a very rare disease. Paul Billings, of Veterans Affairs Medical Center, Palo Alto, California, declared: "As a physician and citizen, I feel for the adenosine deaminase (ADA) deficient child and respect the urge to relieve suffering in this rare simple genetic disorder. In many ways, this is an adequate justification for most measures. *But, there are more scientists studying this condition than children who have it.* I do not think that progress in genetics will likely soon touch the lives of those with *common ailments* fostered by neglect, malnutrition or lack of education.

"There are many similarities between past and contemporary conditions: scientists *exaggerate* the impact of their work, are blinded by their *ambition, profit* quietly from their research; those affected with genetic problems are not forced into sterilization, though this still occurs in some settings, but nonetheless suffer genetic discrimination. The label 'genetic' can mean no health or life insurance, or worthless policies leading to excess morbidity and mortality; no job or the loss of freedom to switch jobs (to move up the ladder); loss of privacy, other rights and entitlements, and prejudice from many quarters. This is a kinder, gentler eugenics.

"But the result is an ever growing *underclass* suffering not helped by the genetic revolution. Who will benefit under the current system from gene therapy? And we still try to explain behavior, crime, and alcoholism with genetic explanations when the structure of our society and social conditions seem so clearly etiological. Isolation and stratification within our nation, often promoted by governments, seems to be increasing."

Billings continued: "I wish Dr. Anderson well as he struggles with what is human and tries to help children with rare simple genetic illnesses. But be not deluded, somatic genetically-based therapy will more often be used for enhancement and to enrich physicians than to relieve suffering from rare disorders. And many even simple genetic

70

disorders cannot be treated in this way because the damage occurs *in utero*. Will we see more fetal manipulations? And even more conditions incur problems too early for *in utero* intervention.

"Genetics has taught this century two great principles for ethicists and theologians to mull over: human variability, and interaction between many factors as the best description of most human conditions. We will never derive the full benefits of progress in human genetics until these principles lead to: a public consensus to study and spend our resources to reduce the *burden of common environmentally induced illness* as well as rare conditions; protection of the right of privacy, the right "not to know," and the right to healthcare; and a populace which rejects being divided on biological grounds, and accepts, fosters, and cares for the diversity, complexity, serendipity, and mystery which is in fact the wellspring of our humanness."

Skepticism about the publicized benefits of the HGP was also expressed by Abby Lippman, an epidemiologist at McGill University, Montreal.

"Genetic engineering is being promoted in North America as the way to cure disease, to understand illness. But whose disease and which illness will be conditioned by prevailing attitudes about individuals, their bodies, and their roles. Developed and practiced in a society that is gendered, racist, classist and systematically discriminates against those with disabilities, it would be naïve to think that how and for whom genetic engineering technologies are developed will not reflect these attitudes. Genetic engineering is itself also imbued with values. For example, to add to or subtract genes with the idea of changing an anticipated phenotype is not only too simplistic biologically, but it is necessarily to view the living organism, ourselves included, as open to design, as (re)programmable. It is to view our offspring as objects for us to fashion, our various diseases and maladies as curable with but a biomedical 'fix.'

"To 'do' genetic engineering, then, is to express values that lead to certain ways of thinking about subjects, objects and the relationships between them.

"If we acknowledge, then, that genetic engineering is more than a biomedical/technical activity, that it is not neutral and that it necessarily influences how we think about and experience ourselves, our children and others, how we devise plans for healing and curing, how we define and deal with what we shall call 'different,' how we interrelate

71

with our surrounding worlds, are we not led to think that it cannot but alter us as humans?"

In summary, while the HGP and related research enjoy the unqualified approval and support of a probable majority of informed and involved persons, there are reservations about its full implications which give pause to such acclaim.

B. Concerns of Women

The preeminent role of females in reproduction is obviously played from the time an ovum, which is large, is fertilized by a spermatozoon, which is tiny, through the nine months of gestation to birth and beyond. From the time of implantation of the zygote in the endometrium of the uterus, this embryo/fetus is truly "a part of a woman's body," even as it develops toward more and more viability and independence. Then comes the usually wonderful but demanding task of motherhood. In a minimal sense, the male's supplying of a sperm cell is all that is required of him. Unhappily, too many men act upon that assumption.

Reflecting upon this commonplace knowledge, we can understand and appreciate the often angry complaint of women that the whole field of human genetics is dominated by men: from the bench-bound researchers to the obstetricians and gynecologists. Not only in the HGP but in general experience, as participants in the Houston Conference said, "The insights and experiences of women are often overlooked, despite the fact that they typically carry a heavier role in decision-making about reproduction and child care and spend more time with children who suffer from genetic diseases." Women's concerns about genetics are not merely a plank in the platform of feminist politics.

Some of the disproportionately smaller participation of women in genetic science is starkly visible; some is subtle. The professional positions of research administrators and team leaders are mainly held by men; that is a clear fact. More subtle and seldom noticed is the way the norms of health and behavior have been defined by research with white males as subjects, and middle-aged ones at that. So declared Ruth Ellen Bulger of the Institute of Medicine:

"Assuming all people are exactly alike, or that one position is the norm and all other positions are deviant, devalues and harms certain individuals in our society. For instance, we are now beginning to recognize that we are obtaining large scale clinical trial data preferentially from one subgroup, the middle-aged white male. It is now realized that acting as if the biological human norm is the middle-aged white male disadvantages other diverse groups. It is not entirely clear whether the use of males as subjects of clinical research resulted from a lack of questioning our unstated assumptions about what is the norm; or resulted from concerns of various parties about liability issues related to the fetuses of women who may be pregnant (especially accented by the lack of interest and knowledge concerning analogous effects of various treatments on male reproductive capacity); or else from the convenience in research design which may be disrupted by the varying hormonal states of women; or from women's care-giver responsibilities; or from a devaluing of diseases of women; or from the fact that the majority of research investigators are white males; or from other unrecognized factors. However, such unquestioned assumptions in health research have led us to use disproportionally the data obtained from male research subjects as standards for care; yet the true generalizability of these data remains unclear. It has left us with a lag between what is known about the treatment of white men and what is known about the treatment of minorities, women, and children. This lag is particularly important since, as a society, we lack adequate mechanisms rapidly and systematically to assess the adverse effects of drugs, treatments, and procedures once they have entered the realm of medical care, hence, moving the risk of liability in the use of treatment more to the physician who treats these populations.

"In her review on the use of male subjects in clinical trials, Rebecca Dresser proposes that an oversimplistic concept of equality might be related to the use of homogeneous study populations since, 'In many social contexts, advancing the ideal of equality requires decision-makers to disregard gender, racial, and ethnic differences among people. If all human beings have equal moral value, then in some sense they are identical and interchangeable. . . . Gender, racial, and ethnic differences that affect health and disease must, however, be recognized if women and people of color are to have truly equal access to the health benefits of biomedical research.'[3]

3. Rebecca Dresser, "Wanted, Single, White Male for Medical Research," *Hastings Center Report* 22 (1992), 24-29.

"Dresser asks: 'Are we making similar mistakes in the area of human communication and human moral development from the same kind of unquestioned assumptions? I believe we are and, therefore, there are important reasons to understand differences in how people speak, think, and determine their value systems.'"

Dr. Bulger places much emphasis upon the multicultural nature of American society. People of various languages, nationalities, classes, races, and cultures clearly constitute the population as never before, and the process of diversification continues apace. All of these illustrate the *e pluribus* aspect of the population, but not the *unum*. Women occupy a very large part of the diverse society, in spite of which they are treated politically and sociologically as one of the minorities. Women and people of all the other categories are contraposed over against white males. The reason for this rivalry is deeper than a shift in social attitudes. It is found in the physical and psychic nature of women, now coming to expression for the first time on a broad scale. Dr. Bulger continues:

"While progress in women's rights has brought about an increase in women's ability to control their reproductive history, some womanists [i.e., feminists] fear that new genetic technologies might become only another mechanism of social control, making women into 'hand-maidens' of society, passive vessels in which the male seed grows. Although the societal decisions affect women on the deepest personal levels, they see decisions being made for them by others, often by those with more power, and who frequently are male. Barbara Rothman notes, 'prenatal diagnosis is also very much a part of the history of patriarchy, men's struggle to gain control over women's reproductive capacities.'[4]

"However, others consider these technologies to be beneficial. Testing can provide data that will help them make better decisions about the conduct of their lives. They stress the positive aspects of knowing the answers that such tests might give, since knowing about the absence or presence of genetic differences or risk factors might provide reassurance during a given pregnancy or help in decision making concerning marriage partners, family planning, therapeutic procedures for the fetus or preparations for the arrival of a baby with special problems, or with the termination of a pregnancy. How can one best balance the qualities of

4. Barbara Katz Rothman, *The Tentative Pregnancy* (New York: Penguin Books, 1986), 23.

caring and responsibility with personal autonomy and rights in a society with institutions frequently characterized by injustice and lack of caring? A variety of insights come from women of differing ages, races, ethnic and socioeconomic groups, and religions."

As has been noted, women's special interest in genetics is not limited to problems of childbearing. There are genetically transmitted diseases which victimize only women. Most frequent and dreaded is breast cancer and its related lethal disease, ovarian cancer. Intensified research related to the HGP has been revealing new evidences of the etiology of the disease and its variations of symptoms and age of onset. Thanks to investigations of data about hundreds of women and their families, Dr. Mary-Claire King of the University of California, Berkeley, and others are learning some of the unique characteristics of breast cancer. They find that it cannot be explained by the simple cause and effect of a single gene. There is a gene on Chromosome 17 which is still being sought as one inherited cause. Its mapping and cloning will be of immense importance, of course, as a major achievement of the HGP. But another cause is non-inherited — namely, genetic mutations which occur in the body cells because of environmental factors. These accompany changes wrought by modern industrialization and the life-styles it has introduced. "Breast cancer is a disease of technological society," writes Dr. King: "women at risk for the disease tend to be well educated, well-fed, healthy women who have hormonally rich tissue."[5] While she cannot fully explain why this is so, she suggests with some confidence: "All we know for certain is that growing up healthy increases one's risk of breast cancer. So do having children later in life, beginning to menstruate early, and entering menopause late — three trends in the industrialized West that extend the period in which a woman's body produces unopposed estrogens."[6]

Commenting on this intensified research, Dr. James D. Watson observed, "Suddenly, we've had to realize that breast cancer may be the most common (inherited) disease there is."[7]

5. Mary-Claire King, "Localization of the Early-Onset Breast Cancer Gene," *Hospital Practice* 26.10 (Oct. 15, 1991), 125.

6. *Ibid.*, 126.

7. Michael Waldholz, "Stalking a Killer," *Wall Street Journal*, Dec. 11, 1992, A1.

Continuing her discussion of women's concerns, Dr. Bulger cites with approval the thesis of Carol Gilligan concerning the distinctive difference between women and men. Her 1982 book, *In a Different Voice: Psychological Theory and Women's Development*, has become a virtual bible for women who write in fields of social ethics and theology.

"She found that women constructed moral dilemmas as a problem of care and responsibility in relationships rather than of rights and rules. She also found that in considering the way women deal with moral problems, absolute judgments yielded to the complexity of relationships. Women, thinking contextually, analyze by context, not rights. Gilligan studied a series of women when they were making a decision about whether to undergo an abortion and then again at the end of the following year. By analyzing their construction of the abortion dilemma she found that the moral problems for women were defined as an obligation to exercise care and to avoid hurting others.

"For Gilligan, the moral imperative for women that emerges is an injunction to care, a responsibility to discern and alleviate troubles of this world. For men, the moral imperative is an injunction to respect the rights of others and thus to protect from interference the right to life and self-fulfillment."

Among theologians since about 1970, there has been vigorous analysis of prevalent behavior of women as contrasted to that of men. Psychological studies, often implicitly interpreted through dramas and novels, have decisively drawn distinctions consistent with Carol Gilligan's insight. Theologians ask whether or not the characteristic differences between the sexes, perceived beyond those of physiology and phenotype, are due to centuries of evolving social habit, or whether the differences were present in creation "from the beginning." Some interpreters of the biblical affirmation of creation "in the image of God" propose the concept of complementarity, as distinct from a "unisex" or androgynous view of humanity. That is, all humans bear the stamp or image of the Creator but not independently of sexual difference. The simple assertion, "male and female he created them" (Genesis 1:27), is taken to mean that God purposed the mutual community of a woman and man to give full expression to their essential humanity. Male and female physiologies and psyches are indeed different, but humanness is a unity.

Could this pre-scientific, biblical anthropology be translated into terms of genetics? That is, is there a consonance between biblical insights about human life and the unfolding knowledge of how human beings are constituted?

The biblical reading of unity in complementarity is rejected vigorously by feminist theologians who, first, disagree with the textual exegesis of Genesis, and, second, insist that full humanness is not found only in the mutuality of male and female. For them and for many others, the ideal of heterosexual marriage as taught by Judaism and Christianity is not an appropriate paradigm for all persons as a matter of nature. It is merely a social construct which combines affirmation of gender difference with a belief in the unitive standard of marriage. Moreover, feminists argue, even though a religious doctrine of complementarity ostensibly implies full equality in personal, social, and political spheres, it has not prevented the continuance of centuries-old patriarchal patterns of social organization. The authority and power of men over women have been operative for so long a time that it has seemed self-evident to many — especially men — that these are genetically rooted in masculinity. This debate is now seen to be of widest personal and social importance.

C. Truth and Consequences

"The truth shall make you free." So goes the most commonly misquoted text of the Bible. This saying of Jesus is misquoted when it is thus truncated and offered as a universal maxim. The first part of Jesus' saying is a condition for the second: namely, "If you continue in my word, you are my disciples, and you will know the truth," and then the truth which comes by faith — this "truth will make you free" from evil, sin, and death (John 8:32). When "truth" is defined as accurate, verifiable information, knowledge of it may not always be liberating. Often it is the cause of troubles.

Truth-telling in the field of genetic counseling and medicine is problematical. So is truth-keeping when it means the protection of privacy and confidentiality. And truth-seeking is a problem when certain persons are trying to gain information about one's genome which can be damaging to reputation or opportunity. We need not be so cynical as the movie producer whose motto was "We have nothing to fear but the truth!" But experience shows plenty of reason to be very careful about the acquisition and uses of information, and also about the exercise of one's right to privacy and defense of confidentiality with respect to the genetic information.

The main cause for concern today is not whether the information one receives about his or her genetic endowment is accurate. Inaccuracy due to faulty diagnostic testing is relatively rare. When it does occur, for example, in examination of chorionic villus tissue or amniotic fluid it can lead to unfortunate consequences such as the aborting of a genetically healthy fetus. Or the converse may happen when a false negative report is given. However, the infrequency of these episodes minimizes fear of laboratory error.

The far greater concern is how the accurate data will be interpreted and employed. In some circumstances the disclosure of true data results only in a satisfactory outcome. Prospective parents can learn that some fears of their infant's manifesting spina bifida or cystic fibrosis are needless after all. Or they can terminate a pregnancy, however tragic that may be, in order to avoid the birth of a grossly malformed or severely retarded baby. We recognize, however, that the definition of a "satisfactory outcome" to a pregnancy varies widely according to differing evaluations.

Some very embarrassing, or even catastrophic consequences may follow the testing of a man's DNA to determine paternity. The accuracy of so-called "DNA fingerprinting" is at least 99 percent. In court cases of inheritance or child custody the testing of a husband's blood sometimes proves that he is not actually the father, as was supposed. Even the wife may not have suspected this unsettling fact, much less the children. The accuracy of DNA analysis for forensic purposes is so well established that courts in many states accept it as definitive. When informed of the nonpaternity of their husbands, some women are reported to have maintained a fretful silence rather than face the adverse consequences for their families.

Genetic identification can be ascertained either *in utero* or at birth. Caskey reports that "3-5% of our genetic referral pregnancies have fathers different from ones indicated by the mother." Two cases are described as examples of the problems requiring DNA fingerprinting.

A 37-year-old female requested prenatal diagnosis for her pregnancy risk of chromosomal aneuploidy. Following counseling and chorionic villus sampling procedure she requested additional consultation. She indicated the pregnancy could be by either her husband or a second partner following an affair unknown to the husband. She would continue the pregnancy if by her husband but not by the second partner. She planned to discuss the decision with her husband.

A 19-year-old female requests *in utero* DNA fingerprinting after pregnancy possibly caused by a gang rape. She had been attempting to purchase crack when she was abducted and raped by at least two men. The event was not recorded with the police and only recently revealed to her husband. She and her husband had been using condoms. They stated that the pregnancy would be terminated if DNA tests showed that the husband was not the father.

In these cases the issue is not confidentiality as such, since the husbands were informed. However, they illustrate the torturing strain on a woman to decide whether to reveal the shame of infidelity or the shame of being victimized. Depending upon her own character as well as upon social factors, the DNA identification provides the exact information on which a difficult choice may be made.

Keeping genetic secrets is a problem in the public sphere as well as in the family. The price paid for services of omnipotent computers which store and process all sorts of data about individual persons and their affairs is the forfeiture of privacy. Medical records, like banking transactions and assets, purchases by credit cards, and tax returns, are all vulnerable to inadvertent disclosure or investigation by public authorities. Some data are legally accessible, others supposedly protected.

This characteristic of our cybernetic society permits the increase of obstacles and threats to genetic privacy. The two contexts that are chiefly discussed in regard to privacy are employment and insurance. They are prominent because a great majority of citizens are, or will be, touched by them. They pose problems that are plain for all to see, requiring neither sophistication nor subtlety. Will I be refused a job because of a known genetic susceptibility to a certain disease? Will I be unable to secure medical insurance for the same reason? The questions obviously arise when a person currently shows symptoms and manifestations of certain diseases, such as diabetes, which do not suppress occupational activity. Some disabilities are evident only occasionally, such as epilepsy; but they appear on medical records and cannot be concealed from examiners. Moreover, the strict rules of insurance carriers against withholding or distorting information about one's medical history when making application make dissimulation very difficult.

Quite different is the matter of confidentiality in cases of pre-symptomatic or late-onset diseases. These are inherited diseases that cause no symptoms before early middle age. Among them are Hunting-ton disease and adult polycystic kidney disease. The possibility that one is potentially afflicted may be suspected or inferred by reference to older family members who have suffered the effects of deteriorating tissues and organs, leading to death. Or else, thanks to recent research and new methods of testing of DNA, the onset can be accurately predicted.

Extremely serious decisions are required of persons, spouses, fami-lies, physicians, genetic counselors, and, perhaps, pastors. If the genetic information is initially known only to the diagnostician, who is then entitled subsequently to know it? The person in question? Yes, but some who take the tests relent and decline the results, preferring uncertainty to constant apprehension. Where results are given to the person tested, the concentric circles of confidentiality need to be defined with respect to the effects on other members of an extended family or offspring conceived out of wedlock. Genetic testing can show which parents, siblings, or near relatives are carriers of diseases; and according to Mendelian calculus it can show what the chances or odds of producing affected offspring will be. As people learn more about genetic science and genetic counseling becomes a more common practice, there will be clearer understanding of which persons should have access to such information.

The aforementioned problems of securing medical insurance and life insurance will remain vexed and debatable until the companies agree on a generally uniform policy, if indeed they will. Insurance companies are not agencies of public service or welfare. They are intended to earn profits. However, they are indispensable to the maintenance of medical care and health, and so must express a sense of public responsibility. Insurance carriers cannot avoid taking risks, but it is the nature of their business to keep risks of pay-out at a minimum. Dependable predictions of the onset of inherited diseases reduce risks for the insurers, and at the same time put insured persons in jeopardy of having to pay higher premiums, accept exclusion clauses, or suffer the loss of any coverage.

These are just a few of the many strands of the national health care insurance knot which must be untied.

According to the dire prediction of Roger J. Bulger, "The genome project . . . raises the specter of differentiating our insurance groupings according to an assessment of genetic risk, a specter so unpalatable and unjust that our society could not tolerate it."[8] An optimistic proposal to avoid so deplorable a situation for the populace is seriously recommended by C. Thomas Caskey, who asserts that "pre-symptomatic diagnosis is *not* disease and therefore should not be considered prior existing condition."[9] This would remove a cause of discrimination against many people based upon conditions expected to occur rather than already in evidence. But its adoption would depend upon some broadly agreed policies in a national health insurance program which allow just and fair profits for the insurers.

From a religious perspective, all these problems of privacy and confidentiality are of high importance and direct relevance. Even though insights and judgments of both secular and religious nature are intermingled and often contribute to the same attitudes toward the uses and abuses of genetic information, religious convictions often give added force and insistency. This can be said of honoring the integrity and autonomy of the individual person by protecting confidentiality; respecting the wishes and well-being of other persons who are affected by disclosure of genetic information; having concern for those who for genetic reasons suffer unjust discrimination in their attempts to gain and maintain both employment and medical insurance.

Such humanitarian and ethical commitments also undergird the state and federal legislation which is intended to mitigate the injustices of a free-market approach to employment and insurance. During the last three decades the tide of legislation and regulation has been rising for the purpose of protecting classes of citizens from discrimination. Along with ethnic minorities, the elderly, women, and persons with disabilities are being shielded from arbitrary exclusion from insurance

8. Roger J. Bulger, "How the Genome Project Could Destroy Health Insurance," *The Washington Post,* August 4, 1991.
9. C. Thomas Caskey, "Presymptomatic Genetic Diagnosis — A Worry for the U.S.," in *Gene Mapping,* ed. George Annas and Sherman Elias (New York: Oxford University Press, 1992), 183.

pools and the job market. Although the disabled are virtually invisible to the majority of Americans, they actually constitute an estimated population of forty-three million. The widening extension of the civil rights movement has specifically embraced persons who experience disabilities or handicaps due to genetic effects or illnesses. Certain states have stricter laws against bias than do others; but all are subject to the Americans with Disabilities Act (ADA) of July 1990. As this law is put into effect by stages until 1994, employers having a minimum of fifteen employees will be obligated to comply with its tenets.

Specifically with respect to genetic disabilities, for example, the ADA prevents employers from requiring pre-employment medical examinations and questionnaires which would cause disclosure of epilepsy, diabetes, hypertension, or other non-apparent diseases or susceptibilities. One can anticipate numerous problems which will arise in the implementing of this law. Disputes, contesting interpretations, and litigation can surely be anticipated. But justice and human and social benefit are the objectives clearly being sought. As a legal expert in these matters, Dr. Mark A. Rothstein, asserts: "To the extent that the Human Genome Project increases the possibility of disclosure of confidential genetic information, coercive genetic screening, invasions of privacy, or genetic discrimination, then I think that we must be vigilant to ensure that the legal system, medical ethics, corporate culture, and public policy clearly and definitively reject such incursions."[10] It could well be added that religious bodies ought to use their immense numbers of members and considerable influence on public opinion to augment that rejection.

As the scope of concern for confidentiality is reduced from the wide social dimension to the personal one, the individual patient and physician come into focus. The question of the most acceptable kind of relationship which should link the patient and his or her doctor generates much discussion and literature, with particular focus on truth-telling. The current consensus would seem to favor tact, candor, and clarity on the part of the doctor. "Tell it to me straight," says the patient in a television drama, and the paragon of a physician does so with sincerity and kindness. Will the kidney keep functioning or is a trans-

---

10. Mark A. Rothstein, "The Genome Project and Employment," *Legal and Ethical Issues Raised by the Human Genome Project,* ed. Mark A. Rothstein (Houston: University of Houston, 1991), 382.

plant indicated? Does the biopsy show the colon to be cancerous? These are typical questions put to internists and surgeons.

Now comes the new practice of genetically-directed medicine, bringing more complexity to the answering of inescapable questions about diagnosis and prognosis. The doctor is challenged not only to disclose true information to the patient for the sake of both the patient's health and the rule of honesty; he or she must also exercise prudence and discernment concerning how much of the known information to share, what to withhold, and with whom else to share it. This caution is in order for two reasons. First, the doctor's primary concern for the "best interest" of the patient may mandate a limitation on "the whole truth and nothing but the truth." Second, the serious concern for other members of the patient's family may impose restrictions. In other words, the medical dictum "Do no harm" can collide with the rule of telling all the facts of a case. However, this collision does not render the physician dumb. Words of information and counsel must be spoken despite the dilemma.

It would be instructive to know what physicians are actually saying to patients and what their attitudes are toward the difficult cases which are presented to them. In order to find out what kinds of counsel are actually given, John C. Fletcher and Dorothy Wertz conducted a survey of more than one thousand doctors in twenty-five centers of genetic medicine in twelve countries. They spoke only with doctors, not genetic counselors with master's degrees. This was not due to any bias against the latter professionals, but only because of the varying credentials required of them in different nations; this would frustrate comparisons. Six hundred seventy-seven persons answered the detailed questionnaires. Since they averaged fourteen years of experience in the field, their responses were considered highly representative. In the Houston Conference of 1990, Dr. Fletcher presented the data as gathered and interpreted.[11]

Regardless of nationality or culture, geneticists recognize the serious difficulties of maintaining confidentiality and their "duty to prevent unconsenting disclosures of the patients' genetic diagnoses and health prognosis."[12] Likewise, they all see that such third parties as

11. The conference presentation was based upon an article by John C. Fletcher and Dorothy C. Wertz, "Ethics, Law and Medical Genetics: After the Human Genome Is Mapped," *Emory Law Journal* 39.3 (Summer 1990), 747-809.
12. *Ibid.*, 763.

insurers, employers, and government agencies which request personal information raise two related questions: should these parties be given the data deliberately for the benefit of the patient or relatives, or should no disclosure be made at all? The typical cases which arise illustrate the dilemmas:

> "(a) The geneticist knows, but a married couple does not yet know, which one has transmitted a disorder to a child;
>
> (b) Chromosome tests reveal that a phenotypical but infertile female has an XY (i.e., male) genotype;
>
> (c) Tests reveal false paternity, and the identity of the biological father is a secret;
>
> (d) A geneticist is aware of previous elective abortions in the context of a marriage and the husband does not know;
>
> (e) Disagreements arise between geneticists about interpretations of laboratory findings and an abortion might occur if disclosure of the disagreement occurs;
>
> (f) Disclosure of a genetic diagnosis to a vulnerable or fragile individual may carry a risk of psychological harm."[13]

Respondents for the most part expressed agreement with the principle of respecting the patients' autonomy in deciding what to do in response to the information given them; they also agreed on the corollary principle of not imposing on patients their own values and judgments. Yet, those principles are inevitably conditioned and qualified in practice by the counselor's own discretion or moral commitment. It would be a discretionary judgment when the geneticist decided not to reveal the paternity other than that of a husband, lest unhappy consequences for the mother, the child, other relatives, and the marriage bond itself should follow. And a moral judgment would be one by which the doctor intended to discourage the female patient from considering an abortion. In other words, the doctor may acknowledge criteria of higher authority than utter objectivity and confidentiality. In fact, the survey revealed that a great majority affirmed these exceptions.

Some hospitals and clinics for women have a stated policy of not performing prenatal diagnosis for congenital diseases or abnormalities

13. *Ibid.*, 764.

unless women agreed in advance that they would terminate an adversely evaluated pregnancy. The ostensible rationale for the policy is to avoid needless use of diagnostic personnel and clinical resources. It is, therefore, interesting to note that 85 percent of the geneticists in eleven countries disputed such a policy and felt obligated to perform the sonograph scan, amniocentesis, or chorionic villus sampling without such a condition.

The traumatic and exasperating condition of a married couple's infertility poses a different sort of problem. Is the doctor's duty fulfilled after he or she has found a genetic reason to avoid childbearing or has explained the physical causes of the inability to reproduce, such as oligospermia or closed fallopian tube? If *in vitro* fertilization would enable the wife to conceive, should this difficult, expensive, and still risky procedure always be recommended? If so, only with husband's sperm, or perhaps with a donor's (usually vendor's)? Or in cases of the wife's inability, by a surrogate's uterus on nine months' contract? There are other variations on the theme of what is variously called assisted, artificial, or noncoital procreation to avoid predicted risks and dangers. The survey revealed wide disagreements among the genetic physicians. Less than half, for example, would counsel maternal surrogacy, except in the United States, where two-thirds would do so. The reasons behind such inhibition are varied. In some countries, though less so in America, the Roman Catholic prohibitions of artificial insemination, *in vitro* fertilization, embryo manipulation, and surrogacy are strongly influential. Many Orthodox and Protestant Christians as well as certain Jews share the Catholic position. But American Catholics exhibit more disagreement with their Church's teachings than do Catholics elsewhere.

A particularly sensitive issue with respect to confidentiality and truth-telling in prenatal diagnosis is that of gender selection. Even many advocates of the so-called "pro-choice" policy do not extend the abortion liberty to gender selection. And Protestant churches which generally recognize the legitimacy of the individual woman's choice nevertheless draw the line of transgression when gender selection is proposed. Here it is not the will of the prospective parents but the inviolable life of the fetus which prevails.

The issue is especially ambiguous and vexing for women with a militant commitment to their rights, solely as women, to make abortion choices. When they learn of attitudes toward female births in China and India, where in some places the reported chance of aborting females is ninety-nine times greater than for males, their sense of human outrage prevails. The ambivalence is not limited to feminists. Dr. Fletcher admits his own change of mind. When gender selection became practicable in 1980, he opposed it on grounds of human value; but then he reversed his attitude on grounds of autonomy. By 1990, however, at the Houston Conference, he was a passionately vociferous opponent of gender selection.

The problem of truth-telling and confidentiality in relation to gender selection rests with the physician. Will he concur with the parents' request to find out what the gender of the fetus is, and then tell them? Or will he, having learned the truth, refuse to answer their questions?

Drs. Fletcher and Wertz, while opposing abortion for gender selection, were nevertheless disinclined to favor legislation against it. This would infringe upon the general legality of abortion choice, they fear; so they propose no rule but a strong admonition to control the practice. "Geneticists have no duty," they conclude, "to cooperate with parental desires to abort for gender selection" for three reasons: "(1) gender is not a genetic disease, (2) equality between males and females is violated, and (3) sex selection is a precedent for eugenics." Moreover, it "discredits the public image of prenatal diagnosis and medical genetics."[14]

In conclusion, the survey data and the researchers' observations make it clear that the problems of keeping genetic secrets cannot be resolved simply by the rule of non-directive counseling and a professed respect for telling the truth. Many cases occur wherein diverse and complex factors mandate discernment and prudence in disclosure. The widening field of genetic medicine substantiates the challenge to geneticists to keep working out the moral implications of this field of practice.

D. A Danger of Knowing Too Much?

Public apprehension concerning the danger of scientists "knowing too much" about molecular genetics is in some sense compounded by the

14. *Ibid.*, 788, 790.

generally low level of scientific literacy in our culture. People who are inadequately informed or poorly conversant with basic science feel both intimated by the expertise of the experts and cut off from any understanding of the relevance of scientific breakthroughs to their own lives.

There are, however, well-informed, articulate, and thoughtful critics of the runaway pace of scientific research; some come from the ranks of scientists themselves. For these, "knowing too much" may indeed pose a serious threat. There are two general causes for anxiety: cost and abuse.

Even the richest nation on earth cannot pay the cost of all possible research and development. Vigorous opposition to certain projects in outer space, however bold, heroic, and potentially rewarding, is prompted by convictions about humanitarian justice in allocating resources. Billions for a space station, and nothing for the essential needs of urban populations? Even the relatively modest budget of the HGP is criticized for this reason. (Much stronger was the argument against the super-conductor super-collider in nuclear research, causing it to be terminated.) "We cannot afford such knowledge," say the critics.

Potential or probable abuse of knowledge is an equally cogent factor, whether in the acquiring or the uses of it. When human values are grossly abused in research, as in the tolerated crimes of German Nazi and Japanese medical scientists fifty years ago, most contend that we cannot pay the moral cost. The same may be said of research for developing chemical and biological or even atomic weapons. Writers of science fiction imagine stories of disasters caused inadvertently, or by fiendish intention, using techniques of genetic engineering. But we do not need the caricature of "the mad scientist" to teach us the dangers inherent in trying to know and do everything of which our most prodigious minds are capable. This is why regulatory agencies are needed to assess and oversee biological research funded by the government. Likewise, ethics committees and institutional review boards are needed to protect human subjects of experimentation; animal subjects are now strictly protected, too.

The idea that limits should be set upon knowledge in the human biological sciences is in continuity with an ancient intuition. The primal prohibition, or taboo, imposed upon Adam and Eve was against eating the fruit of the tree of knowledge of good and evil, lest they "become like God." The Greek myth of Prometheus proscribed human efforts to seize the energy of divine fire rather than the power of moral discernment. Like "man's first disobedience" in Eden, the stealing of fire from the gods represented the human creature's presumption to be god-like. In both myths, the punishment came swiftly and decisively: expulsion of Adam and Eve from the garden and chaining of Prometheus to an island rock under pounding waves. Warning stories about the dangers of an excessive thirst for knowledge are in fact ubiquitous in Western culture. In medieval legends of "the philosopher's stone," people are enticed with the (futile) hope of a knowledge which would allow them to transmute lead into gold. And Marlowe's Dr. Faustus gambles his soul's eternal destiny for the fulfillment of a quest for knowledge — and loses.

These familiar stories have taken on new meaning with the rise of modern empirical science, attaining unprecedented relevance during recent decades. If the appetite for knowledge became ravenous during the Renaissance in Europe, it has been insatiable in the modern era. Then, the largest library, that of the Vatican, contained about sixty thousand volumes plus manuscripts. Now, the Library of Congress numbers books in the millions and journals in hundreds of thousands. In addition to the quantity of knowledge preserved in print, the amount stored in computerbanks defies imagination. The future of knowing seems to be boundless.

In the temples of science it is regarded as brash, heretical, and, for some, enraging when one proposes that boundaries be set. Is it not axiomatic that the human intellectual quest should be pursued without constraint? Quite simply, no. And in the special case of genetic science either regulation or voluntary restraint is bound to be necessary. So suggests an astute writer, Marc Lappé, in his essay entitled bluntly, "The Limits of Genetic Inquiry." Because the uses of scientific information are seldom well known at the successful conclusion of a first stage of initial research, he writes, "there will continue to be a struggle between those who want science to march forward without restraint and those who would monitor its direction in order to assure utility of the data acquired or to minimize its adverse consequences."[15] Lappé's intent is clearly not to impede or fetter genetic science as such; rather, it is to

15. Marc Lappé, "The Limits of Genetic Inquiry," *Hastings Center Report* 17.4 (August 1987), 6.

deflate some excessively pretentious claims for genetics' variable success in overcoming diseases. "Possibly because of a deep-seated need for diagnostic certainty," he observes, "most people seem to view DNA probes as offering a virtually fail-safe diagnosis." They make decisions on procreation or therapy, therefore, "on a false sense of absolute predictability."[16]

There may indeed be a valid case against presumptuous or poorly supported claims of genetic knowledge and what can be accomplished on the basis of it. As a group which is both well informed genetically and critically reserved about the HGP declared: "The most that the complete sequence of an organism's genes can tell us is what proteins that organism can make. Such a list of ingredients cannot tell us how they will interact and operate together."[17] This judgment is true insofar as it pertains to the physical status of an organism, such as a human. But it leaves open for investigation and discussion the important question of genetic effects upon human behavior.

The Nobel laureate in genetics, Walter Gilbert, predicts a time when all the information necessary to a complete, comprehensive description of an individual human will be micro-recorded on a compact disk. A person will hold up a CD and say, "This is me." But Gilbert writes, "This will be difficult for humans. We look upon the human race as having not only tremendous variation but also infinite potential. To recognize that we are determined, in a certain sense, by a finite collection of information that is knowable will change our view of ourselves."[18] Gilbert's prediction of a total-information CD of one's genome is conceivable. But his belief that everyone's individual persona can be reduced to the function of genes is vulnerable to serious refutation.

The Archbishop of York of the Church of England, John S. Habgood, addressed the Houston Conference on the provocative subject,

16. *Ibid.,* 8.

17. Council for Responsible Genetics, "Position Paper," *Issues in Reproductive and Genetic Engineering* 3.3 (1990), 293.

18. Walter Gilbert, "A Vision of the Grail," *The Code of Codes,* ed. Daniel J. Kevles and Leroy Hood (Cambridge: Harvard University Press, 1992), 96. Gilbert's bold predictions are elaborated in "Sequencing the Human Genome," *Human Genome Project: Ethics* (Bilbao, Spain: B.B.V. Foundation, 1991), 45-51.

"The Perils of Trying to Know Too Much." He was bemused by Walter Gilbert's early and frequent use of the Holy Grail as an analogy of the HGP (The "Holy Grail Project"?).

"Borne up by such rhetoric it [the Genome Project] became the unstoppable quest, the ultimate search for the essence of humanity, the blueprint for understanding human biology. No doubt a certain amount of hype was necessary to persuade the politicians to fund it. But there is a quasi-mystical element in the way it was presented which made the word 'grail' strangely appropriate. The grail of medieval legend was indeed symbolic of the quest for the secret of life. It was also about magical powers. It has strong moral and religious overtones. But above all the grail was systematically elusive; it was the quest for it which became significant rather than the hope of finding it. I wonder how much search for the grail of human genetics will in time be seen to share these same characteristics — both good and bad."

Dr. Habgood was a biologist and pharmacologist early in his career, and has written perceptive books on the relation of science to theology. For more than a decade he chaired The World Council of Churches' program on social and scientific issues referred to in our first chapter. Concerning the HGP he said: "I am not technically equipped to discuss the pros and cons of complete sequencing. I can see the value of building up a vast data base as a kind of reference map, despite the frequent claim that only about three per cent of it will convey useful genetic information. But, against that, I can also see that the larger the data base the more difficult it is to devise ways of handling it, especially when, as now seems likely, parts of the work are going to be contracted out to commercial interests. I can see the challenge of climbing the equivalent of a biological Mount Everest 'because it is there.' But then, I am also conscious that the best science has about it a certain elegance and economy, which the mind-blowing tedium of large-scale sequencing at present seems to lack. I can see the point of postponing much of the sequencing work until the technology is available for it to be automated. But if in the meantime attention is focused on those parts of it which are medically and biologically most important, I wonder how much will be lost if the full work is never done. That ninety-seven per cent of the DNA sequence now labeled 'junk' worries me. Does the fact that no function has been found for it mean that it has no function? And if so, what sort of evolutionary explanation might there be for such a high level of redundancy?

"I believe it is healthy that the aims of the exercise should change as it progresses, not least so as to keep in view those human questions about its purpose which are apt to drop out of sight when a scientific project begins to turn into a technological race. The accumulation of massive amounts of information is not knowledge, though it may provide a basis for knowledge. Knowledge is more than an abstract pattern in the mind or in the computer. It is an understanding of what to do with such patterns, how to use them. It is a claim to be able to take responsible decisions about some more or less reliable bit of the natural world. And where that knowledge relates to human beings, it is important that its connections with other aspects of human life are not broken or ignored.

"The point I am making applies to specialized knowledge in general. It is always part of a larger human-based understanding and set of purposes. But genetic knowledge has its own additional and peculiar problems in that the significance to be ascribed to it in the life of the complete organism is seldom totally clear. Where there is a one-to-one relationship between some identifiable genetic characteristic and some specific human trait or disease, then obviously that genetic information can be profoundly significant for that human life. But, as we know, most relationships are not of that kind. The combined effects of multiple genes in both normal and abnormal development rapidly blur the ability to trace exact connections. Even more important is the fact that genes are not simply creating structures, but controlling process. The history of an organism, therefore, both in terms of the interactions between its parts and in terms of its interactions with its environment, is an irreducible factor in its having become what it is. There are historical connections to be traced, which cannot merely be subsumed into descriptions of chemical and physical causation, any more than the story of evolution can be reduced to such terms. And what is true of organisms in general is uniquely true of human beings."

The archbishop used schizophrenia as one possible example of the complexity of factors causing full manifestation of the inherited genetic disposition. The information about the gene's presence and location must be conjoined with knowledge of conditions and attitudes within the family and immediate society. Religious beliefs are often influential.

The onset of the illness is then determined by "an interaction in which personal history and social relationships play an indispensable part." He explains further: "What therefore does our genetic knowledge give us? Merely one factor in a long and tangled story. In some instances it may be the decisive factor. Central to the work done hitherto is the list of diseases in which genetic abnormalities seem to be life-determining. Even so, it is quite a short list. As it is extended to include a wider range of diseases, and still further to include normal human traits and characteristics, the lines of communication between genetic chemistry and human consequences seem increasingly tenuous. At every stage there are interpretations, interactions, and historical processes, so much so that the idea of drawing a clear dividing line between heredity and environment seems not just increasingly unreal, but increasingly irrelevant. Our knowledge of the basic chemistry of life undoubtedly tells us something. In assessing its significance, however, we need to be aware also of what we do not know, and in the nature of things cannot know. High-sounding language about the essence of humanity confuses the building's blocks with the finished product. The fact that we share ninety-eight per cent of our genes with chimpanzees does not mean that there is only a two per cent difference between being chimpanzee and being human."

There is no peril in knowing the very astonishing fact that a comparison of human DNA and chimpanzee DNA shows so little difference. This is well attested and accepted. The peril, such as it is, is in attempting to quantify human nature. Take away certain genes which constitute one-fiftieth of your DNA molecule and you are a chimp! Add forty-nine chimp genes to one human gene and *homo sapiens* results! Frivolous as it seems, this mode of thinking about human identity is not unusual. Some philosophers assert that a fetal human has no more value than a fetal pig — and they *do* resemble each other. One may as well say that the eight- or sixteen-cell zygotes of many species are of equal worth because they look alike.

The magnitude of differences among species may be greater or less than external appearance and behavior suggest. The same may be said of variations within the human species as a whole. Responding to Dr. Habgood's address, Ronald Cole-Turner said we must be prepared to be not only informed but wise about interpreting new genetic data. The research under the HGP "will give us a molecular norm by which to measure genetic differences precisely. We will learn not just that there is a 1-2% difference between human beings and chimpanzees, but just how much genetic difference there is among human beings, differences of gender, of ethnic groups, and within groups." He asks, "How will we absorb this research into a new cultural synthesis, especially in an atmosphere of revived ethnic hostility and crimes of hate?" Like other new knowledge, genetic knowledge can have a destabilizing effect upon human societies. Some people therefore have fears about the social implications of genetic information. Yet, risks of acquiring knowledge must be taken. The final word about human nature and behavior has not been spoken."

Dr. Habgood's own address concluded with the observation: "In the study of human life the confusion between building blocks and finished product is particularly disastrous. One of the most striking characteristics of human life, as actually lived and experienced, is its open-endedness. To be human is to be unfinished and free. This is a theme well explored in Christian theology. 'It does not yet appear what we shall be, but we know that when he appears we shall be like him, for we shall see him as he is' (1 John 3:2). St. John's whole epistle is a profound exploration of the intimate relation between human life and God's life, of the idea that human beings find fulfillment and complete- ness only in loving and being loved, and that overarching our human loving is the infinite love of God. We cannot know what we are in any final sense until at the end we meet that love face to face.

"This consciousness of unfulfilled potential is not an exclusively theological one, however, though I believe theology enormously illumi- nates it. All human beings, whether religiously aware or not, try to reach beyond themselves. All of us are shaped by our histories and live, whether we believe it intellectually or not, as if we were free to create our own future. All of us live in a variety of relationships with other people and have to acknowledge that what they are makes us in part what we are. A theological perspective enables this openness and these influences to be recognized in their ultimate form as receptiveness to the incessant creative activity of God, the God who holds us and all things in existence. If we want to know where to find the essence of our humanity, this surely is the right place to look. All the different dimensions of what it is to know a human being, from knowing their DNA sequence to knowing their personality, meet in this all-

93

encompassing relationship with God. To see them this way sets them in perspective. The peril in not seeing them this way lies in imagining that we know more than we do."

As an avocational scientist himself, the archbishop revealed no intention of minimizing, much less obstructing, genetic research. He was not, as some do, attacking scientists for their professional arrogance. Despite their extraordinary ability as pioneering explorers in the strange, uncharted land of DNA, he observed, most maintain a respectful modesty: "Scientists themselves — apart from a handful of publicity seekers — are, for the most part, fairly humble about the extent of their knowledge, and that humility needs to be the starting point in decisions about its use. A sense of the inherent limitations of knowledge in this field should make us cautious about how such knowledge as we have is put to practical use."

CHAPTER FOUR

Concepts of Human Nature

A. Old Questions, New Evidence

ONE DOES NOT need to be a philosopher to ponder the question, "Who am I?" A theological education is not a prerequisite for asking, "Am I really a child of God?" From the day of one's birth the inevitable issues of moral responsibility will become more and more insistent. The reality of disabilities, sickness, suffering, and mortality will at times nag everyone's self-conscious mind. People have always thought deeply about these and similar issues of human existence. Their responses are inevitably conditioned by differing cultural and religious conventions, traditions, and teachings, as well as by individual experiences in particular families.

It would be an exaggeration to claim that recent, rapid revelations of the function of DNA give us a master key to unlock all the mysteries of human nature, which until now have been obscured. But there is no hyperbole in the assertion that the genetic revolution is opening new and unprecedented perspectives on traditional concepts of the nature of human persons and communities. We can seriously ask, How do the emerging data of genetic science affect some traditional theological concepts of human life, human behavior, and moral responsibility? Would such changes of theoretical and theological concepts merely indicate a more sophisticated scientific knowledge on the part of religious thinkers about the constantly immutable human organism? Or is a changing concept needed to account for a changing, evolving phenomenon called human life?

There is a familiar French proverb which tells us that "the more things change, the more they remain the same." It gives succinct expression to the idea that evolution, change, and progress are merely an illusion. The great wheel of Fate turns very slowly and eventually returns to its previous position. As the gloomy Hebrew preacher ruminated, "The thing which hath been, it is that which shall be; and that which is done is that which shall be done; and there is no new thing under the sun" (Ecclesiastes 1:9).

Many people of faith have been satisfied with a rather passive and pessimistic view of God and creation. The God of their theological concept is immutable, infinitely remote, and divinely static. They dwell in a created world of nature which changes only in the direction of corruption and chaos. As the old hymn expresses it:

"Change and decay in all around I see;
O, Thou who changest not, abide with me."

It is this prevailing pessimism which through the centuries has caused many church bodies and their members to be resolutely conservative. Believing that they were faithfully conserving divinely revealed truth, they have derided scientific theories, tried to stifle research, and blocked the advance of experimental science. So the astronomy of Copernicus and Galileo was denounced as heresy, as were the geology of Lyell and biology of Darwin. Michael Servetus first demonstrated the blood's circulation in the vascular system in the 16th century, even before William Harvey; but his science was quashed by the judgment of strict Calvinists who burned him at the stake in Geneva. Pope John Paul II's sincere but tardy exoneration of Galileo and the Presbyterians' penitential monument to Servetus at Champel have not quite nullified the religious mentality which sought to silence unorthodox views with unilateral decrees rather than wrestling honestly with new knowledge.

There is, of course, another prominent theme in the Bible, one which is optimistic, hopeful, and open to the future: a theme of creativity, novelty, innovation, discovery, movement, transformation. "Remember ye not the former things. . . . Behold, I will do a new thing," says the Lord (Isaiah 43:18-19); "They that wait upon the Lord will renew their strength" (Isaiah 40:31); "I create new heavens and new earth" (Isaiah 65:17); "Be transformed by the renewal of your mind"

(Romans 12:2); "Old things are passed away; behold, all things are become new" (1 Corinthians 5:17); many similar promises and expectations can be cited.

Two strikingly variant attitudes toward the purposes of God and the meaning of human existence have thus been adduced historically from biblical sources. The first type typically discounts, and is discounted by, science. But, surprisingly, modern science itself is partly dependent upon the second type of religious belief.

Historians of Western science have long theorized that the rise of empirical research and experimentation was more encouraged than inhibited by this latter emphasis of biblical religion. Two reasons are given for this interpretation. First, all of created nature was desacralized, human bodies included, because they were created by God and claimed no divinity for themselves. Pantheistic taboos concerning natural elements and organisms were repealed so that all natural phenomena became open for investigation. Second, the hopeful faith in a God who continues to create and to be involved with his creation provided impetus and attraction to scientists who could hope for a better future.

People who adhere to a religious faith that teaches a static view of nature and a pessimistic view of human history are not disposed to expect beneficial results from the modern life sciences. Their stance is defensive against the findings, in particular, of the palaeontology and developmental biology of the human species. Data which suggest an evolution of humans from primordial aeons to the present and beyond are seen to pose a threat to their religious doctrine. Still more dangerous may be the probing of chromosomes or mapping of genes.

The kind of biblical religious faith which has actually facilitated the rise of modern experimental science also enables persons to be tolerant of change and hopeful for the future. Here there is no weakening or diluting the belief in God as primordial Creator and continuing Sustainer of the cosmos. Neither is there surrender of conviction that humanity is uniquely God-related and primary among all other organic creatures. These beliefs make room for evolving modifications of human life, whether by natural or humanly contrived causes. And they generate an expectant, positive anticipation of progress in improving both individual and social life through the contributions of fruitful research and judiciously employed technology.

Sudden change cannot be easily assimilated, however — not even by persons who are open and friendly toward science. As whole fields of medicine, agriculture, and industry are being transformed by applied genetics, most of us who are not scientists sense a strange mixture of exhilaration, admiration, and conceptual shock. The exhilaration comes from realizing that we belong to the first generation in all human history to know so much about the effect of genes and heredity upon our bodies and lives. The admiration is felt in the presence of the data themselves and of the remarkable researchers who reveal them. But the conceptual shock affects our sense of who we really are as human persons and why we act or behave the way we do.

New genetic data may in fact occasion a greater sense of disorientation regarding our unique and sovereign human identity than did the questioning of human origins by Charles Darwin and A. R. Wallace more than one hundred thirty years ago.

In 1858 and afterward, religious people of all communions reeled from the shock of evolutionary theory and geological findings. They struggled both passionately and frantically to defend the biblical description of instantaneous creation of every species and of human uniqueness. That struggle, for many, still continues. It may take the form of direct counter-attack, as in the demand to teach so-called "creationist science." Or it persists in the minds of numerous people who are unable to resolve their inner conflict between mature scientific knowledge and a naïve, almost childish religious faith.

Evolutionary theory has been but one of a series of modern shocks to traditional Western notions about human nature. Sigmund Freud's analytic depth psychology was a shock to religious and moral sensibilities, and to our understanding of behavior. The cybernetic inventions of computers since 1948 have been a shock to our confidence in the uniqueness of human intelligence. Now genetic researchers tell us that 98 percent of the DNA material which makes up the cells of our bodies — from toenails to neurons to kneecaps — is identical with the genes of our nearest animal relative, the chimpanzee, and consists of the same chemical structural units of all other living organisms. The shock effect of this news has not yet been fully manifest.

The molecular geneticists have already opened a large window, so to speak, on the microscopic double helix of paired nucleotides which constitute the DNA molecule. Their research exposes a vast panorama of the estimated one hundred thousand genes in each human cell. Speaking in Boston at the 1988 meeting of the American Association for the Advancement of Science, Dr. Victor A. McKusick of Johns Hopkins University made a trenchant remark about the effect of the gene-mapping project. He said that from the time of Vesalius of Padua until now — 400 years — we have known human physiology only by empirical description. Now we can have a physiological knowledge consisting of genetic information: no longer only the body's physical characteristics and chemistry, but its cellular constituency and genetic potential. Just as the marvelous new electronic scanning and magnetic resonance imaging machines give us an inside view of parts of the body, the gene mapping and sequencing will afford a look inside the cells and inside the chromosomes where genes reside.

It is almost impossible to visualize one of the 100,000 genes on that chain; it is still more difficult to conceptualize the inherent power of those genes to determine what kinds of organic cellular life they will produce. We describe them in popular parlance as "building blocks" of life, or "blueprints" of organisms, as being "programmed" or "wired" to produce protein for any one of the countless differing parts of the body. But those metaphors illustrate the gene's purposes very poorly and explain their activity not at all. Building blocks after all are crude and lifeless. Blueprints are just the expression of the architect's intelligence and imagination; they can achieve nothing by themselves. And the computer analogy of programming is again reductively mechanistic.

It is no wonder that the unfolding mystery of the gene is stimulating a new era of philosophical and theological thinking about the nature of organic life in general and of human life in particular. The question which humans have asked wistfully for as long as there has been self-conscious reflection is, "What is life?" In general, two kinds of theory have been offered to that question. We call one "materialistic"; we call the other "spiritual" or "idealistic."

The materialistic concept of life was advanced in ancient philosophy by Democritus among the Greeks and Lucretius among the Romans. They believed that all organic systems and the power of living consisted essentially of hard, material atoms. They invented the word *a-tom,* to say that it was irreducible; it could not be cut any finer. The spiritual idea of life is more venerable, possibly originating in India; it was given enduring currency in the West by Plato and a long succession of philosophers called Neoplatonists. The core of this view is the belief that the essence of life is the soul, the spirit, or the mind. These are eternal. The physical manifestations of the body are only transitory appearances.

To the present day, biological research and philosophical biology have been pursued within the contrary tension of these two notions of life. The story of that tension and of the attempts to resolve it is a red thread of continuity in the history of scientific endeavor, as well as in the related disciplines of philosophy, religion, theology, and ethics.

Today, considering the explosion of scientific research and technology — especially in the fields of biotechnology and medicine — most people acknowledge that the materialistic theory of life has been well demonstrated, and thus it prevails. Convinced materialists greet this acknowledgment with a sense of triumph; others with perhaps a grudging acquiescence. Those who are adamant and intransigent in their adherence to pure spirituality as the sole reality are simply dismissed from the scientific conversation.

But the emerging data of genetic science itself have begun to reveal a more complex picture. Research in molecular biology and biochemistry is rapidly discovering heretofore unknown and surprising characteristics of the DNA molecule as the quintessential unit of organic life. And the new knowledge apparently gives support and comfort to both the materialists and the idealists, while equally preventing either one of them from claiming to have the true concept of life.

No one can reasonably disagree with the explanation of the structure and activity of the DNA molecule as the interaction of chemicals. Just as our entire written language is based upon the alphabet — A, B, C to Z — we know that the units of living matter have a four-lettered alphabet: A for adenine, G for guanine, T for thymine, and C for cytosine. Combined with a sugar and a phosphate group, these compositions of atoms of carbon, hydrogen, nitrogen, and oxygen produce the twenty amino acids, which in turn are the elements of proteins.

Deeper than the chemical structure of cells and genes is the emerging knowledge of atomic physicists about the very source of energy. So it would seem that the materialistic, or mechanistic, concept of life has been given a double warrant by the molecular biologists and the nuclear physicists. All may be reduced to physical-chemical energy. Moreover, as is widely claimed, whatever happens at the atomic and molecular level is simply due to random chance. There is no plan or purpose in nature. In this reductionist view of life, all biogenesis, mutation, evolutionary development, morphology, health or disease, sensibility, behavior, mental activity — everything reduces by descending levels to the elementary electrical energy of the atom, be it a wave or a particle.

And yet — the "and yet" is extremely important — the very physical theory of energy which is being worked out today gives strength to the argument that energy and matter are themselves the expressions of an inexplicable force. We hesitate to call it a spiritual power or a metaphysical reality. And we must be cautious, whatever our faith and piety might be, about invoking too readily the name of God or presence of divinity, while still leaving open the possibility of that invocation.

The new genetic science thus gives the same signals to both the mechanistic materialists and the absolute idealists, or spiritualists; namely, there is a probable truth in the intuition that human life is an inseparable admixture of material and spiritual dimensions. They constitute a unity in the human being which has come to be expressed in medical terminology by a single adjective: "psychosomatic." "Psychosomatic" means the unity of soul and body, of spirit and matter, in the whole person. Used as a medical term, it is rather new. But its meaning is ancient, going back mainly to the Bible, and to the Hebraic insight which is set forth in the Old Testament and developed in the New. This was an insight about life which differed sharply from both Greek materialism and ancient Indian and Greek spiritualism. For more than two thousand years it has been the third option between those extremes. In lands and cultures shaped largely by the biblical religions of Judaism and Christianity, the psychosomatic unity has prevailed. It has survived the emerging findings about the *psyche* during the rise of modern psychology; and it has accommodated new knowledge about the *soma* derived from biomedical research. (The competition has been, and remains, exceedingly strong from the opposing sides: on one side, scientific materialism; and on the other, the dualistic temptation to divide *psyche* from *soma* to the negligence of the material body, while giving almost exclusive value to the spirit, soul, or mind.)

Biblical anthropology, then, has provided a model of the human person which has prevailed in Western civilization. It is still considered normative by a probable majority of people of this heritage. According to this view, a generic human, man or woman, consists of the physical body, in the head of which is a brain of large size and almost limitless capabilities. The brain is the locus of the mind; but somehow the mind transcends the physico-chemical activity of the brain and the neurosensory system of the body. This transcendence is palpably demonstrated by the voluntary exercise of the will in making decisions and directing the actions of the body. The relation of brain to mind is thus described by some as interactionism, though the concept has been disputed. New research in endocrinology of the brain as well as in psychic phenomena seems to strengthen the notion of mind-brain interaction. Beyond both brain and mind, however, in this traditional, biblically informed view, is the unique soul of each individual person, wherein the deepest attributes of selfhood are to be found. The soul is also believed to be the living link to metaphysical reality and intelligent power. In personal and theistic terms, this reality is called "God."

Whether one holds the view of human nature as existing independently of a soul or some metaphysical power or, instead, believes that humanness is a uniquely divine gift and attribute, the existence of evil is of central importance. In general, evil may be regarded in two ways: as ontological and as moral. Conditions, occurrences, and experiences which disrupt, frustrate, or prohibit the realization of well-being and health have adverse, negative effects upon people and their lives. This evil is ontological because its end result is to destroy the very *being* of a person; it leads to death. Disease is such an evil. Conditions, occurrences, and experiences which allow, induce, or coerce people to bring injustice, suffering, and death to others represent moral evils of varying gravity. Evil actions may be prompted by malevolence, greed, or inexplicable compulsions. Both kinds of evil exhibit many faces, which need not be depicted and analyzed here. The relevant point is that genetic research is bringing to light new factors which account, in greater or lesser degree, for both kinds.

In the category of ontological evil are the diseases which we carry in our genes. Everyone has at least a few of these, or their mutations, which potentially cause debilitating or deforming illnesses. Unlike infectious diseases or accidental injuries, these belong to us as part of our individual natures. More than four thousand (estimates vary) of such diseases are known.

In Western civilization the displacing of ignorance and superstition about the causes of disease began less than two centuries ago. The role of ill winds, vapors, humors, evil eyes, maledictions, and divine retribution for sins were discounted once microbes, bacteria, and viruses were discovered. Pasteurization and the washing of doctors' hands replaced amulets, incantations, blood-letting, and numerous remnants of folk medicine. Sterilization and antiseptic measures were augmented in mid-twentieth century by the amazing success of antibiotic medicines and immunizations. As for congenital diseases, they could be traced in family histories and current relationships. But the real causes of these diseases remained hidden in the as-yet-undecoded DNA molecules.

In order to appreciate the brightness of the genetic revolution in medicine, one must remember the slow progress from the dark age of the nineteenth century to the dim age of the mid-twentieth. While family studies are still indispensable, diagnosis and prognosis now are made possible by sophisticated methods of linkage analysis and mutation detection. Prenatal analysis of maternal and fetal tissues is rapidly expanding to confirm or refute genetic predictions and to discover abnormalities which could not have been predicted. The list of these discoverable and predictable diseases keeps growing as researchers in the Human Genome Project succeed in finding their deleterious genes: cystic fibrosis, Duchenne muscular dystrophy, dwarfism, adult polycystic kidney disease, sickle-cell anemia, retinoblastoma, alpha-antitrypsin deficiency, neurofibromatosis, PKU (phenylketonuria), Lesch-Nyhan syndrome, the hemophilias, Huntington disease, and colon cancer.

Beyond the manifest diseases as such are the *susceptibilities* to fifty certain diseases. The famous oncogenes give clear indications of vulnerability to various cancers. Other tests show dispositions to cardiovascular disease, arthritis, diabetes, as well as such neural and mental disorders as manic depression and schizophrenia. Unlike the clearly defined genetic diseases which are heritable, and which usually manifest themselves during fetal and newborn stages of life, these susceptibilities can be predicted to appear eventually toward the middle or end of life.

If genetic diseases belong to our nature and being as ontological evils, the moral evils of behavior are also partly influenced by our genomes. Less certain to geneticists than diseases are the predictable *dispositions* toward various kinds of abnormal *behavior*. These are not diseases in the strict sense, but identifiable patterns of personal behavior. Some are of a psychopathic nature, such as schizophrenia and manic depression. They are not morally reprehensible, as though a result of deliberate choice; and yet they are on the border of behavior for which our society tends to hold people responsible. There are other types of behavior which are morally decried by the arbiters of a good society, but toward which the person may be genetically disposed; or, more strongly, these may be genetically determined. Alcoholism is one of these; homosexual aberration is another. Some researchers suggest that kleptomania, compulsive stealing, may have genetic causation. And even suicide may be caused. Compulsive inclination toward violent and criminal activity — the notorious XYY genotype — has recently been debated by geneticists and moralists. Controlled studies of identical twins, reared in differing environments but behaving in identical ways, give some credibility to these theories, if not yet certainty. Debates are intense because sensitivities about social values and morality are at stake.

The challenge which confronts us when we consider what is normal and morally correct about humanity becomes ever clearer. To what extent are the pathologies of personal behavior due to free choice? To what extent due to our genomes? Does objectionable behavior belong to the same categories as abnormal physical structure, congenital diseases, and susceptibilities to disease? Or, to turn the question from negative to positive values: is good behavior something to be learned only by environmental and cultural influence and practiced as a matter of mature will and free choice? Or is goodness, such as altruistic behavior observed in humans or sea gulls or termites, genetically determined so as to ensure the survival of the species? As the sociobiologists have expressed it: the only purpose of genes is to reproduce more of the same, whatever the organisms may be. Some claim that genetic determinism of behavior is so complete that there is in fact no human free will. For most geneticists this is far too extreme a position; as James Watson observed, in an international genome conference in Spain, "[E]ven given the sum of our genetic and environmental heritage, I don't think there is anyone here in this room who feels that in some sense or other he or she doesn't have free will."[1]

---

1. James D. Watson, "Genetic Polymorphism and the Surrounding Environment," in *Human Genome Project: Ethics* (Bilbao, Spain: B.B.V. Foundation, 1991), 27.

Sociobiologists have simply carried to extreme lengths the theory of genetic influence on behavior which is widely accepted with respect to physical characteristics and diseases. From the observed behavior of insects, birds, and mammals, they have extrapolated the principle of determinism and applied it to humankind. Of course, like all others who study biology, they have to take account of the influences of environmental factors on growth, health, and behavior.

The most doctrinaire theory of sociobiology has been advanced mainly by the noted zoologist, Edward O. Wilson. The gentility and sincerity of his writing and personal manner conceal a hard-line dogmatism concerning the way all human behavior is predetermined by chemical messages of DNA within each cell. The logical conclusion derived from this dogma is that our traditional concepts of human free will, voluntary choice, decision making, and ethical rectitude — that all these are merely illusions. Even religion is based upon the function of genes, according to this theory. Wilson writes: "I am suggesting a modification of scientific humanism through the recognition that the mental processes of religious belief . . . represent programmed predispositions whose self-sufficient components were incorporated into the neural apparatus of the brain by thousands of generations of genetic evolution. I suggest further that scientific materialism must accommodate them on two levels: as a scientific puzzle of great complexity and interest, and as a source of energies that can be shifted in new directions when scientific materialism itself is accepted as the more powerful mythology."[2]

To reject this extreme ideology, with all of its inhumane implications, does not make us blind to the demonstrated truth about the range of genetic effects on human behavior. Just as rapidly expanding knowledge of the genes which cause diseases is driving researchers to devise methods of gene therapy, so also the emerging knowledge of genetic causation of morally deplorable behavior is an enlarging factor in the search to understand personal and moral therapy of the whole, psychosomatic person. The task is as mandatory as it is awesome.

The number of attempted suicides, especially among young people, is alarming. Self-murder is usually condemned as immoral by

2. Edward O. Wilson, *On Human Nature* (Cambridge: Harvard University Press, 1978), 206.

religious teaching. We temper the condemnation by sympathy and mercy. Yet, we ask, are suicidal inclinations so compelling that people cannot resist them?

We often define humanhood by rationality: the capacity to think, to learn, to reason, to speak. But many people seem unteachable. They have puzzling disabilities such as dyslexia, and dreadful ones like autism. Illiteracy is very common in our nation. For many it results from lack of educational opportunity. For many others, a basic lack of rational capability. What is the genetic source of such a disability? Does severe mental retardation caused by X-linked genetic anomalies deprive human beings of the quality of personhood?

Addiction to alcohol and other drugs is a curse of the worst kind in human society everywhere. No doubt a large proportion of addicted persons can be held accountable for what they do. Certainly, in each case, there can be found social and environmental factors which drove them to the habit. But what of those who honestly claim that they cannot help themselves avoid dependency upon marijuana, crack, cocaine, and — most prevalent of all — alcohol? They are like St. Paul in his personal struggle with obeying the moral law of God. The good, which he wants to do, he cannot do; and the evil he wants to avoid is just what he does. "Oh, wretched man that I am!" He found what he called "another law" at work in him. He called it "the law of sin and death" (Romans 7:19-25). We may wonder — because we do not know — whether that "other law" leading to morally pathological behavior is found in some genes. And, if so, what kind of therapy or restitution can be found? The problem baffles the experts.

B. Human Reflection of Divine Image

James Bachman, in a paper prepared for the 1992 Houston Conference, pointed out that: "The Human Genome Project may be leading us toward a more detailed understanding of whatever the ontological core of the human person is. But many religious communities are likely to argue that, however detailed our understanding of the scientific, physical basis of human life may be, we must recognize that some other substance or essence ("life principle" or "soul") that eludes chemical capture is crucial to a full understanding of who the human is."[3] To speak of the soul does not contradict the concept of human nature as a psychosomatic unity. The body is ensouled and the soul is embodied; but they can be discussed in separation. This does not imply dualism in the Platonic or Gnostic sense of the term. When speaking about the chances of altering humanness by genetic engineering, Dr. W. French Anderson declared that such is not possible because of the soul, which he could not define but only designate as "that non-qualifiable, spiritual part of us that makes us uniquely human."

The question of human nature as the presupposition for understanding the theological and human significance of modern genetics was the burden of a Houston Conference address by James M. Gustafson.[4] It is a question which most theologians find unavoidable and with which many scientists want to wrestle. Gustafson says of the inquiring scientists: "They have moral beliefs and aspirations grounded in part in their scientific work which to a scholar of religion function much like myths, doctrines, and practices of religion in various human cultures." So he asks, "How do geneticists and other biologists, who move beyond the strict entailments of their science to explore the meaning and purpose of human life, support those moves from biology to what are religious affirmations, or at least the functional equivalents of them?" In a real sense their scientific profession drives them virtually to become natural theologians or theologians of nature and the nature of human life, even though they may disclaim the titles. At issue is not an intellectual proposition without ethical consequences. Considering the possible effects of genetic technology and medicine upon persons, this is a practical, ethical matter. In the long perspective, the concept of human nature may be more pressing and consequential for geneticists than for any other scientists. While it is a philosophical and theological matter, it is not merely an academic one.

The inevitable and implicit content of the issue is the traditional pairing of nature or/and grace, reason or/and revelation, autonomous humanity or the enduringly personal image of God. Gustafson character-

3. James Bachman, "The Human Genome Project: Issues for the Religious Communities," Conference on "Genetics, Religion and Ethics," Houston, 1992. Unpublished.

4. All quotations of James M. Gustafson are from his (unpublished) conference address, 1992.

izes, first, a class of thinkers and theologians "for whom genetic knowledge is, if not a source of knowledge of God, at least one body of information that has to be taken into account in a modern interpretation of God." They are "naturalistic theologians, in a double sense of naturalistic: (1) they do not depend on special revelation as a source of knowledge of God, but rely in some sense on the classic "Book of Nature," and (2) nature, if it does not become God, is at least that in which God is immanent, or indwelling." Among these thinkers whom Gustafson has in mind are Ralph Burhoe, Phillip Hefner, and Karl Peters, as well as advocates of the Whiteheadian process school. The issue here is not to "prove" God through natural science, but to conceive human nature in relation to our knowledge of God, so as to warrant a valuation of human life in the context of genetics. If one holds firmly that human nature is related to God and God's creation in a way which is "higher" but not essentially unique among all creatures, then the generally prevailing Christian belief about nature can seem to be arrogantly anthropocentric. This complaint is often made today by advocates of animal rights and environmental protection against human exploitation, and is used also in debates about using nonhuman DNA in genetic technology applied to humans.

Gustafson's class of natural theologians also includes those whom he describes as follows: "given the theological conviction that there is a divine ordering in and through nature that directs it to good ends . . . genetics and other aspects of biology provide a modern description and explanatory account of that divine ordering. Put more generally, if one accepts the fundamental assumptions of a theological natural law, and if one judges that in Thomas Aquinas and the classic Catholic tradition that law was explicated in terms of Aristotelian science, including biology, then it is possible to introduce modern biology and genetics to replace the Aristotelian elements of the past." In addition to these diverse ways of accommodating a theological anthropology to current knowledge of molecular biology, Gustafson discusses ideas of a Catholic, Stephen J. Pipe, and a Protestant, Edward Farley;[5] and he identifies his own theocentric emphasis with their versions of natural theology and ethics.

5. Stephen J. Pipe, "The Order of Love and Recent Roman Catholic Ethics: A Constructive Proposal," *Theological Studies* 52 (1991), 225-88; Edward Farley, *Good and Evil: Interpreting the Human Condition* (Philadelphia: Fortress Press, 1990), 79.

The second class of views on human nature, different from the naturalistic, was most vigorously expressed by the late Swiss theologian Karl Barth. For him, the prime source of knowledge of human nature is divine revelation in the Bible and thus particularly in the person of Jesus Christ. He distinguished between the "phenomenal human" and the "real" one. "The phenomenal human (read 'nature') is what is informed by various naturalistic explanatory accounts of life. Genetic science is opening new knowledge of phenomenal man. Knowledge of the real man, however, comes from the revelation of the divine goodness toward the human in Christ, and from the human capacities to be responsive and responsible in relation to God."[6] The biblical teaching of *imago Dei,* the image of God, is the first and most important indication of human nature. However diversely the image may be interpreted, it means that the dignity, value, and sanctity of each human life and all humanity inhere essentially in the relationship to God as Creator. In the terms of the New Testament, moreover, the image in fullness is shown in Jesus Christ, to whom all of us as bearers of a fragmented and provisional image may ultimately be conformed (2 Corinthians 3:18).

In this context, Gustafson cites an interpretation of the *imago Dei* proposed by the present author: "In what is the most *biblically* theological treatise on bioethics that I know, J. Robert Nelson writes: 'Humanness is the distinctive quality implied by the symbol of the image of God, the image in which everyone is created and which is the presupposition of life's meaning: everyone's unique identity is the creation and endowment of God.'"[7] Gustafson comments, "I think for him, and for most authors who invoke the biblical symbol, it functions to posit a reality in each human that gives him or her intrinsic value, or infinite respect. It is invoked generally as a limit to human intervention, backing an ethics of restraint." But he is not persuaded by the usefulness or validity of this way of reasoning. "If God is spoken of in terms of gracious goodness for humanity in a Barthian sense, the parameters within which intervention is permitted will depend on inferences drawn from what is the divine good for the human. In many

6. Karl Barth, *Church Dogmatics,* vol. 3, part 2 (Edinburgh: T. & T. Clark, 1960), 198.
7. J. Robert Nelson, *Human Life* (Philadelphia: Fortress Press, 1984), 130.

instances, I believe, the use of the idea of the image of God with reference to ethics becomes tightly circular; what God is imaged to be is what is distinct about the human, or what is claimed to be distinct about the human is projected onto God." He is not, of course, the first to observe this self-referential tendency to "make God in man's image." Historically, it has been called "idolatry." But faith in Christ as the "proper" or "real" human counteracts this inclination to make normative human nature out of relative, transitory concepts. Conversely considered, the criterion for testing how well people express the "real" human nature is the way they are active "imagers" of God in all personal relationships and moral behavior, as well as in stewardship of the earth. As the biologist Hessel Bouma III and colleagues say, bearing the image of God implies the obligation "to image" God (using the word as a transitive verb).[8] Why that is often so difficult to do constitutes the profound and perennial problem of sin and evil: the image of God is defaced and broken.

Is humanity's capacity to be an imager of God being demonstrated by the prodigious achievements during the twentieth century? Is there evidence today for asserting that the divine image can justly be understood to mean that we are *co-creators* with God? The early successes of genetic research and technology are commonly proclaimed as demonstrating god-like creativity. Cartoonists have altered Michelangelo's famous "Creation of Adam" on the ceiling of the Vatican's Sistine Chapel to show the extended fingers of God and Adam meeting on a DNA molecule. Even as he is the creature of God, Adam is also co-creator with God. Apart from the cartoon humor, is there serious philosophical and theological thought supporting it?

The idea of co-creation is not new. But it has been given wider currency than ever before because of advances in molecular biology. Research and applied technology in atomic physics, computers, artificial intelligence, laser beams, and extraterrestrial space exploration have also gone far beyond the technological dreams of Renaissance humanists and nineteenth-century mechanists. Poets, musicians, and artists have also heard their "creations" evaluated as signs of human co-creativity with God. "The soul of Man must quicken to creation," wrote T. S.

8. Hessel Bouma III et al., *Christian Faith, Health, Medical Practice* (Grand Rapids: Wm. B. Eerdmans, 1989), 27-34.

Eliot. "Out of the formless stone, when the artist united himself with stone / Spring always new forms of life. . . ."[9]

There are numerous ways to illustrate human creativity, but none excites more enthusiasm for the notion of co-creatorship than the methodical manipulation of genes or the popular talk of "creating life in a test tube."

The Houston Conference summary statement alludes to divided opinions about two concepts of humanity's relation to all the non-human components of the created world. One view sees humanity in the role of steward; the other in the role of co-creator. Are they just different words for the same thing? Or really in mutual contrast?

Stewardship has enjoyed a long history in religious thought, especially in biblical tradition. God has created the world and called it "good." Humans are permitted to use everything for their livelihood and culture, always with two attitudes: thankfulness to God and prudential care of the earth. That this double mandate has often been ignored and violated is the grim historical fact which accounts for our grave ecological crisis throughout the world. Jesus told stories about unjust and unfaithful stewards; and taught that we should all be faithful, responsible stewards (or managers) of God's creation and gifts. But however expansive its application, the term has always implied that human creatures remain creatures, even in our best, most responsible enactment of stewardship. Only God can properly be called Creator.

The recent cascades of intellectual, scientific, and technological achievements in many fields have convinced some religious thinkers to abandon the biblical and traditional modesty about human capabilities. They employ the doctrine of synergism, or co-working, with God, arguing that it in no way minimizes God's supremacy as divine Creator to assert that we have become co-creators. The distinguished British biochemist and theologian Arthur R. Peacocke has chosen to use this term repeatedly and emphatically. In biblical terms, he points out, stewardship means to be God's vice-regents, managers, or trustees in exercising dominion over creation.[10] But beyond these generally accept-

9. T. S. Eliot, *Collected Poems, 1909-1935* (New York: Harcourt, Brace and Co., 1936), 206.

10. Arthur R. Peacocke, *Creation and the World of Science* (Oxford: Clarendon Press, 1979), 297.

able, and still significant, terms, Peacocke commends the nomenclature of *co-creator* (or *co-worker* and *co-explorer*) with God. For God's continuously creative presence in the world is characterized by being open-ended and emergent, so that man can now exercise his own created free creativity consciously in cooperation with the Creator."[11] The words "created free creativity" do guard against suggesting that the creature is the Creator. Therefore, Philip Hefner, in agreement with Peacocke, urges the more careful designation "created co-creator" in a well-reasoned defense of the same. "We humans, then, can claim no arrogant credit for being co-creators. We have been created as co-creators. Put in scientific terms, we did not evolve ourselves to this point; rather, the evolutionary process — under God's rule, I am arguing — evolved us as co-creators."[12] Such is God's decision, he concludes, not ours.

A heavy weight of emphasis is given to the concept of co-creator by the Division of Mission of the United Church of Canada, responding to the Royal Commission on New Reproductive Technologies, 1991. "We are called to be co-creators with God, working for wholeness in our communities and in each person. . . . Anything less is to deny our worth and our role in world Creation."[13]

Two Roman Catholic authorities, Kevin O'Rourke, O.P., and Benedict Ashley, O.P., are critical of the concept of stewardship because they see it as reflecting a static view of creation in which humans have no original creativity at all. Because God the Creator is generous, they argue, humans are encouraged to share in a continuous creation with God: the extension of evolution through seeking to unleash the potential within nature.[14]

The use of "co-creator" in relation to genetic engineering or gene therapy remains somewhat problematic, however. What is literally meant by "creator?" One who applies labor and thought to existing materials?

11. *Ibid.,* 315.
12. Philip Hefner, "The Evolution of the Created Co-Creator," in *Cosmos as Creation,* ed. Ted Peters (Nashville: Abingdon Press, 1989), 227.
13. "A Brief to the Royal Commission on New Reproductive Technologies," on behalf of The Division of Mission in Canada of the United Church of Canada (January 17, 1991), 14.
14. Kevin O'Rourke and Benedict Ashley, *Health Care Ethics: A Theological Analysis,* 2nd edn. (St. Louis: Catholic Health Association, 1982), 324.

Even beavers "create" dams and termites build earthen towers of habitation. Are beavers co-creators with God? No, it may be said, because only humans are mentally able to be consciously deliberate in both their creativity and their faith in God. Then, one asks, do intention, capability, and faith constitute co-creatorship? Something seems to be missing from that equation. Perhaps it is the prepositional phrase *ex nihilo*.

In all languages the Christian creeds confess God as "Maker" and "Creator" of "all things visible and invisible." The classic text of Genesis has been taken to mean either that God brought order out of chaos or that God brought the cosmos (all things) into existence out of absolute nothingness. The question applies not only to nematodes, dinosaurs, redwoods, and galaxies, but in a special way to human persons. To human minds, which keep asking "How" and "Why," creation is a baffling yet inescapable concept. Over the centuries of pondering and debating the issue, Jewish and Christian thought has favored the out-of-nothing alternative. By this strict reasoning, a team of researchers who are synthesizing a batch of insulin, treating human dwarfism, or patenting a mouse with unique cancer resistance, however worthy of admiration, cannot literally be called creators, co-creators, or created co-creators.

Just as the classical definition of creator cautions against casual use of the term co-creator, so too does the classical biblical emphasis on the sovereignty and transcendence of God. The Christian creeds declare faith in the one God who is solely omnipotent, all powerful as Creator. "To whom then will you liken God?" demands the Hebrew prophet (Isaiah 40:18), ridiculing idols and putting down pretentious human creatures as grasshoppers. To be sure, there are current ideas advanced by theologians of a limited God, a developing, questing God, who must explore possibilities along with his human creatures. In such terms, God is part of the cosmic evolutionary process. If God is demoted, in theological acknowledgment, from absolute to relative being and power, the co-creator concept is consistent.

But the term "co-creator" may be misleading in another way. As Ronald Cole-Turner ably contends, such language is unrealistically optimistic about human motivation, activity, and achievement. "One never reads of co-creation and sin in the same sentence."[15] What are

---

15. Ronald Cole-Turner, *The New Genesis* (Louisville: Westminster/John Knox, 1993), 102.

the moral or ethical assumptions behind the usage? Are all the manifestly imperfect and often harmful or evil "creations" of humans to be counted among the works of "co-creators?" If genetic science is considered a human creation, does this imply that its results and uses are invariably good — i.e., in harmony with God's good purposes for humanity and creation? No one is *that* optimistic about any branch of science or, indeed, of any type of activity, despite the many ways in which scientific endeavor has been congenial to well-being and puta-tively in harmony with God's will. The concept of stewardship seems to avoid the ambiguity while preserving the need for a relation of responsible agency in communion with the Creator.

C. Can We Go beyond Gene Therapy to a Changed Nature?

Many people are dissatisfied with their present condition of body, mind, spirit, soul — the whole person. They enroll in classes to learn self-actualization and personality enhancement. They exercise vigorously, hoping to become not only healthy but socially acceptable and sexually attractive. They pay plastic surgeons to rebuild chins and noses and carve thinner waistlines. Athletes use steroids to enhance their already impressive muscles. Cranial hair is dyed various colors, while wigs cover what is left of hair, or else hairs are implanted like shoots of rice. Cosmeticians cover natural blemishes and wrinkles, while permanent, indelible skin decorations are executed by the tattooer's needle. Foot-binding of women in China and elongation of heads and flattening of lower lips in Africa are virtually obsolete, but modern surgery is capable of effecting even greater change not only of appearance but of actual and legal identity: namely, changing a man to a woman. If so many kinds of change are familiar to us, should we not welcome the new possibilities of altering our bodily characteristics by genetic engineering?

Already in use commercially since 1985 is the artificial human growth hormone, a cousin to the one for cattle called bovine soma-totropin. The human growth hormone is effective when taken regularly before puberty. By supplementing a deficient natural supply it can cause the child eventually to reach normal height (though not deliberately to become a giant; it is not prescribed for mature basketball players!).

Smallness of stature or actual dwarfism need not be called a disease, but it is considered a serious disadvantage socially, economically, and, for some, psychologically. The matter of stature poses a question which may well become increasingly real as research progresses. Let us assume the truth of two propositions: first, that tallness is a desirable asset for a person, and second, that scientists will discover how to produce a growth hormone which will be effective beyond puberty and able to control growth to specified heights. Would the hormone be used for therapy or for physical enhancement, or both? What is the difference, if any?

Many writers and some policy statements have strongly opposed genetic enhancement. They remind us of the danger of falling into the trap of the eugenic ideology of super-people ruling over inferior classes: the alphas over the betas, gammas, and deltas like the nobles over the serfs and slaves of earlier cultures. Bernard Davis warned of a day when there might be unbearable commercial competition in society for the procreation and production of highly enhanced children. But have no fear "for the foreseeable future," he wrote, because "there is a technical safeguard: the number of genes affecting each of these traits is large, and so it will be difficult to manipulate or even identify them."[16] His assurance may be justified, or maybe not. Genetic technology is irrepressible. If the manipulation of human germ-line cells should become feasible in clinical practice, the present opposition to it on moral grounds might be eroded. Advocates of modifying these sex cells during *in vitro* fertilization will commend both the therapeutic benefits of eliminating diseases and the values of enhancing certain traits.

For the sake of illustration at the Houston Conference, LeRoy Walters proposed four hypothetical scenarios involving enhancement. Improving the body's immune system, first, would strengthen resistance to breast cancer and prostate cancer as people grow older. Second, the body's need for sleep would be reduced by, say, half the present time, "without loss of attentiveness during waking hours." The power of memory, third, might be doubled from the present retention of ten percent of experiences to twenty percent. Fourth, behavioral tendencies to be aggressive and ferocious could be much reduced, being replaced

16. Bernard D. Davis, *The Genetic Revolution* (Baltimore: The Johns Hopkins Press, 1991), 257.

by generous and peaceful tendencies. In each case, Walters speculates on the benign and desirable consequences of these genetic changes. As one imagines them, the personal and social effects would be numerous. Would they be so beneficial as to overcome present inhibitions concerning this taboo subject of both therapeutic and behavioral enhancement? Walters has had long experience at the Kennedy Institute of Ethics as both scholar and government adviser on genetic engineering. He quickly added that he does not now advocate these forms of enhancement; neither does he suggest that they represent "a quick technological fix to social ills." Many other environmental factors are involved in the enhancement of both personal health and a good society. "My only plea is that, while we are working on these other fronts, we should not lose sight of the potential contribution of gene-mediated enhancement to the welfare of the human race."

The professional and public debate over manipulating sex, or germ-line, cells in noncoital procreation has been seething for more than a decade. Despite the agreement of scientists with Bernard Davis that the complicated problems of managing multigenic determinants of physical and behavioral traits have not been resolved, the discussion continues. The predominant view among geneticists and religious ethicists seems to be that the risks of harmful mutations would be too high, whether elimination of genetic disease or enhancement of traits be the objective.

It is good to avoid confusing the differing aspects of gene manipulation by defining them. *Somatic (body) cells* of individuals can now be altered for *therapy,* one gene at a time. There is very little cause for opposing this. *Germ-line (sex cell)* DNA might be changed with respect to single genes for the purpose of *eliminating* diseases, but the method is not yet perfected. The method of manipulating *multigenic* DNA in order to *change traits* remains unachieved. And the question of modifying *human nature* is wide open because of its philosophical and theological as well as biological dimensions. The guarded conclusion of *Splicing Life* (1982) stands: "At most, it can perhaps be said that this technology may eventually allow some aspects of what it means to be human to be changed."[17] The proverbial saying, "You can't change

---

17. *Splicing Life,* The President's Commission for the Study of Ethical Problems in Medical and Biomedical and Behavioral Research (Washington, D.C.: Government Printing Office, 1982), 70.

human nature" may, in light of recent genetic research, yet be challenged.

For Dr. W. French Anderson, the implications of genetic tampering with human nature are profoundly unsettling. As the first person ever to have applied gene therapy to a human being, in treating girls with ADA deficiency, his opinion deserves respect: ". . . Hanging over all this excitement is a fundamental question," said Anderson, because "the technology exists to put a gene into a human for any purpose." He asked, "Is there anything wrong with that?" And answered, "Yes, I believe that there is." His enthusiasm about gene therapy becomes more than cautionary when one speaks of altering physical and behavioral traits. Having now the basic technology, which awaits further refinement, he asks, "Can we alter our humanness by this kind of manipulation? Can we alter what is uniquely important to us as a human race by engineering our genetic machinery?" After some decades, or perhaps centuries, the momentum of many manipulative processes could carry the human race beyond the point of no return. In the case of "smog-filled air, polluted rivers, contaminated ground water, defective nuclear power plants, the disappearing ozone layer," he declared, "there remains the possibility of reversing the damage. If we inadvertently contaminate our genetic heritage, the damage may not be reversible."[18] He is not the first major geneticist to warn against the irrevocability of changes made in heritable genes of the germ line. Such protest cannot be dismissed as stemming from ignorance or anti-scientific bias.

It is argued from the other side, nevertheless, that scientists, ethicists, and those who set public policy reject the argument that there are "perils in knowing too much." If genetic changes are irrevocable, so also is the march of research and technology unstoppable. The tension between these two views is not likely to be relaxed.

18. These remarks formed part of Dr. Anderson's address at the Houston Conference, 1992.

CHAPTER FIVE

Personal Religious Positions Individually Expressed

How DO my practice and understanding of religion influence my attitude toward genetics? How does my knowledge of genetics affect my religious faith, theology, and ethics? These two questions complement each other. Most people will say flatly that they have never even thought about the relationship between the two fields. Many may admit ignorance of one field or the other — if not both! But persons who are likely to be readers of a book such as this will find both questions pertinent and worth trying to answer.

Certain participants in the "Genetics, Religion and Ethics" project were asked to address themselves to the two questions. Members of the Washington, D.C., study group prepared a detailed questionnaire with ingeniously nuanced questions. Two of the more comprehensive responses are quoted extensively in the following pages, as are extracts from shorter responses, which were presented orally at the Houston Conference and thus limited by time. These do not constitute a systematic survey of all possible positions and perspectives, of course, but represent a valuable sampling. They invite a continuing, more widely representative study.

The generalization which seems most evident is this: there is no uniformity within the major categories of Jewish and Christian faith. In each religious community, communion, or denomination there are extreme poles of conservatism and reformism with variations in between. It is apparent that persons who adhere most closely to the distinctive traditions of their particular faith are recognized as the most authentic representatives. They are also the least likely to make concessions in the direction of recognizing scientific, materialist explanations of human nature and behavior.

JUDAISM

Rabbi Barry Freundel

The most extensive response to the questionnaire was made by Rabbi Barry Freundel of the (Orthodox) Georgetown Hebrew Congregation in Washington, D.C. It is here reproduced in its entirety.

Section One: Background Issues on Creation/Co-Creation Related to the Human Genome Project from a Theological Perspective

To answer appropriately a number of the questions from a Judaic perspective, one must understand a basic premise of Judaism's legal and moral structure. As a religion of law, commandment, and imperative, we premise virtually all moral discussion on the issue of responsibilities. Who is responsible to whom? What must I do in a particular case? What must others do? Rights are derivatives of responsibilities, generally speaking, and not the other way around.

(1) G-d as Creator and G-d's Creation All beings of human parentage are deemed to have a soul and, thus, to enjoy full rights of protection and preservation of fundamental human dignity including, especially, the absolute right to every G-d-given second of life. (The commandment against pronouncing the Holy Name is acknowledged in English by writing G-d.) Within Judaism every soul is infinitely precious. Judaism teaches that one who saves a single soul has performed an act equal to saving the entire universe. This is not simply homiletic teaching. The Talmud teaches that in a case where brigands demand that a

120

city turn over one unnamed member of the city's choosing to be killed or all will die, no choice may be made and all must die. The subset is equal to the whole. Each person is infinitely valuable.

(2) Understanding of Human Being as Creature or Creator   Any post-maturity male (13 years plus) or female (12 years plus) is responsible for all areas normally considered part of their respective legal categories.

There are, however, exceptions. Children do not carry any re-sponsibilities, nor do the insane or mentally deficient. However, reach-ing maturity or return to normal mental capacity brings on or restores obligation to one's full set of responsibilities. In no case and at no time, it must be noted, does lack of responsibility in any way diminish the infinite value of the human being. This remains true whether the capacity and requirement for responsibility is there or not. Put another way, our responsibilities to the person do not change, though the person's capacity to carry out his responsibilities, and, therefore, his responsibilities, can change.

(3) Understanding of the World   When we move from the realm of law to that of philosophy, Jewish thinkers have long sought to find that quality of the human being that represents, in the real world, the manifestation of *imago Dei* with which man was created. Maimonides claimed to find it in man's intellect, Martin Buber in man's capacity for love, S. R. Hirsch in his ability to make ethical choices, and A. I. Kook in his creative faculty. Most radical in this regard was Mai-monides, who saw divine providence and one's share in the world to come as dependent on one's intellectual capacity and the perfection of that capacity through study and contemplation during one's lifetime. Despite this philosophical history, any real world conclusions of this type are left, even by Maimonides, to areas solely in G-d's control.

(4) The Relationship of G-d and Human Beings to the World
One must also add to this the question of whether human life can arise without human parentage (other than Adam and Eve). Here analysis turns to the Golem stories, which describe artificial, humanoid life being created by a mystical adept. (These stories, which served as the inspiration for Mary Shelley's "Frankenstein," usually end with the destruction of the Golem, often by the adept himself or another rabbi. The lack of moral

concern in such destruction is understood to mean that the Golem is not a human being. Were this creature to be considered human, his life would have been as infinitely precious as anyone else's.)

Significantly, it is not the lack of human parentage that robs the Golem of his human status. It is his inability to speak, which for medieval Jewish philosophers represented the quality facilitated by the human soul that indicated its superiority to that of the animal which only provided the capacity for movement. Should such life be created at some point in the future, I suspect that Judaism would be very open to offering protection and preservation status to such beings because of the overriding Jewish view of the preciousness of life. I would expect a lively debate as to what requirement such life would have to fulfill what specific responsibilities, with the more rational schools in Judaism arguing for greater responsibility on scientific grounds and the more mystical schools arguing against, on the grounds that the granting of a human soul is G-d's department, not man's. This mystical-rational split will appear on a number of issues within the purview of the Genome Project.

Section Two: Key Concepts on Genetics and Humanhood

Concept I: Personhood/Humanhood   (1) Are there theological reasons to equate humanhood and personhood? Is humanhood a species concept only, or does it also imply the capacity for consciousness, feelings, values? Where theological distinctions refer to differences between our species and other species, what does biology/genetics have to say about those differences?

Based on the above discussion, then, biology/genetics can speak to some of the criteria cited above, such as parenthood, at least in terms of which species parented a particular offspring, and, perhaps to capacities such as speech, ethics, creativity, etc. For some purposes and in some contexts this may be determinant. However, the soul is beyond scientific evaluation. This area will forever remain the purview of the theologian. Whether a strongly exclusivist view of the entire question or a more synthesized position such as is presented here will become dominant over time depends on many factors, not the least of which is the question of what issues manifested in what way become "real-world" and not just theoretical problems. It is ultimately possible and perhaps likely that a mixed response will emerge, with the more scientific conclusions being adopted where such are felt to be appropriate and the more "theologic purview" style responses holding sway when these are perceived to be more in keeping with Jewish values.

(2) Does biology — particularly genetics — have anything to add to or clarify the definition of personhood?

This question again uses terminology and carries assumptions which do not mesh with Judaism's conceptualization of the issues. Again, personhood is there for any human descendant, at least in terms of how such an individual must be treated. Beyond defining who is whose biological parent, it would not seem that biology/genetics would have much else to say.

In terms of the fetus, its status is a protected one but not co-equal with an already functioning human being, i.e., the mother. Therefore, should the fetus pose a physical danger or, according to many authorities, a psychological danger, its life would be forfeit. Three rationales are offered. One speaks of the fetus as a "pursuer." Under Jewish law one who pursues another with intent to kill forfeits his own life to anyone in a position to save the potential victim's life. The fetus is an inadvertent pursuer; nonetheless, the fetus's life is forfeit. It is clear that this line of reasoning bears no relationship to genetic personhood.

A second line of reasoning deals with the level of viability of the lives involved. We are sure that the mother's life is viable; we cannot be sure about the fetus. In all cases where one must choose between certainty and doubt, certainty wins out. Again, this line of reasoning is not influenced by genetic considerations.

Finally, the third argument describes the fetus as less fully human than the mother, and therefore, more appropriate to be sacrificed. Although this sounds like an argument to which genetic information might be valuable, it probably is not. The fetus's diminished status is probably a function either of its dependence on the mother for life or on the question of the time of entry of the soul into the body. The former is obviously not subject to genetic scientific information, though it would seem that, based on our previous discussion, the entry of the soul might be. Yet, it too is probably not. All of the qualities mentioned — speech, intellect, etc. — are manifestations of the presence of the soul, but not the same as the soul. The soul is, for Judaism, a metaphysical construct and not subject to scientific measurement.

For the reasons cited above, then, abortion is generally prohibited except in cases of need to preserve the life and, possibly, well-being of the mother. The quality of life of the potential child is never an acceptable criterion for abortion. The fetus is valuable either as the repository or the potential repository of the human soul. It is a living thing and must be treated with respect.

Jewish law does recognize developmental changes in the status of the fetus. During the first forty days after actual conception, it is referred to as "merely fluid." At nine months, it is considered viable, and once 51 percent of the baby has emerged from the birth canal, it is considered co-equal with the mother. In the stage between six weeks and the ninth month, it is in a sort of intermediate state. The impact of this legal structure is to make the rationale for permitting abortion less restrictive the earlier in pregnancy that the woman is. However, at least some serious problem must exist for an abortion to be permitted at any stage. Again, in this analysis, since the concerns are developmental and not genetic, the latter type of information will not impact on this issue in any way that I can foresee.

It is probably important to add one caveat to the above, by way of responding to the more general question. The Genome Project may discover the genetic sites of the various aspects of human personality suggested as manifestations of the soul's presence. That in itself would not be troubling as it would be seen as uncovering the mechanism of G-d's creation. Great concern, however, would exist about tampering with such sites either in terms of damaging something fundamentally human or in terms of potentially diminishing free will and individuality. However, Jewish thought would probably await the final form of the knowledge gained and the shape and impact of the potential interventions before offering a final response to the issue involved.

Concept II: Parenthood   Is there any special theological significance to genetic parenthood? Are some methods of conception theologically more "correct"?

Genetic processes are submicroscopic, and Judaism will often exclude things that are not visible to the human eye from legal consideration. (The judge only judges according to what his eye can see.)

For example, it is hard to imagine any opposition to the removal of the gene for Tay-Sachs or Down syndrome and its replacement with a healthy germplasm no matter what the source of this replacement gene. It is, likewise, hard to imagine this action affecting the parentage of the child. Even the more mystical communities would probably go along with this analysis because of the health benefits involved.

The more interesting question would arise in circumstances where large amounts of genetic material from different parents would contribute to the genetic makeup of the child. At least one writer on the subject has suggested that parentage, at least on the mother's side, would be determined by the womb in which the child grew. Precedent for this position arises from Jewish agricultural law. For the first three years that a tree produces fruit, the fruit cannot be eaten. If a 20-year-old branch is grafted on a two-year-old trunk, is the fruit 20 years old or two years old? In all cases, Jewish law follows the source of sustenance, not the genetic origin. So, too, one may be able to assign parentage to the mother whose womb provided sustenance. Though arguments and sources exist that would dispute this conclusion, the majority of Jewish authorities accept it.

On the father's side, there is a predisposition in Jewish law to maintain family ties and integrity even against circumstantial evidence to the contrary. In cases of extended absence (longer than nine months) of the husband, pregnancy was attributed to the action of demons delaying the husband's sperm. In cases of racial anomalies appearing in children, imaginative genetic theories are advanced to explain and maintain the integrity of the family. I suspect that similar rationales would be used in this type of case perhaps with even greater ease, as no act of even suspected adultery exists here, though this was clearly a concern in these earlier cases.

There are, however, several other considerations that will enter into Jewish discussions of creation of life of this type. Parenthood and awareness of parenthood and familial relationships are very important to Judaism. At a certain point this awareness disappears. Parenthood is probably not, strictly speaking, the same as genetic relationship in Judaism, though genetics is one component. Acting to achieve procreation, nurturing the fetus in the womb, birthing and raising the child are part of the definition as well. The more these other processes are severed from the actual creation of life, the more the objections will grow. Therefore, the critical question is not which type of parentage is acceptable, but rather the reason and circumstances for the alternative road to parentage will be extremely important. Is the question being raised for reasons of dealing with infertility, promoting health or well-being, or other, similar, types of concern? If so, the response will tend to be positive. If, however, it is being advanced for anti-family or exploitive reasons, it will likely be opposed.

Judaism recognizes that there is a reality beyond secular and religious law that must be given credence. Even if legal arguments can be presented to maintain the parental bond in the face of circumstantial or scientific evidence to the contrary, the reality must be faced. There is, therefore, a predisposition in Jewish law to using Gentile germplasm or gametes in such procedures where donors other than the legal parents are involved. The reason for this preference is to avoid the possibility of the child so produced marrying a half-brother or sister. Since inter-marriages are prohibited and since conversion into Judaism severs all family relationships as the convert is seen as born anew, use of non-Jewish genetic material avoids the real-world problem of possible incest.

One final point: the status of a child produced by any method of parentage will not differ from those produced in the normal fashion (see above). However, Jewish law specifically requires men to procreate. Donation of genetic material may constitute fulfillment of the obligation. Jewish law speaks of women becoming pregnant in baths or from sperm left on bedsheets. The biological father in such cases does fulfill his obligation. Interestingly, no claim of incest or adultery is raised as no sex act is involved. However, Jewish law is concerned that the child which results may lose knowledge of his or her family relationships.

Finally, there is a raging debate about consciously initiating such a procedure as in artificial insemination by donor, which centers around the seemliness and appropriateness of such an action. Concerns for appearances of adultery and stress within the family are also raised. This debate is probably paradigmatic of what will emerge as each new technology reaches the public domain. If the positive values of the procedures are demonstrated they will probably be found to be acceptable to most segments of the Jewish (even Orthodox) community.

Concept III: Kinship and Lineage   Can biology help define the limits of a "family"? Or is the concept of "family" ultimately meaningless in

biological terms? Are there special biological and/or theological obligations owed to persons of shared lineage? What issues are posed by the
incidental genetic determination of non-paternity? Should such non-
paternity be revealed?

Judaism in its laws of inheritance, laws of incest, and requirements
for procreation, among other areas, has a very finely developed sense
of family relationships and their importance. However, evidence sufficient to establish kinship and family under Jewish law will vary depending on the circumstances. For example, incest prohibitions which
can entail capital offenses require testimony of two witnesses and other
stringent parameters, while inheritance disposition, which is only a
monetary matter, may well be resolvable by genetic tests. Further,
maintaining a presumption of innocence may be possible through
scientific evidence, while determining guilt may not be. In addition,
establishing a parent-child relationship for purposes of the financial
and personal service obligations thus involved (which in Judaism work
both ways depending on age and physical and financial circumstances)
could probably be accomplished by genetic testing. Therefore, the
answer would appear to be "sometimes" if one is asking whether biology
can determine the limits of the family. Obviously, then, "family" is not
a meaningless term for us, in either the scientific or theological arena.

As to other imperatives, Judaism, as indicated, posits a whole
range of responsibilities and obligations based on lineage. Genetic
testing or information might well play an important role in defining
where these obligations and responsibilities might lie. In this regard, a
person seeking to discover familial relationships should be aided in his
quest by whatever genetic testing or information is available.

However, there is an important caveat to all this. As indicated
above, Jewish law acts to maintain existing families whenever possible.
Further, Judaism has a concept of illegitimacy — a child resulting from
an incestuous or adulterous relationship — that precludes an individual
so stigmatized from ever marrying (or having any of his descendants
marry) within the community. Because of the devastating nature of
such a stigma, Jewish law works to preserve legitimacy, even in the face
of circumstantial evidence to the contrary. For example, if one knows
information about a family previously thought to be legitimate that
would question its legitimacy, one is enjoined against coming forward
with that information. On this basis, a recent author has argued that

Judaism would not permit use of a genetic test for the purpose of determining family relationships that would lead to inadvertent disclosure of illegitimacy. Such test could only be applied in cases of overwhelming need such as medical necessity. Particularly relevant in this regard is the present practice of routinely revealing to patients who are genetically tested that their stated biological father is not, in fact, their biological parent according to the test. Jewish law would preclude such revelation except where absolutely necessary. Genetic counselors operating under Jewish law would keep such information confidential and would only reveal the medical and biological conclusions (e.g., susceptibility or nonsusceptibility to a particular illness or condition) without explaining why the particular determination had been reached. Given that such patients are not actively seeking information about parentage, nor are they even aware that there is any such information to be sought, such revelation is deemed inappropriate both for the harm it might do to the patient and his familial relationships, and for the dampening effect it might have in keeping others from coming for testing when such testing is both necessary and desirable.

Concept IV: Human Diversity and Human Equality (1) How does contemporary biology speak to the moral value that theology gives to human diversity and equality?

This question again uses terminology foreign to Jewish thought and certainly to genetic applications within Jewish thought. Judaism does not view itself as either a race, a religion, an ethnic group, or a nationality but as a total way of life, though other groups in society are generally free to define their groupings in any way that they choose. Further, outsiders may join (convert to) Judaism by agreeing to share in Judaism's historic destiny and by accepting the obligations incumbent on one who lives a Jewish life (Halachah or Jewish law). Finally, salvation (in Jewish thought, "a share in the world to come") is available to the moral Gentile as it is to the Jew who fulfills his obligations. Given this background, diversity is assumed and accepted. There is no agenda to proselytize the world or anyone in it and make them Jewish. In certain circumstances, such as encountering an individual of different racial appearance after not having had such an experience for a while, a blessing is recited praising G-d for creating diverse types of people in his world.

(2) What can it say about the concept of race, the value of biological diversity, the correlation of specific disorders or capacities with particular populations? Can we be different and still be "equal"?

As stated, race as a concept essentially does not appear in normative Jewish thought. Even in the blessing just described, it is appearance, not genetics, that determines whether the prayer is to be said. In any case, as indicated, diversity is assumed and assumed to be a blessing of G-d's bountiful gifts to the world and a reflection of his Glory. "G-d made man from one mold (Adam) yet all the coins (human beings) so minted are different," say the rabbis in describing one aspect of G-d's capacity to transcend human limitation. Diversity is seen as intrinsic to G-d's creation and running of the world.

(3) Are any of its contributions on these points relevant to the moral significance of diversity and equality? What are the theologically significant aspects of "equality" when biology tells us that our capabilities are very different?

Moving on to equality, again as indicated above, Judaism does not have a concept of human equality but of human infinite value. All people are of infinite value. However, all infinities are not equivalent. Equality exists within similar groups in regard to responsibilities, but people do not need equivalent talents to fulfill their obligations. In fact, diversity may allow for these responsibilities to be completed with greater creativity and in different, spiritually meaningful ways by diverse individuals. Genetics may tell us who falls below the minimum capacity to fulfill basic obligations but macro-behavioral tests would probably be more direct, accurate, and cost-effective.

Finally, disorders and capacities of particular populations were known to Jewish thinkers and were generally seen as part of G-d's functioning through natural law to bring diversity, justice, challenge, reward, and punishment to this world.

Concept V: Identity, Integrity, and Uniqueness (1) How does an organism's identity as an integrated individual depend on its genome? Or, alternatively, on how much of its genome does an organism's identity depend.

Identity relates to the soul which exists in a realm beyond the genetic and scientific. It also relates to qualities of humanhood such as intellect, love, capacity to make ethical choices, creativity, etc. The

129

genome will affect these, and interventions that affect these areas would be rigorously regulated. In addition, other changes would have to be examined carefully for fear of potential impact on these areas. However, since the genome is submicroscopic this divorces it, at least somewhat, from the usual macroscopic judgments in Jewish law. Reactions to interventions that change the functioning of an organism, human or otherwise, might be very different from judgments about doing genetic manipulation which led to the initial creation of an organism. Also mystical vs. rational debates will probably emerge in this area, with the mystic communities being less accepting and more restrictive out of concern that this activity might be distorting G-d's plan for the harmony of the universe.

(2) Are there objections to genetic testing/screening for untreatable diseases?

It is important here to state explicitly a point implied in some of our previous discussion. Knowledge is value-neutral in Judaism. There is no "right to know" and no automatic good in knowing. Rather, knowledge is judged by the impact it has and the use to which it is put. As such, testing/screening for untreatable diseases, if the uses and consequences of the information are morally appropriate, should be performed. If not, not.

(3) For your tradition, what are the implications of the "banking" of DNA? How does that influence the implications of DNA banking for purposes such as immortalized cell lines, future disease testing, future forensic identification for military, for crime?

Once again, no overall answer can be given. Uses that are positive within Judaism's system of moral belief would be fine, those which are not would be prohibited. As DNA is submicroscopic, its preservation poses few, if any, problems, and "immortalized cell line" will, for this reason, have no significant legal or theological meaning. Further, though privacy is an important value for Judaism, health and justice considerations are often more significant. Determination of how to proceed in particular cases would not seem to be particularly complex as these issues and their relative worth are fairly well defined in Jewish law.

As indicated, the submicroscopic nature of DNA makes its usage and ownership a moot question. Further, Judaism has a legal principle that in a circumstance of "one benefiting while the other loses nothing," the one may benefit without permission or consultation. Since DNA might be collected from hair follicles left behind after a meeting, it certainly fits this latter category.

It would seem that only two concerns remain. One is method of procurement, which might involve surgery or other procedures that require regulation. Second, if life were created from the DNA that is harvested, the issues of parentage and lineage discussed above would then become matters to be dealt with. However, these concerns would seem to be ancillary to the central question raised here.

I should note that mystical Jewish sources do ascribe certain human essence or extension as well as demonic activity to nails and hair. Such concerns may manifest themselves here as well. However, if the DNA in question were being used for positive purposes, this should overcome any objections of this type even in the more mystical communities.

Concept VI: Health and Disease (1) Since health and disease are given different theological interpretations by different traditions, and as more physical conditions are understood to be conditioned by the presence of inborn, inherited genes, what do these interpretations imply about the people involved, about concepts of determinism, about concepts of blameworthiness and taking responsibility for one's health, about definitions of health and disease, and for policies of social eugenics?

I have trouble accepting the premise of the question. Infectious disease is certainly not genetic, and even the specific conditions listed in the question seem clearly to be affected by behavioral and environmental factors. At most, a genetic propensity for a particular condition may exist, but date of onset and, perhaps, even response to and course of the disease are subject to human intervention.

Approaching the question's premises from the other end — the religious side — Judaism accepts the idea that disease is not always a direct act of divine providence and intervention. "All is in the hands of heaven except for cold winds and heat (and the diseases they bring)," says the Talmud.

Meeting the question on its own terms, Jewish tradition understands that death is part of life. A person is granted a certain number of days (perhaps the mechanism is genetic) that will be subtracted from or added to, depending on one's living up to G-d's expectations. Since the genetic processes described go on outside the scope of human

131

observation, on an individual basis there is plenty of room for G-d to intervene.

Further, how early a cancer is detected, and whether one is near help or not when a heart attack occurs are typical of the random factors that leave a great deal of room for G-d to intervene when and where he chooses to do so. In this regard, then, genetically determined life spans pose no theological problem. Similarly, length or shortness of days makes no statement about the moral character of the individual. Further, Judaism does not hold simple moral mechanistic views on illness so that these questions do not pose theological problems for us.

The term "eugenics" sets Jews on edge because of its association with Nazi atrocities. Nonetheless, from earliest Jewish tradition, people were advised not to marry into families in which particular diseases and medical conditions existed out of an understanding that such things were hereditary. Action that would serve to remove such conditions from the human family that did not prevent anyone who wanted to from procreating would be viewed favorably. Since all life is precious, even life with illness, and since all men share an obligation to procreate, no license exists for preventing this process.

(2) What are the biological and theological implications for diversity and equality when doing good for a person in the instance may produce bad consequences in the larger group?

As indicated above, all life is precious, even life with illness. Further, Jewish law generally deals with that which exists in the present reality and assumes that, since many factors may change before "tomorrow" comes, we can most effectively deal with the future by dealing with the problems of the present. A person who is ill today is to be helped to the extent possible. What results in later generations will be dealt with then.

(3) What is our responsibility for unanticipated/unpredictable effects or loss of valuable associated characteristics? Are defective genes somehow critical to being human?

Human beings do the best that they can. If our best cost/benefit analysis says go ahead, we go ahead. If facts change our analysis we change our procedures. "G-d protects the simple" is a Talmudic principle that allows us to assume that when we do our best G-d will take care of what we could not foresee or anticipate. If things do not work out, the theological question is G-d's to answer, not ours.

Judaism does not view human beings as flawed (it has no doctrine of original sin). Defective genes are items to be repaired as we fulfill our divinely ordained task of Tikun Olam (Healing the World).

Section Three: Questions on Creation/Co-Creation Related to the Application of Theological Perspectives on the Human Genome Project

Part A: Acceptability of the Human Genome Initiative Itself

(1) Do you believe that genetic research is a form of inquiry that can yield information that is valuable and true?

(2) Is the mapping and sequencing of the human genome objectionable, either inherently, because of the interventions involved in obtaining that knowledge, or because of the danger that this knowledge will facilitate improper intervention?

Though one author, writing from a Jewish perspective, has equated genetic analysis with the biblical tree of knowledge as prohibited, his concern centered primarily on the fear that no adequate safeguards exist to prevent creation of an "Andromeda Strain"–type virus. Though this is certainly a concern that must be addressed, it does not go to the core of the question. As indicated above, Judaism views knowledge as value neutral. The question is always, What use is being made of the knowledge? Given the great potential for good that the Genome Project brings with it, responsible, ethical research is certainly in keeping with Jewish values. Judaism views this world as having been created unfinished. Man's task is to use the raw material of this world to bring it towards perfection. Genetic material is just as much appropriate raw material as anything else.

Part B: Acceptability of Intervention in Humans

(1) Are there acceptable forms of technologically-assisted reproduction within your traditions? If certain forms of assisted reproduction are acceptable, are there objections to artificially creating human lives with genetic alteration? If certain forms of assisted reproduction are acceptable, are there objections to cloning?

Procreation is G-d's first commandment. Life is precious. Jews are a small minority that recently lost one-third of their people to the

Holocaust. With that as background, it is no wonder that Judaism sees positive value in bringing children into the world. Though the natural method will always be preferred, alternate methods, used when difficulties arise with nature's way in a particular case, are seen as a positive good. Particular methods need to be examined and some may be rejected because of problems associated with them, but the overall stance remains positive.

In vitro fertilization is a good example of the above. The general concept is perfectly acceptable. Concern comes from the possibility that some fertilized eggs may not be implanted. Discarding them is tantamount to abortion. Present techniques allow for freezing and later implantation. This, among other considerations and approaches, can serve to mitigate the concern and make this procedure completely acceptable.

Artificial insemination by husband (AIH) is universally seen as acceptable, though there are better and worse methods of procuring sperm. Insemination by donor (AID) is very controversial, with concerns ranging from appearance of unseemliness to the potential of siblings with the same biological father inadvertently marrying. Despite this, some recent responses have taken a permissive stance while offering solutions to the potential incest problem. For discussion of cloning see above.

(2) Are there objections to the kind of somatic gene therapy now being conducted on a small scale, which involves the genetic alteration of cells taken from, and reintroduced into, living people?

Somatic gene therapy is no different from any other medical procedure with the possible advantage of being submicroscopic and thus not subject to some restrictions that may exist in other therapies (see above). The individual therapy suggested would therefore be judged by the same risk/benefit criteria used in analyzing any other medical or surgical procedure.

(3) Does the stage of development at which somatic alterations are introduced make a difference?

Fetal life, and to a lesser extent infant life less than thirty days old, might allow for slightly higher risk factors as these stages of life are, in the first case, not seen as fully human, and in the second case occasionally not proven as fully viable.

(4) Are there objections to *any* kind of germ-line therapy?

Such involvement needs to be for positive reasons to be acceptable. Therapeutic considerations would certainly allow for such procedures. Interestingly, the Talmud even allows prenatal intervention for intellectual-ethical and even for esthetic reasons. Talmudic rabbis believe that the thoughts of the parents at the time of procreation affect the child. A certain Rabbi Johanan used to sit on the road from the ritual bath so that women passing that way could see him. This ritual bath is required seven days after the end of a woman's menstrual period. For the onset of her period until this immersion, sexual relations between a woman and her husband were prohibited. Now, at a point in time which is often a woman's most fertile period, sexual relations resume.

This story of Johanan on the road appears twice in the Talmud. In one instance, the reason for his action is explained by his hope that women who might conceive that night would be thinking of him and thereby produce Jewish scholars of his stature. The second citation offers a different rationale. Johanan was a very handsome man and he wanted the children conceived to be as good-looking as he was. Cross-generational intervention for positive purposes is, therefore, permitted.

(5) Are there objections to specific kinds of genetic alteration? Does the objection depend on whether the alteration is somatic or germ-line?

Those elements that touch on fundamental human qualities as described above would need to be treated with greater delicacy. Further, fundamental alteration of personality would seem to threaten destruction of the individual and would raise "Brave New World"–style fears. Nonetheless, positive modification to solve a particular problem would seem to be appropriate in any area. Genetic modification would not be different in this regard from psychological or behavioristic ones.

(6) Are there objections to eugenic alterations? Do your traditions make a distinction between negative and positive eugenics?

Again, eugenics is a very frightening word for Jews. As such, there would be great hesitation and concern in such projects. Therapeutic activity would certainly be sanctioned, but improvements of characteristics would raise doubt as to whether the individual was being done away with and whether certain types of people were being defined as undesirable. It would take some doing, though it might be possible, to overcome these concerns. How the process is used, and the results of its use, will be very important in answering this question.

(7) Are there objections to combining human and nonhuman genetic material? To blurring the boundaries between humans and other life forms? To reducing the physical, cultural, or psychological diversity among people?

Man is seen as different and unique in Jewish tradition. Blurring these lines would, I suspect, be intolerable to the Jewish community. Similarly, reducing cultural or psychological differences genetically would raise both the concerns cited above and the fear that human free will was being diminished. This would be anathema to Jewish tradition. Altering physical differences would raise the eugenics fear before such a project got very far.

(8) What connection, if any, do the religious traditions you are representing make between the right to create and to destroy life? Do concepts of stewardship or co-creation play a role in your traditions?

Parents create life but cannot kill their children. Only G-d has such rights. Creating life is a positive good, destroying it without sufficient reason is an abomination. Life is a precious value.

Stewardship and co-creation are central to Judaism. The Human Genome Project is a new area filled with great potential in which such stewardship and co-creation can be carried out. The task is for us to make it proceed along the most ethical and moral path that we can construct. In this way, the project can be another important building block in our task of finishing G-d's plan for creation begun by him at creation and carried forward by us in our partnership with the Divine.

Fred D. Ledley

How a Jewish geneticist perceives his dual role as a religious believer and a molecular biologist was explained by Fred D. Ledley, M.D., of the Baylor College of Medicine faculty.

I am not a scholar in Judaism, and it would not be appropriate for me to expound Jewish doctrine as Rabbi Freundel has done in his scholarly commentary on the Orthodox perspective. I would like to describe four images which may provide a montage of my views as a Jew on the Human Genome Project.

The first image must be the remembrance of the Holocaust, which continues to haunt Jewish experience, theology, and practice. I believe there is little veritable connection between the Human Genome Project and the atrocities which were visited upon my families half a century ago. In fact, I believe the project is more likely to prevent such abuses in the future by demonstrating the inherent variability and homogenization of humanity. Nevertheless, since it is impossible even in retrospect to understand how the paranoid ideation of the fascist state came to be endured by the world community, it is impossible to be sanguine about the potential abuse of the Human Genome Project. The remembrance of the Holocaust teaches that it is essential not only to consider how the project will affect rational individuals, but also how it may be used by the irrational.

The second image is that of the *bris,* the ceremony in which a Jewish child is entered into the Covenant of Israel eight days after birth. The *bris* is a celebration of life and the ineffable wonder of human creation. Judaism has no doctrine of original sin. Men and women are understood to be created in God's image, essentially good. The process of conception and birth is the fulfillment of the first biblical commandment, and is perceived to be an embodiment of the role men and women play in the continuing process of God's creation. The notion that men and women have the ability and responsibility to continue God's creation is central to Judaism. This view has its technical roots in the rabbinical theology which teaches that the revelation of the Law at Sinai is not complete, but continues to this day through the instruments of the rabbis and teachers and the exposition of the oral law.

The third image is that of the process of revealing the oral law — the process of Halachah. The oral tradition in Judaism provides a process of analysis and accommodation, which is capable of distinguishing right from wrong and sacred from profane. This tradition involves a process of discourse, debate, and even disagreement. The deliberations of the great rabbis over the past three millennia have been canonized in the Mishna and Talmud, and continue today in the form of response between rabbis and their congregations in which congregants ask questions of their rabbis and receive rabbinical interpretations.

In Judaism, right and wrong are understood to be God-given principles which can be revealed by rational individuals appealing to religious commandment, to relevant circumstances, and rabbinical interpretation. It is understood that the judgments of two men, two

137

rabbis, or even two Talmudic sages such as Hillel or Shammai, may disagree. It is understood that there may be competing interests and conflicting interpretations, that the principles of Jews and gentiles may not be the same. It is also understood that the law must be reasonable and humane. A law that cannot be followed, the rabbis teach, is inappropriate.

The final image is that of God. God in Judaism is at once whole, ineffable, transcendent, and beyond attributes. God's very name in Hebrew is unpronounceable and remains a mystery. Yet the Jewish image of God is also enigmatic. God is a creative force that could conceive the world from the void, yet still pause to argue with Abraham and Moses. God is the omnipotent author of life and death who expresses regret over the devastation of the Flood and the destruction of Israel.

If men and women are truly created in God's image, then Judaism teaches that they are created in the image of the Lawgiver and the Creator. Jewish religious practice focuses on understanding and propagating God's Law, thus continuing the process of revelation. I would suggest that by engaging in the Human Genome Project, and in the attendant study of our ethical and moral responsibilities, we may in a practical and spiritual sense not only learn more about ourselves, but also learn more about the divine image in which we are created.

So what does all this mean? It means that as a Jew I approach the Human Genome Project with expectation and wonder at coming better to understand the ineffable mystery of God's creation. It means that I maintain an assiduous suspicion of anything that seems even remotely eugenic, and aware of the possibility that even the noblest of sciences can be perverted for racist, antisemitic, or nationalistic purposes. I believe it is possible to exercise the knowledge gained from genetics to enhance both God's creation and the well-being of mankind.

Two teachings are central to Jewish bioethics. If you can save a human life, the rabbis teach, then all prohibitions may be violated except for blasphemy, murder, and incest. If you can save a single life, it is taught, it is like saving the entire world. In this context, the Human Genome Project is not only our opportunity; it is our creative responsibility.

ROMAN CATHOLICISM

Albert S. Moraczewski, O.P.

The Dominican scholar Albert S. Moraczewski is not only a respected expert in theology and medical ethics but also a pharmacologist.

On October 23, 1982, while addressing those participating in a study week sponsored by the Pontifical Academy of Sciences, John Paul II made the following remarks regarding gene therapy:

"It is . . . to be hoped, with reference to your activities, that the new techniques of modification of the genetic code, in particular cases of genetic or chromosomic diseases, will be a motive of hope for the great number of people affected by those maladies.

"It can also be thought that, through the transfer of genes, certain specific diseases can be cured, such as sickle-cell anemia, which in many countries affects individuals of the same ethnic origin. It should likewise be recalled that some hereditary diseases can be avoided through progress in biological experimentation.

"The research of modern biology gives hopes that the transfer and mutations of genes can ameliorate the condition of those who are affected by chromosomic diseases; in this way the smallest and weakest of human beings can be cured during their intrauterine life or in the period immediately after birth.

"[While] . . . I approve and support your worthy researches, I reaffirm that they must all be subject to moral principles and values which respect and realize in its fullness the dignity of man."[1]

In a 1983 address to the World Medical Association Convention, the Pope distinguished carefully between a "strictly therapeutic intervention" and those "interventions aimed at improving human biological condition."[2] Therapeutic interventions, that is, those aimed at correcting a defect, at healing a malady, are "considered in principle as desirable." Such interventions are viewed as restoring a structure or

---

1. Pope John Paul II, *Origins* (Nov. 4, 1982).
2. *Origins* (Nov. 17, 1983), 388.

function, e.g., repairing a broken leg or stabilizing cardiovascular function by means of suitable pharmacological agents. But the norm or standard by which the restoration is directed is the healthy human person. Presumably, by extension and application of the above principle, the Pope would see gene therapy aimed at the cure of a disease or disorder, such as sickle-cell anemia, Duchenne muscular dystrophy, cystic fibrosis, as a movement towards the norm so long as such gene therapy "tends to real promotion of the personal well being of man without harming his integrity or worsening his life condition."[3]

"Integrity" in the papal statement refers to conserving structural and functional wholeness of the human body-person. Should the genetic intervention result in a new disability, or aggravation of a pre-existing disorder, such consequences would be viewed as a worsening of the individual's life condition. The risk of such results would need to be carefully weighed against the level of the reasonably expected benefits.

Pope John Paul II in this address does not condemn out of hand any genetic intervention "aimed at improving the human biological condition." But he does place requirements or conditions that would need to be verified before such genetic manipulation could be considered as morally acceptable.

When genetic manipulation is directed at improving the human biological condition, rather than correcting a defect, the issue is different and of more profound theological significance. The stated aim is to improve the human biological status. But, one may ask, what would constitute an improvement? Greater resistance to disease? Better memory? Higher intelligence? In this connection a novel by Dr. Robin Cook entitled *The Mutant* provides some interesting — even if at present fictional — possible consequences. Would increased mental powers be necessarily accompanied by greater moral sense and behavior? If not, high intelligence would be very destructive, as the novel illustrates.

The necessary conditions to be met, as stated in the papal address, include the following:

(1) "The biological nature of every human as a single substance composed of two principles, body and soul, should be respected." Thus one, for example, would violate this condition if an attempt were made to attach a human brain (or head) to a totally synthetic body (see C. S.

3. *Ibid.*

Lewis, *That Hideous Strength*), or control the brain's activity by direct connection of the brain with a computer (see *The Terminal Man* by Michael Crichton).

(2) In the procreation of a new human person or in genetic intervention, that new human life must be accorded the basic rights inherent in all human persons. This means that the developing human embryo at any stage may not be used experimentally, i.e., not directed to the therapeutic benefit of the individual but aimed at producing some predetermined qualities.[4]

(3) Modification of the genome (or the "genetic store") may not be directed "to create groups of different people, at the risk of provoking fresh marginalizations in society."[5] This concern recalls to mind the alpha, delta, and gamma groups of people visualized in Aldous Huxley's 1932 novel, *Brave New World*.

Not to be overlooked are the remarks of the National Conference of Catholic Bishops (NCCB) made in 1977 regarding recombinant DNA Research. While praising the potential benefits, it expressed caution in regards to the then yet unknown hazards associated with genetic engineering:

> "Because the technology has the potential to modify all forms of life, it requires full exploration of the ends it serves and the means to these ends. Serious, thoughtful reflection on these matters as well as responsible collaboration between scientists and the public are morally and pragmatically imperative. . . .

> "Simply stated, the dilemma is this: investigation involving recombination DNA promises great theoretical advances. Moreover, this technique may have practical applications (*e.g.,* in medicine and agriculture). At the same time, because the research is new (in some cases involving pathogenic substances and sometimes new organisms) it may involve unknown and potentially grave risks."[6]

4. See the Vatican *Instruction on the Respect for Human Life in its Origin and the Dignity of Procreation,* Congregation for the Doctrine of the Faith, Feb. 22, 1987.

5. *Ibid.*

6. National Conference of Catholic Bishops, "Statement on Recombination DNA Research," May 2, 1977.

Clearly, there is not only an order in the universe which must be respected but there is one in the microcosm of each individual person. The exceedingly complex interrelationship of the multitudinous cells, tissues, and organs as well as the innumerable biochemical systems which are involved in the development, functioning, and homeostatic processes of the human body, render any experimental genetic elimination or addition a very hazardous enterprise. Perhaps an old axiom may be applicable here: "If it works, don't fix it."

Beyond these concerns is a more fundamental theological consideration, an anthropology, which may be underlying the Pope's response. But I must emphasize that the following is my speculation, partially based on the Scriptures and partly on a comment made by the English scholar, C. S. Lewis. In brief, I believe that a fundamental issue is the view that Jesus Christ stands as the Alpha and Omega of the entire universe (see Revelation 1:8). The author of Colossians reflects a similar view:

"He is the image of the invisible God, the first born of all creation. In Him everything in heaven and on earth was created, things visible and invisible . . . all were created through Him and for Him." (Colossians 1:15-29)

In other words, he is the norm, the standard, in whose specific, concrete image the human race was fashioned. Ordinarily, Christians think of Jesus as a model of human behavior. And that is certainly true. But to see him as a norm for human bodily structure and physiological activity is rarely considered. Of course, I am not saying that all humans must be male. Genesis made it clear at the very beginning that: "God created man in his image; in the divine image he created him; male and female he created them" (Gen. 1:27).

The human race may be viewed as being created in two images: *Imago Dei* and *Imago Jesu Christi*. The thrust of the two creation accounts in the Book of Genesis is that humans are made in the image of God. We humans, then, are images of God inasmuch as we have received a delegated dominion over the earth and its creatures. But one can ask, parenthetically, does that include a dominion over our bodies?

The second image in which we are fashioned is that of Jesus Christ. In this case the imaging is more specific, namely, the humanity of Jesus Christ. Our bodies now are like his. The Letter to the Hebrews notes that Jesus was like us in all things except sin (4:15). This could also be conversely stated: we are like Jesus in all things except for our sins.

Furthermore, St. Paul notes that our resurrected bodies will be fashioned after Jesus' glorified body (see Philippians 3:21). So it seems fitting that our preglorified bodies remain as his was prior to his death and resurrection. That is the point which C. S. Lewis makes in his novel, *Perelandra:* since the second Person of the Most Holy Trinity has personally united to Himself a human nature — soul and body — that psychophysical unit has been elevated in dignity above its mere created nature. If this is so, can we freely alter what God has so blessed as no other creature on earth has been?

Whatever evolutionary steps may have preceded the appearance of our species, *homo sapiens,* does not present a problem here. If our paleoanthropological record is correct, our prehuman ancestors went through considerable anatomical changes before the evolutionary development produced — albeit with false starts and dead-ends — our present species.

Jesus Christ was born a member of that species and by that fact has "consecrated" it. He is the perfect human exemplar in his basic psychophysiological structure and in his behavior. To be sure, no assertion is being made here about a photographic image: sex, color of skin, eyes or hair, size, weight. Rather, what is important are those psychophysiological elements genetically determined which are shared by all human beings regardless of their race or condition. Ultimately, what must be protected in any genetic alteration of the human being are the cognitive-affective powers, including the capacity to make free choices. It is the human intellective power coupled with free will which makes possible human beings to share in God's dominion over the material world. It is also these same powers that give humans the capacity, the opportunity, to share in the resurrection of Jesus Christ and to be divinized by the gracious gift of God.

Finally, as a personal conjecture, the fact that the Son of God took on personally this human nature — that is, became a member of *homo sapiens* — has granted to it a consecration which prohibits any substantial genetic alteration that would generate a distinct species or individual whose intellectual and volitional capacities were compromised even to the point of not being able to share in the glory of the Resurrected Christ.

Kevin O'Rourke, O.P.

An additional observation on Roman Catholic teaching made by the Reverend Kevin O'Rourke, O.P., of the Center for Health Care Ethics of St. Louis University is here summarized.

There is essentially no difference or conflict between science and faith or reason and revelation, since all truth is one. This emphasis of St. Thomas Aquinas is ignored by many who have also forgotten the wholeness and unity of each person. Likewise in society, or human community, unity and wholeness is violated by all kinds of unjustified discrimination or neglect. The HGP should benefit not only the affluent in Europe and America, but all people. This is implied by a theologically motivated concern for justice without discriminatory limits. To be sure, justice in medical services and scientific benefits is not a moral province peculiar to Christianity; but the strong emphasis on the personal integrity and value of each one is distinctive in the Church's ecumenical mission.

Father O'Rourke again asserted his defense of the concept of human beings as co-creators with God, a view necessitated by the advance of science and accompanied by requisite changes in traditional, pre-scientific, and pre-genetic doctrines of God and creation.

EASTERN ORTHODOXY

Stanley S. Harakas

The contributions of Eastern Orthodox Christian thought to religious ethics and medicine are becoming better known in North America, due largely to the writings of the Reverend Stanley S. Harakas.[7] He is a professor at the Holy Cross Greek

7. Stanley S. Harakas, *Health and Medicine in the Eastern Orthodox Tradition* (New York: Crossroad Publishing Co., 1990) and "Eastern Orthodox Bioethics" in *Theological Developments in Bioethics: 1988-1990,* ed. B. Andrew Lustig (Dordrecht and Boston: Kluwer Academic Publishers, 1991), 85-101.

Orthodox School of Theology, Brookline, Massachusetts. In addresses at the Houston Conference and the 1993 meeting of the American Association for the Advancement of Science he explained the implications of genetics for his tradition.

The Eastern Christian theological anthropology shares in significant ways some presuppositions of genetics. There are perspectives in Orthodox teaching about human nature that provide "coincidences" with genetic understandings and methodologies that are not highlighted by other Christian theological traditions.

Though in this earthly life growth toward God-likeness can be continuous, it is never completed. In the Eastern Christian worldview, the eternal Kingdom of God provides a transcendent referent for everything. Within this eschatological context, the goal of human life is understood to be an ongoing process of increasing communion with God, other persons, and the creation. This forms the matrix for Eastern Christian ethics and provides it with the materials and perspectives for articulating the "ought" dimensions of the Church's teaching.

Among the more important aspects of these teachings for our topic are:

(1) Supreme value of love of God and neighbor;
(2) A view of nature as fallen, yet capable of providing basic norms of living;
(3) Close relation of material and spiritual dimensions of human existence and their appropriate relationship and integration;
(4) Self-determining ability of human beings in moral settings;
(5) The movement toward God-likeness.

All these are acknowledged within the framework of time, history, and eternity: i.e., in an eschatological frame.

Concern for the health of the body, though not central, has a significant place in Eastern Christian ethics. The Eastern Christian mind-set calls for "a healthy mind, a healthy spirit, with a healthy body." The body is not merely an instrument, nor is it simply a dwelling place of the spirit. It is a constituent part of human existence. The body requires attention for the sake of the whole human being. Practices that contribute to bodily health and well-being are ethically required. Adequate nourishment, proper exercise, and other good health habits are fitting and appropriate, while practices that harm the body are considered not simply unhealthful, but also immoral. Abuse of the body is morally inappropriate. Both body and mind are abused with over-indulgence of alcohol and the use of narcotics for nontherapeutic purposes. Eastern Christian teaching holds that persons who might be attracted to these passions need to exercise their ethical powers to overcome their dependence upon them and to control the condition and its impact upon their lives. This discipline becomes, then, an aspect of their growth toward God-likeness.

When illness comes, there is an ethical duty arising from the Eastern Christian perspective that directs human beings to struggle against sickness which, if unaddressed, can lead to death. The moral requirement to care for the health of the body indicates it is appropriate to use healing methods which will enhance health and maintain life.

For Eastern Christianity two means are used concurrently for healing illness: spiritual healing and different forms of medicine. The first is embodied in nearly all services of the Church, but in particular, the Sacrament of Healing, or Holy Unction. There is also a continuing tradition of multiple forms of prayer and saintly intercessions for the healing of body and soul. Yet, the Church does not see the spiritual healing approach as exclusive nor competitive with scientific medicine. St. John Chrysostom (4th century), one of the great Church Fathers, frequently referred to his need for medical attention and medications.

Consequently, from this theological perspective, there is a dynamic understanding of human nature created with a certain givenness, yet open to growth and development.

How does such a theological anthropology relate to what might be understood as a genetic anthropology? A genetic understanding of human nature? I believe, as I said earlier, that there are certain coincidences between genetics and this theological perspective. I would like to treat them briefly under five headings: Determination, Development, Distortedness, Therapy, and Synergy.

(1) *Determination.* In both the genetic and the theological understanding of human nature there is an understanding of givenness in the human condition. For theology it is creation in the image of God. In genetics there is the understanding that human physical characteristics are the products of a complex chromosomal chemical structure.

The genes function in interrelation with each other and in relationship to the somatic dimensions of human existence to define aspects of human life and existence. Comparing the genetically-defined human eye with the genetically-defined eye of a fly reveals significant dimensions of identity in each. The whole complex of the human person then is seen, at least in some dimensions, as pre-defined and as determined in some ways. I do not think that to say this is to adopt a "deterministic" stance. It does mean that from either perspective there is content and specific meaning to the term "human being."

(2) *Development.* In both views, the "givenness" of human nature is present, but incipient. It needs development. In both cases, there is perceived to be a *"donatum"* which includes within it its own end. One could say that there is both in the concept of the image and likeness of God and the genetic "code of codes" a built-in *telos,* a sort of Aristotelian *entelecheia* which provides a predefined end toward which the process leads. There is a goal that can be described in both understandings, and fulfillment means at least in part the realization of that end, and no other, provided that conditions favorable to development and growth are present and active. Human nature, though defined by some parameters, is not static but dynamic in its formation.

(3) *Distortedness.* In the Eastern Christian understanding of "original sin" the human condition is at the center, not guilt. Broken relationship with God means a distorted human condition. While all the aspects of the divine image remain in empirical human beings, they are all distorted, weakened, and broken to some extent. Intellect is darkened, self-determination weakened, creativity distorted, ethical sensitivity in some measure corrupted. Genetics has discovered a similar distortedness in the human gene pool. As I understand it, no individual human being is without some damaged or distorted genes. The givenness of human nature defined by the human genome also suffers from some distortedness that eventually may produce what human beings define as genetically caused illness.

(4) *Therapy.* The Eastern Christian understanding of the redemptive work of Christ is often described precisely in therapeutic terms. A common designation for Christ in Eastern Christian liturgy is "the physician of body and soul." Though as a science genetics does not necessarily imply a therapeutic intention or interest, since as a "pure

science" it functions descriptively, seeking to map out the human genome, there seems to be an assumption that this knowledge is destined for therapeutic purposes. Of course, there are also biologists who see this knowledge as a tool for dominating others and creating a new world determined by genetic manipulation. But those geneticists involved in the discussions of the relationship between genetics and religion seem to assume, rather, a therapeutic and healing stance.

(5) *Synergy.* The assumption is that human nature needs human self-determining action to realize the potentialities given it. In theology, this means the cooperation and communion with God. Humanity conforms through a moral and spiritual struggle for authentic human existence and against forces which destroy or weaken the image of God in human life. This self-determination on the part of the human being is precisely required to affirm some dimension of what it means to be human. Similarly, genetics increases understanding of the human genome, its functioning, and its possible manipulation for therapeutic purposes. The geneticist is not just an observer. By his very study and intervention the geneticist becomes a synergist in the process.

By emphasizing these five commonalities, or coincidences, I in no way confuse these two approaches to human nature. Rather, I wish to affirm their differences and their integrity. In this discernment, I would also seek to give to theological anthropology a vision that transcends that of the geneticist, which can contribute to addressing issues and problems that confront the geneticist once he or she steps out of the laboratory. Thus, the following concluding comments.

Genetic counseling seeks to provide information to a couple before they conceive children so that potentially serious conditions in newborns can be foreknown. Genetic counseling is related to genetic screening of population groups that might be carriers of particular genetic illnesses. Genetic screening refines and makes more accurate the earlier practices of the Church and society that sought to reduce the incidence of deformed and deficient children, through the restriction of consanguineous marriages.

As a procedure that would reduce the number of persons entering into marriages with dangerously high chances for the transmission of genetic illnesses, these procedures ought to be strongly encouraged. Genetic screening of young people with Mediterranean backgrounds before marriage might guide them in the selection of spouses. This would help them avoid the tragedy of illnesses such as Cooley's anemia and Tay-Sachs disease in their progeny.

Genetic engineering as a topic of ethical concern provokes conflicting reactions among Eastern Christian ethicists. The potential therapeutic possibilities are looked at somewhat positively, but the potential for misuse and abuse makes Eastern Christians very cautious.

Since the Church strenuously opposes abortion, information indicating the prospective birth of a genetically deformed child cannot justify ending the life of the baby in the womb. Instead, this information could be used to prepare the parents to receive their child with the love, acceptance, and courage abundantly required to care for such an exceptional baby.

The common denominator in all these issues is the high regard and concern of the Church for human life as a gift of God. Eastern Christianity takes a conservative approach to these issues, seeing in them a dimension of the holy and relating them to transcendent values and concerns. Only an intense respect for human life can curb the modern tendency to destroy human life before it begins and as it approaches its end. The human person, from the very moment of conception, is dependent upon others for life and sustenance. It is in the community of the living, especially as it relates to the source of life, God in Trinity, that life is conceived, nurtured, developed, and fulfilled. The trust each person has in others for the continued well-being of his or her own life forms a basis for ethical norms. Eastern Christian ethics, consequently, functions with a pro-life bias that honors and respects the life of each person as a divine gift which requires development and enhancement.

George J. Pazin

Who is a "layman?" In the field of medicine Father Harakas is called a layman. Conversely, in relation to theology and the Church's ministry George J. Pazin, M.D., a specialist in infectious diseases, is a layman. Dr. Pazin is a professor at the University of Pittsburgh School of Medicine and member of the Orthodox Church. He expressed some personal views on genetics.

I recognize that my religious beliefs clearly influence my teaching. Indeed, with regard to my teaching about HIV infections and AIDS, I sense a calling to expose misleading and misguided "education" foisted on the public by educators who feel we have a primary responsibility to avoid alarm and calm hysteria. I feel that my primary responsibility as an Orthodox Christian physician is to be truthful and trustworthy. "Thou shalt not bear false witness."

As I turn to consider the influence of my Orthodox Christianity on my views of genetics, I automatically feel a responsibility not to bear false witness. Two thoughts come to mind. First, scientifically, we have not accomplished something until we have accomplished something. Therefore, although we have an obligation to project into the future, we should be most careful not to exaggerate our projections. I tend to prefer genetic presentations such as that presented by Dr. C. Thomas Caskey which deal with "what we can do today" rather than futuristic presentations which may present exaggerated predictions. Secondly, I remind myself that a scientist defines the circumstances of an experiment and then carefully observes the results.

Although we may develop insightful expectations, we must honestly subject the null hypothesis to experimental scrutiny and verification through rejection. We must remember that scientists do not create nature's behavior; we observe nature's operation.

I do have a concern that in our enthusiasm to help humanity we may oversimplify the prospects for treatment and downplay unrecognized potential for injury or damage. We may look to progress and fail to anticipate injuries which might result from improper, unjust use of knowledge to discriminate unfairly against people because of their unfortunate and heretofore secret inheritance. Unintended side-effects of genetic therapeutic interventions are not given serious enough consideration. As a physician, I am skeptical of presentations which suggest that the treatment has no side-effects. I do not believe there is forbidden knowledge; rather, I am apprehensive that we may abuse or misuse knowledge.

My knowledge of genetics enhances my religious beliefs, first, by expanding my sense of wonder and astonishment at God's creation. I cannot help but ask why specific genes are located at specific locations. It is apparent that we are only touching the surface of true genetic knowledge. Nature, God's creation, is awesome.

My knowledge of genetics also enhances my religious beliefs because I am strengthened by the knowledge humanity is capable of acquiring through observation and reasoning. It is almost as though God has created a remarkably beautiful mechanism for progressive improvement of humanity, has enabled humankind gradually to acquire an understanding of his creation.

Thirdly, my knowledge of genetics enhances my religious belief that God is a merciful God, inasmuch as genetics may be an avenue though which some genetic diseases may eventually be cured and suffering may be relieved. This is particularly significant because I look upon genetic diseases as diseases which are not the result of human abuses. It is comforting that human efforts to understand creation may be rewarded by a reduction in human suffering. Having seen several patients recently with sickle-cell anemia, I look forward to the time when the suffering of these unfortunate patients may be relieved. It is regrettable that public health measures to reduce the incidence and prevalence of genetic disorders are seemingly delayed by sociopolitical considerations.

I am all in favor of repairing God's creation with the genetic tools that we have discovered, but I shudder to think of our trying to improve upon the creation. I agree that somatic or germ-line genetic interventions to treat genetic diseases are appropriate, but eugenic attempts to enhance physical or mental traits should not be endorsed. The latter suggests an element of dissatisfaction with normal humankind. I re-emphasize that we have serious limitations in our ability to appreciate unintended side-effects of genetic interventions. The repair of adenosine deaminase deficiency is obviously beneficial and appears to exceed the risk; but I am not sure that making me or my progeny taller, faster, or smarter is necessarily beneficial. Reducing sleep requirements for humankind might be a curse. Deleting the "ferocity complex" sounds dangerously like performing a frontal lobotomy or performing "therapeutic" castration.

PROTESTANTISM

Roy J. Enquist (Lutheran)

The Protestant Reformation of the sixteenth century in Europe produced two large families of churches with distinctly different doctrines: the Lutheran and the Reformed (Presbyterian). Their differing styles of evaluating the HGP and responding to its implications are well exhibited in the following passages. The Lutheran writer is Roy J. Enquist, a professor at Gettysburg Theological Seminary. He responds in general to the same questionnaire which prompted Rabbi Frankel's exposition of faith and genetics.

Section One: Protestant Principles

Protestantism is distinguished by its double concern: the primacy of the gospel of Jesus Christ, and the salience of that Word for the moral life. The diversities with this tradition — confessional, denominational, cultural, partisan — are obvious and well known. More fundamental, however, is the basic loyalty which Protestants share: a faith in the saving power of God in Christ and its ethical significance. Protestantism's preoccupation with ethics as transcendently based has made it vulnerable to criticism. But society's growing awareness of the indispensable importance of moral values for human life suggests new opportunities for people of faith to be of service to other communities in modern life.

The Protestant belief in "the priesthood of all believers" implies that all people need to have access to the sources of faith and virtue. It also indicates that no one can speak in matters of faith for all others without their consent. The acknowledgment of such a restriction has not served to discourage advocacy of particular theological/ethical argument, but rather to stimulate it. The present statement thus speaks only for its author, a Lutheran, but attempts to be faithful to the Protestant spirit and perspective.

A third core belief is the primacy of Scripture as the authoritative written record of the witness of Israel and the apostolic Church. That message is heard to center in Jesus Christ, who himself is the Word of God in human form, a Word accessible to the faithful by means of the work of the Spirit in the present and historic life of the community. The intellectual, spiritual, and moral experience of that community and its members provides the matrix within which the Word is heard and obeyed. Faith thus is both passive — an openness to the splendor, mystery, and love of God — and active — a disciplined responsiveness to the divine imperative which orders lives of love, justice, and care. That imperative is understood to have an intellectual dimension. Paul writes, "I appeal to you therefore, brothers (and sisters), . . . be transformed by the renewal of your mind, that you may prove what is the will of God, what is good and acceptable and perfect" (Romans 12:1-3).

One way in which caring for the creation is disclosed is found in the churches' current study of the interplay of theology and bioethics, including the discussion of the moral significance of genetic engineering. The balance of this essay is a response to the invitation to reply to the conceptual and methodological issues raised in the document "Religious/Theological Attitudes toward Genetic Intervention and Alteration of Life-Form."

Section Two: Key Concepts on Genetics and Humanhood

Concept I: Personhood/Humanhood   Humanhood and personhood are frequently used interchangeably. However, closer attention suggests a necessary distinction. Humanhood, understood as membership in *homo sapiens,* is in part a biological concept. Such capacities as consciousness, self-consciousness, psychological and physiological feelings, and ability to recognize and articulate values are commonly accepted as distinguishing marks of human identity although they are not exclusively human. Clearly they are not equally accessible for empirical analysis even though a human being deprived of such capacities would be recognized as significantly deficient. Historical attempts to deny human beings the power to utilize such capacities appropriately meet with outrage and revulsion. The theological ground for this consensus is focused in the classic Hebrew concept, humanity as created in the image of God *(imago Dei).*

Within Protestantism, the *imago Dei* doctrine serves to affirm the universal moral dignity of all human beings. The biblical tradition does not assume that all human beings know the reality of God, but it holds that all humankind possesses moral capability and responsibility. Adam and Eve are pictured as the universal human prototypes who are morally accountable. Indeed, that accountability is the point of their adventure in Eden. The New Testament lays even stronger emphasis on the universality of moral accountability as the distinguishing mark of what it means to be human (Romans 1:18-19, 1 Corinthians 15:22). From its beginnings, Protestantism has argued that the human moral dilemma roots not in the abstract possibility of an amoral life but rather in the conflict between alternate loyalties so that the human project is characteristically marked by a struggle between competing values.

At the same time, the newer of the creation narratives in Genesis (chapter 1) articulates a fundamental continuity between the human and the animal creations (cf. Psalm 104; Job 38). The contrast between the created order (human and nonhuman) and the transcendent ground and source of all things is unmistakable. The solidarity of all creatures is presupposed and consistently affirmed.

Personhood is a theological rather than a scientific concept. It always implies the presence of a relationship between persons, since personhood does not exist in isolation but only in the interrelationship of persons. Thus, while personhood and humanity are closely related, they are not identical. Humanity is that sector of the biological order which, among other criteria, has the capacity for language and for moral judgment. Personhood presupposes humanity as here understood, but it also implies a dimension of transcendence which may not always be present in human consciousness. Personhood, for example, always presupposes self-consciousness as well as the consciousness of others as persons, while humanity does not always demonstrate this capacity. Thus, rather than speaking of persons as having the capacity to become moral agents, it is the moral agent which has the capacity to become aware of a personal life. (In the Scriptures, persons do not *have* souls, they *are* souls; they are interrelated, inter-subjects, beings addressed by an ultimate order which is actually personal.)

Biology and genetics, as scientific concepts, appear to regard conception as a process rather than as a moment. This scientific preference is theologically important, for it illumines the ethical judgment that

154

humanness (and certainly personality) are better understood in terms of process than in terms of one moment. The tendency to trivialize humanhood by reducing it to a moment is theologically dubious.

Concept II: Parenthood Theologically understood, parenthood is modeled by the revelation of God as Parent. Genetics did not enter into that formulation since God is not the biological parent of humankind. Genetic parenthood thus is not theologically significant. Personhood, as we have seen, is critical to human value formation but is not itself a scientific concept.

The Jewish and Christian picture of God as Father and, to a lesser extent, Mother, has not only served to humanize the doctrine of God, it has also given incalculable emphasis to the role of parent as an image of divine self-disclosure. Psychoanalysis has shown the ambiguous power of that image even in secular cultures. In the Bible the parent is the life-giving nurturer, not necessarily the biological parent. There are those who hold that there is a "natural order" which requires that the act of procreation be expressive of the mutual love of husband and wife; any intervention threatens a God-given order and is to be rejected. A more typical response holds that the God of the Bible is a God of history who calls humanity to be coworkers by exercising responsible dominion (another aspect of the *imago Dei*) on earth. Biological science can enable childless couples to assume the blessings and responsibilities of parenthood. The basic issue in this view is not the legitimacy of using technology but the question of purpose. Why have children? To prove one's manhood (or womanhood)? To have someone to give one's own life meaning? A profound investment of love, care, and nurture is essential for the raising of children. The method of conception thus is not ethically critical, but the capacity to assume responsibility for the child-to-be-born is.

Concept III: Kinship and Lineage Theologians and the laity generally need to be aware of the sociobiological understanding of kinship and lineage. Human identity in terms of personal and cultural life has a sociobiological base. While terms like "family" and "race" appear in sociological literature, their scientific character is debated. They are of major importance in some religions while in classical Christian theology they are of minor significance. From its beginnings the Christian tradition has been engaged in conflict with those who would raise family or race to levels of theological significance. Jesus' rejections of the claims made on him by his family, his (and the prophets') denial that ethnic/national considerations enjoy divine approval, are well known. The protological and eschatological visions of the Hebrew Bible and the New Testament alike are rigorously inclusive of all human categories: race, tongue, gender, tribe.

It does not follow that persons of shared biological lineage do not have the right to receive pertinent genetic information. The general moral right to obtain access to the truth concerning one's physical-social origins is incontestable. Individuals have the right to get information concerning nonpaternity and other relevant genetic data. It is the withholding of the truth from the subject that is difficult to defend. Who decides who is best served by nondisclosure?

Concept IV: Human Diversity and Human Equality In showing that race is a social construct rather than a scientific fact, biology can assist theology in the latter's emphasis on the unity of humankind. The biblical creation stories, for example, make no allowance for racial differences as having any moral significance. Given the biblical writers' awareness of major racial and cultural differences in their time, this indifference represents a strong moral bias in favor of inclusivity.

Biological diversity is a given which theology can generally affirm and celebrate. The diversity of the creation, reflecting the Creator's judgment that it is good in its very diversity and order, gives metaethical support for the natural diversity and order everywhere demonstrated.

Nonetheless, in a fallen world, it is also clear that some forms of diversity are ethically troubling. One study indicates that genetic disorders appear in more than 66,666 infants out of every million born each year in the United States. Genetic disorders account for thirty percent of the children and ten percent of the adults who are in hospitals. The ethical task is to encourage the development of strategies for overcoming those forms of genetic diversity that diminish the quality of human life.

In particular the problems relating to diversity and equality appear in discussions regarding genetic intervention. The tendency is to champion either diversity or equality. Protestantism historically has a strong interest in affirming both values. This emphasis on the correlation of diversity and equality can be contested philosophically, but an exclusive emphasis on either value is even more vulnerable. Theologically considered, human beings are equal before God even as they are diverse by God's design. This is particularly clear in other areas of ethics. Racism fails in its incapacity to account for the unity of humankind on either scientific or religious grounds.

An adequate strategy in bioethics will seek to do justice to both human equality and human diversity, knowing that a double perspective will more likely bring us to the whole truth. With respect to the correlation of disorders and capacities in particular populations, the moral temptation is to discriminate in the light of genetic differences (sickle-cell anemia; Tay-Sachs disease). Theology can provide a critical service by showing that justice is not grounded in the demonstration of actual equality by subjects, but that a transcendent perspective enables one to affirm a necessary polarity: e.g., limitations of capacities centered in particular populations require rather than invalidate the moral obligation to affirm human equality.

Biological data can be morally confusing in that evidence can be garnered from "science" to support both democratic claims of equality and totalitarian claims of inequality. Theology can be called on to make the value judgment (that science, as science, cannot) that (1) truth is both philosophically and morally necessary for the human moral life, and (2) truth, in this instance, encompasses a basic polarity: equality of humans and diversity among humans.

Concept V: Identity, Integrity, and Uniqueness An organism's identity is dependent on its genome. However, of fundamental importance too is its social environment. The identity of a human organism will be shaped, if not determined, by family, social history, language, and culture (including religion). But what is most significant is the subject's reception, rejection, and transformation of any or all of this. Thus, it is possible to overestimate the importance of an organism's genome by a process of biological reductionism.

While there would appear to be no objection in principle to genetic testing for currently untreatable diseases, the rationale for such research should be published in the scientific community.

The "banking" of DNA for future use as well as its being used for diagnostic and forensic purposes does not appear to raise ethical

157

problems. The cloning of cells in perpetuity would be discouraged as lacking a recognizable moral base. In all of these cases it would be important that the research be conducted according to generally accepted scientific and ethical guidelines. The information gained could be abused, as could all valuable data.

Concept VI: Health and Disease   Complex polygenic disorders present new challenges to theology's understanding of creation and can serve to move us to a more profound understanding of our humanity. Early Protestantism strongly emphasized creation as a continuing reality *(creatio continua)* and gave primary focus to its personal meaning for human subjects in their relation to the whole fabric of the cosmos. This existential understanding of creation equips the tradition to deal with issues of health and disease in a morally significant way. One's health is a concrete sign of the goodness of God's creation. One's disease is a sign that, in the words of Jesus' parable, "an enemy has done this." One's status as a creature is seen as a dynamic: we are constantly being created, dying, and being born again. Holy Baptism is seen by the reformers as a daily act — not that the sacrament would be repeated but rather that its generative significance (from death to life) could be experienced anew each day. One's physical death is therefore not the final or ultimate evil. It has been swallowed up in the death of Christ and transformed by the power of the resurrection. Accordingly the modern belief (often unwittingly encouraged by the medical community) that the significance of human life can only be judged by its longevity is unacceptable. The whole point of the primitive Christian gospel was that in Christ the power of death has been broken and that they who live in him need not fear it (John 11; Romans 8). Similarly, one of the major "meanings of salvation" in the Scriptures is healing, restoration to wholeness of life. In the Gospels, Jesus is pictured as one empowered by God to heal the sick. Accordingly, within the history of the church, caring for the sick, whether or not recovery can be contemplated, has been a traditional ministry. The separation of the medical arts from spiritual care is a relatively recent development, historically understandable but not altogether salutary.

(1) The theological meanings of health and sickness continue to demand investigation of several issues.

(a) The people involved. All persons have inherited genes which

are only partly understood and which are not all fully desired. Thus, the recognition that no one creates oneself, that we are all the creation of Another and not self-generated, shows the myth of the self-made man to be an illusion. We are not totally responsible for what we are, for what "we make of ourselves," or for what happens to us. The theological interpretation of human life as being constituted primarily by its relationships find its analogue in the social connections of one's genetic inheritance.

(*b*) Determinism. In spite of idealist and existentialist calls for us to create ourselves, science powerfully reminds us of our massive indebtedness to factors quite beyond our control. Increasingly the moral problem we face is how one is to establish a credible ground for belief in freedom, in responsibility, given the reality of determinism. Mature religion typically finds it possible to affirm both freedom and determinism (destiny/predestination) however illogical that may seem initially. Such religion need fear no new demonstrations for determinism. It need only show how that is not the whole truth. Freedom is still possible.

(*c*) Blameworthiness and responsibility. The polarity of freedom and determinism makes it possible to assert responsibility. This polarity makes it possible to assert responsibility for one's health even while honestly recognizing one's inability to determine one's genetic inheritance. Folk wisdom has always recognized this strange phenomenon: through courage and integrity one can triumph over apparently insuperable odds. No one is given an ideal life situation (or genetic legacy). What we do with what we have been given is the disclosure of our moral character. The scientific age has changed the terms of this drama, but the drama itself, with a new cast of characters, appears to have settled in for a permanent run.

(*d*) Health and disease. Definitions need to be dynamic rather than absolute. Religion's traditional insistence on a holistic understanding of human life appears to be increasingly recognized as critical — even if it is philosophically unclear, scientifically imprecise, and ethically troublesome. In the biblical tradition, health is understood in terms of such concepts as peace, salvation, resurrection, redemption, forgiveness, righteousness. The eschatological vision is of the death of disease and the victory of life. As we think today of health in terms of wholeness, well-being, social justice, ecological coherence, we are close to classic

Judeo-Christian thought and have a valuable dialogical base for deliberation with the medical and political communities.

(e) Social eugenics. In a democratic, pluralistic society, it is extremely difficult to determine a common social policy for health care. A fundamental question yet to be resolved regarding social eugenics is whether and to what extent eugenics is desirable. Those religious traditions which see human beings as being empowered by God to be co-creators believe they have not only permission but a responsibility for defining eugenic policy. Obviously, abuses can occur. This suggests the need not for an abandonment of eugenics but for the development of more careful and just processes by which the human family can be sustained. The pagan belief that Chance is king is unacceptable. Equally specious is a biologism that denies a morally responsible use of scientific knowledge.

(2) Implications for diversity and equality in so-called dysgenic medical practices. Traditionally, one confronts a basic moral problem whenever either the individual or the group is understood to have rights that are absolute and that therefore may undercut the rights of the other party. Both individual and group values and rights are valid and should be affirmed. At the lowest level, this implies a method for determining a compromise whereby both the individual and the group are recognized. At a higher level, a method is required which will so enhance the values of the individual and the group that they can find themselves fulfilled in each other.

Soldiers or priests give their lives not as signs of self-abnegation nor self-rejection, but as a means for fulfilling the self by transcending the limitations of the self. Again, a community that encourages its individual members to fulfill the personal potentialities for the common good is stronger and more viable than one which repudiates individual dignity. Totalitarianism in the twentieth century has proven less stable than even flawed democracies.

To take an example from medicine, persons with Type I diabetes can be encouraged to consider how to express their sexuality and their desire for parenting without themselves providing genetic material for the next generation. Christianity does not hold that anyone has an absolute right to reproduce oneself sexually.

(3) Responsibility for the loss of associated characteristics. Such responsibility is grave indeed. The ethical dilemma is clear: intervention

in the form of genetic therapy can result in unanticipated consequences for which, in spite of our ignorance, we are in some sense responsible. The problem, however, is hardly unique to the medical community. Lacking prescience, human beings never know as much about the consequences of their actions — for good or ill — as they frequently pretend. In the case of genetic research, scientists cannot claim nor be expected to demonstrate fatidic or moral perfection. The presence of unpredictable negative consequences in a procedure must be acknowledged, not to prevent the project from going forward, but to enable the community to acknowledge its own need to recognize its limitations in the face of the unknown. Humility does not prevent moral tragedy but it frequently serves to diminish its likelihood. On the other hand, being genetically "flawed" is no index of moral dignity. Humanity is not defined by the absence of defective genes. In any case the range of possible defects is staggering. Moral judgment would need to address each case in terms of the factors relevant to it.

Section Three: Questions on Creation/Co-Creation Related to the Application of Theological Perspectives on the Human Genome Project

Concept I: Acceptability of the Human Genome Project itself   Ethicists in the Protestant community generally hold that genetic research is a form of inquiry that can yield information that is both valuable and useful. The mapping and sequencing of the human genome is not objectionable inherently but there is danger, of course, that this knowledge can be used to facilitate improper interventions. Clearly, knowledge is better than ignorance. Yet knowledge is not unambiguous morally. Its capacity for abuse requires its deployment in a matrix characterized by life-enhancing, humanly enriching values.

Concept II: Acceptability of interventions in humans   The theological community has just begun to explore the ethical implications of genetic intervention in human life. Relatively little has been done to familiarize its public with the prospects and problems. Much remains to be done. Here we can only offer general guidelines for discussion and revision.
   1. Technologically assisted human reproduction. When for a

161

variety of reasons insemination through intercourse is problematic, artificial insemination using semen obtained from the husband (AIH) is permitted as presenting few legal, social, or ethical problems. Artificial insemination by a donor (AID) other than the husband, however, is to be resisted. While the desired end may be praiseworthy, the means are inappropriate since AID separates procreation from marriage and thus violates the marriage covenant. The biological presence of the donor is contradicted by his social absence — a grave act of irresponsibility on his part which can only create psychological problems for the couple and the child. While some single women may contract for semen from a donor, the mother's deliberate exclusion of the child's father from the child's life cannot be morally justified. Little attention has been given to the ethical implications of the cloning of human life. It is likely, however, that most ethicists would resist the procedure if it meant that a human life would be created without provision for the nurture, care, identity, and relationships typically provided in family life.

2, 3. Most ethicists would probably not object to somatic gene therapy which involves the genetic alteration of cells taken from and reintroduced into living people. Nor would the state of development at which such alterations are introduced make a difference except, of course, that in the case of a child or adult the appropriate consent would need to be obtained. In all cases, the dignity, value, and integrity of the human person would need to be recognized as paramount.

4. Germ-line therapy involving genetic alterations to gametes that would be passed on is deeply troubling since the results are not predictable. Undesirable sequels could occur which prove devastating. Again, serious objections would be raised to specific kinds of genetic alteration of genes which contribute to emotion, gender, and intellectual ability. The objection would hold whether the alteration is somatic or germ-line since too little is known about either at the present time.

5. Both negative and positive eugenics, genetic manipulation to eliminate debilities or to improve talent, are unacceptable to many. Similarly, ethicists generally would object to combining human and nonhuman genetic material, particularly if this were done to reduce the physical, cultural, or psychological diversity among peoples. The character of the objection is not completely clear, but many would argue that such intervention is precluded by our present lack of adequate scientific knowledge, social understanding, and, indeed, moral accountability.

6. The suggestion that there may be ethical connections between such issues as capital punishment, abortion, and justifiable war theory, on one hand, and genetic engineering on the other is provocative. There are those who argue for a "seamless garment" inclusive of abortion and pacifism. More typically, however, each issue is viewed separately, and different styles of argumentation are usually employed. Thus Protestantism is traditionally supportive of justifiable war theory with an important minority urging pacifism; the former argument usually is consequentialist and the latter deontological. Probably, for the foreseeable future, the attempt to build a "consistent ethic" will prove fragile. On the other hand, the care with which the major Protestant communions have dealt with the biological/cultural/ethical issues in the abortion debate may provide a clue as to their interest in biomedical issues generally. Christians who are inclined to read the Bible contextually and those who seek to read it literally usually differ in their judgment regarding abortion. That difference in method will likely lead to similar differences in their approach to bioethical issues for the foreseeable future.

Gerald P. McKinney (Reformed)

Traditional, or "confessional," Protestant theology has for nearly five hundred years emphasized the abyss separating divine omnipotence and human, creaturely dependence and frailty. Calvinists have been more rigorous than others in teaching this gap, which can be bridged only by grace from God's side. The permeating influences of the Enlightenment, rationalism, romanticism, humanism, idealism, and scientific, empirical method have modified the beliefs and views of many Christians. Among other ways, these influences have promoted a more optimistic estimate of human potentialities and a less austere notion of God's mandatory requirements. An exemplary exposition of a modern Calvinist theology in relation to genetics is offered by a religious scholar of Rice University, Gerald P. McKenny, Ph.D.

A. How has genetics influenced my views about religion?

Genetic knowledge gives persons a sense of fate, or for those who are carriers of or are affected by serious conditions, a sense of being victims of fate. This surpasses the historical or social senses of being conditioned. Why this sense of fate? And why is it more pronounced than senses of being conditioned by socio-economic forces, or socio-biological imperatives, or the unconscious, or language itself — all familiar to theologians? I believe the reason is due to the confluence of three factors.

First, genetic knowledge holds the promise — or the threat — of explaining human uniqueness and conditions and characteristics of individuals with a high degree of precision. Second, the explanations offered by genetic knowledge may be able to locate particular conditions, and perhaps eventually human characteristics, to more or less particular sites. However diffuse these sites may turn out to be, and however limited the capacity to locate complex human characteristics, the metaphors of map and site imply a greater efficiency and thoroughness of human explanation than has ever been accomplished before. These factors will force upon us a much deeper awareness of the sheer givenness of human life and its utter imperviousness to the deep illusions that we are naturally the products of our own making. But these two ontological factors are even more complicated by a third. We now know that knowledge, though distinguishable in the abstract, is in reality inseparable from the techniques and practices that concretely constitute it. The capacity to map the human genome and to locate particular genetically based conditions and features is thus inseparable from everything that enables and follows it, ranging from institutional structures to our own self-understanding. The more genetic knowledge advances, the more it controls what we do and who we are. Taken together, these factors may result in a sense of being fated that is rivaled in theology only by doctrines of predestination.

At the same time, genetic knowledge gives persons, especially those who are carriers of or affected by serious conditions, a sense of hope. Again, and for largely the same reasons, this hope exceeds the theologies of hope among some Protestant thinkers both in its scope and in its potential for at least partial realization. The prospect of overcoming and even eliminating from the germ-line certain types of human suffering is, like all other eschatologies, both appealing and frightening. Aside from this, and from the various possibilities of enhancement of human traits, the offering of a precise explanation for genetic diseases and the possibilities of therapy are a source of hope to many who suffer, even when they do not themselves expect to be the beneficiaries of gene therapy.

These two intertwined affections of fate and hope surfaced repeatedly among the genetic counselees interviewed by the Houston group during the preparation for this conference. They give theologians plenty to reflect upon.

B. How has my religious faith influenced my views about genetics?

When we speak of genetically based conditions, two interesting assumptions are often present. One is that a person's genetic makeup is random. We use terms like genetic lottery. The other is that human intervention can be rational. As a Protestant, I am uncomfortable with both assumptions. As one schooled in the thought of John Calvin, I hold three convictions: that God's purposes are never identifiable with nature but also never fully separable from nature, including our genetic inheritance; that God intends human good, though not only human good; and that there are serious limits — due to both finitude and sin — to the capacities of human beings to cooperate with God by finding the human good and the good of other creatures in nature.

How do these convictions apply to genetics? The first conviction means that I have to find God present in the so-called genetic lottery, even if God is present only in God's absence, as a riddle that I cannot avoid. I cannot exonerate God from genetic tragedies, but this does not mean that I have to identify such tragedies with the will of God. God's grace is present in our grief or anger at God's absence.

The second conviction holds that human beings are allowed and even required by the best means at our disposal to participate in God's accomplishing of the human good in and through nature, and this includes genetic interventions.

The third conviction implies that, despite our pretensions to rationality, our finitude assures us there will be folly as well as wisdom in these endeavors. Overestimations of our ability to know the human good are inevitable, as are underestimations of the costs and dangers involved in achieving it. Some of this will be serious folly indeed. Our sinfulness assures us that there will be not only folly but perversion as we seek to impose our ideas of normality upon nature and use our discoveries and interventions to exercise power over ourselves and others.

We struggle with God as we face the agonies of genetic fate, face our illusions about being self-made, refuse to exonerate God from involvement in nature, and find traces of divine grace in the absence of divine meaning. We participate with God in the transformation of fate into hope. And finally, we face our limits with respect to God in our admissions of failure and in our resistance to power of knowledge to control and define us. If Protestant faith bears witness to these three tasks, it will have made its modest contribution to genetics.

The numerous divisions and subdivisions of the Christian churches made it impossible to present them all by representative individuals at the Houston Conference. Also unspoken were the particular perspectives and commitments of persons of whatever denomination whose understandings and attitudes have been ineradicably influenced by factors of ethnic identity, cultural experience, economic status, or physical disabilities. Religion is never limited to privatized belief and experience. It is socially defined in many ways, and some of the social factors have a definite bearing upon the appreciation of genetic science, technology, and medicine.

The major religions of Islam, Hinduism, and Buddhism are likewise subject to divisions of a philosophical or theological kind, as well as to cultural and national diversities. Largely because genetic science is most advanced in English-speaking nations and Europe, the religious thinkers of Muslim, Hindu, and Buddhist nations have not as yet been obliged to reassess their beliefs in the light of this science. The Japanese have begun to do so.[8] Nevertheless, the Houston Conference heard personal testimonies of two eminent scientists of non-Western religious traditions.

8. Darryl Macer and Norio Fujiki, *Human Genome Research and Society* (Tsukuba: Eubios Ethics Institute, 1992).

ISLAM

Hassan M. Hathout

The Islamic faith was represented at the Houston Conference by Hassan M. Hathout, M.D., Ph.D., of the Islamic Center and The Genetics Institute in Pasadena, California. He is a physician, a scientist, and a Quranic scholar.

As a book is proof of an author, creation is proof of the Creator. This is my reaction to the modern vistas of genetic science, for the more we decipher the creation the more we appreciate the Creator. He himself speaks in the *Quran* — that we Muslims believe is his very word: "We shall show them Our signs in the horizons and in their own-selves until it becomes manifest to them that this is the truth" (*Quran* 41:53). In Islam the pursuit of knowledge is a duty on all men and women, and in juridical terminology scientific research is given the technical name of "Revealing God's tradition in his Creation." Never was there a schism between science and religion in Islam, and it is no wonder therefore that the *Quran* says: "Amongst his subjects, the learned heed Him most" (35:28).

Amongst creation, humanity stands out in distinction, for we are endowed with four characteristics that take us beyond biology and make us human: the mind capable of growing knowledge; the concept of good and evil; the ability to exercise our choices; and accountability for the choices we make. Whether these features represent genetic structure or are like electricity that flows in a wire, but is not of the wire, is so far not possible to tell. In any case, they make us responsible beings, freedom and responsibility being the two faces of one coin. Perhaps at the top rung of the ladder of responsibility stand scientists, for, as the *Quran* says: "Are they equal — those who know and those who don't?" (39:9). For indeed science is two-edged, with the potential of doing good or evil, and genetics is no exception. When the atomic bomb was dropped over Hiroshima, Oppenheimer said: "This day physicists have known sin." And it behooves geneticists to watch their step as they fathom the incredible potentialities of neo-genetics.

Used to stem, cure, or ameliorate disease, or to help feed and clothe a growing global population, genetics is indeed a commendable and rewardable charity. But used for vain or deleterious goals, or to manipulate the human personality or undermine its individuality or eligibility for individual accountability is unlawful. Research is free, but between discovery and application there should be a filter of moral acceptability.

But who is to decide what is morally right and what is wrong? In the Godless society it will be a human decision with its proneness to inconsistency, suggestibility, and an ever-changing yardstick. As Dostoyevski said, "without God, everything is possible." The human mind itself admits its limitation, or else it would have ceased to research and we would have spared the research budgets. It is no wonder, when the human mind is the ultimate moral arbiter, to see the immoralities of yesterday becoming the moralities of today and the moralities of yesterday becoming today's immoralities. Under belief in God, on the other hand, we formulate our decisions against the background of accountability to him, and adjudicate to his moral code, which remains constant and consistent along his messages up to and through Judaism, Christianity, and Islam.

HINDUISM

George E. C. Sudarshan

A general survey of medical practice and bioethics in India, published in 1991 by editors related to The Institute of Religion, made no mention of genetics.[9] Many outstanding genetic researchers have made their reputations in Great Britain and North America; their numbers in India and the limited scope of research there indicate that deliberations on the ethical and religious issues of genetics are yet to begin. Even so, enough is known about the most ancient culture-religion of Hinduism, with its variety of schools, to anticipate what some considerations

9. Prakash N. Desai, "Hinduism and Bioethics in India: A Tradition in Transition," in B. Andrew Lustig, ed., *Theological Developments,* 41-60.

will be. The representative speaker at the Houston Conference was a noted scientist, but a physicist rather than a biologist. Professor George E. C. Sudarshan, Ph.D., teaches at the University of Texas. His recorded remarks may be summarized as follows.

In the Hindu way of looking at life and human nature, the norm is always the highest value, namely, the happiness of living. Happiness and health need no explanation, therefore; it is unhappiness and illness that must be explained. If the body is ill, how is it to be understood? The body is really the expression and artifice of an individual's spirit.

Hinduism, being a nontheistic religion, has no notion of blasphemy. A person can say quite bluntly and yet modestly, "I am God." The best in me is not an image or reflection of the divine. It *is* divine. I am God. Divinity functions through me. At the highest level of experience there is no difference between God and man. This does not mean, he said, that I can raise my hand and part the Red Sea! Neither do I have complete knowledge. But I need not desire to possess all knowledge. Indeed, there are many things we now know which it would be good *not* to know: examples in technology abound.

As a matrix for philosophizing about human nature and genetics, therefore, Hinduism is very different from other religious systems and cultures. The reality of life, the essence, is spiritual. Thus, the key concepts which characterize our lives, all human lives, all living beings and the world are: harmony, devotion, surrender, knowledge, action. In Hinduism there is no basic separation or conflict between religion and science. Their unity is taken for granted. The all is one.

To the popular but uninformed notion that all religions are essentially alike the diverse religious views expressed by individuals in this chapter bear a contrary witness. In spite of much writing and numerous conferences on the subjects germane to genetics, only a small number of Christian denominations and ecumenical clusters have defined their positions for public exposure. These are presented and discussed in the next chapter.

CHAPTER SIX

Official Religious Positions

CHRISTIANITY may seem to many to be "resolutionary" rather than revolutionary. Of the drafting, debating, revising, and recommending of resolutions there is apparently no end. These are not laws so much as official recommendations. Almost none of them is enforceable, as are certain canon laws, the breaking of which may lead to disciplining, punishment, or even expulsion. Even in cases of such resolutions as are believed to be expressions of the will of God there is much reluctance to impose punishments. Resistance and disobedience among Roman Catholics to formal declarations on contraception and abortion are well known. Other communions exhibit differing degrees of rigor and laxity. And in most denominations, we may safely assume, there are official pronouncements on moral, social, and political issues which are wholly unknown to large numbers of laity — and clergy!

Are these pronouncements worthless? Not at all. At the least, they express the sincere concerns and beliefs of the general membership: the *consensus fidelium.* They provide guidance for people's thinking on various main problems of understanding and conscience. However divisive the issue may be — e.g., euthanasia — it is reassuring to know that these moral counsels and policy statements have been drafted by knowledgeable persons who have labored diligently in preparing them; and they have been adopted by synods or assemblies "decently and in order."

The authority of statements made by interreligious, interdenominational, or ecumenical bodies is even more problematical. For many people, these lack cogency because those persons do not have any sense of obligation to such organizations. "What do I care what the council says?" Conversely, others regard ecumenically produced formulations as having highest authority because they are derived from the widest, most representative sources. "What Geneva says" may be less formidable than "what Rome says," but there is an inherent and palpable authority there. It can best be measured by the manner and extent to which the truth of the document comes to be recognized and received.

In respect to genetics, then, we can pay serious attention to a small number of statements which have been ratified and commended by ecclesial bodies. Two are ecumenical; four are denominational.

A. Ecumenical Statements

1. World Council of Churches

All types, traditions, and families of Christian churches are member bodies of the World Council of Churches. The three-hundred twenty-two member churches having voting rights in the assembly are in the general categories of Eastern Orthodox and Protestant. Though not a member, the Roman Catholic Church is well represented in studies and deliberations carried on by the Council. It is literally global in representativeness, which means that delegates from more than one hundred countries and most cultures take part.

The Council's interest in molecular biology, described above in Chapter One, reached its peak in 1989 at its meeting in Moscow. A study group, chaired by Archbishop John Habgood and served by Wesley Granberg-Michaelson, prepared an extensive paper on bio-technology.[1] First drafted by a small working group, the paper was read by one hundred persons, of whom forty wrote substantial criticisms and amendments, before it was ready to go to the Central Committee for action.

No attempt was made to undergird the practical proposals which the document recommended with a theological rationale. This was a

---

1. *Biotechnology: The Challenge to the Churches and to the World* (Geneva: World Council of Churches, August 1989).

deplorable lack and a departure from the Council's studies ten years earlier for the 1979 conference at M.I.T. In an epilogue there are brief suggestions of how the Christian confession of faith might encourage, inform, and validate the draft's resolutions. Even these, however, are cast only in the somewhat sloganish formula of "justice, peace, and the integrity of creation."

Speaking as a worldwide body, the Council shifted attention away from concerns felt mainly, or almost exclusively, in the technologically advanced nations. At present, both the hopes and fears prompted by genetic developments are felt mainly by the richer, technologically equipped countries. However, the Council's inclusion of member churches from virtually all the poorer and so-called developing nations necessitates sensitivity to the aspirations and anxieties of the "two-thirds" world. They, too, want someday to enjoy the medical benefits of genetically engineered drugs and vaccines; but they fear unrestrained exploitation where, e.g., there are no regulations to control experimentation on human subjects; or they resist "dumping" of ineffectual or dangerous pharmaceuticals.

The Council's governing body approved eleven recommendations and proposals of a practical nature. They are to be studied and implemented as each member church might choose. Since the Council has neither the authority nor means to implement them directly, its role in evaluating the probable impact of biotechnology has been fulfilled for the present by this study.

The first group of seven recommendations deals with human genetics; the other four relate to animals, plants, environment, and politics. The member churches in their own ways are asked "to take appropriate action in their own countries to draw these matters to public attention, and to help governments, scientists, universities, hospitals, and corporations to develop suitable safeguards and controls."

(1) The prohibition of sex selection based on prenatal genetic testing, and warning "against testing for other forms of involuntary social engineering."

(2) Resistance against "unfair discrimination . . . in work, health care, insurance, and education" based upon an individual's genome.

(3) Promoting "pastoral counseling for individuals faced with difficult reproductive choices as well as personal and family decisions resulting from genetic information."

(4) Banning "experiments involving genetic engineering of the human germline at the present time" and "developing future guidelines in this area; and urging strict control on experiments involving genetically engineered somatic cells."

(5) Likewise "the banning of commercialized child-bearing (i.e., partial and full surrogacy) as well as the commercial sale of ova, embryos or fetal parts and sperm."

(6) Urging "governments to prohibit embryo research: any experiments, if agreed, only under well defined conditions."

(7) Keeping informed "on how new developments in reproductive technology affect families, and especially women"; and providing pastoral counseling for those experiencing problems in using such methods.

(8) Opposing governmental patenting of genetically altered forms of animal life.

(9) Urging internationally operative controls on how genetically engineered organisms may be tested, lest there be inadvertent environmental damage.

(10) Advocating a worldwide ban on using genetic technology to produce chemical or biological weaponry.

(11) Supporting international consultations by scientists, governing officials, and church representatives on how genetics can be used with maximal justice and benefit.

What do these eleven recommendations say to millions of members of the churches and to the members in particular who are professionally active in biological research, medical practice, biotechnology, and governments? What do they say to people in these fields who constitute an interested public outside the general membership of the churches? Perhaps without really intending to do so, the Council sends a very negative message. In a prologue to the statement it is asserted that "the potential dangers as well as the potential benefits of many forms of biotechnology" are recognized. But where are the benefits actually identified? Only in the last words of (11) is a hope for benefit expressly stated. The Council counsels caution in (2), (3), and (7), where social discrimination, reproductive choices, and protection of families and women are the issues. The seven other recommendations use the language of control, banning, and prohibition.

In terms of theology, the positive possibilities of genetic medicine, both diagnostic and therapeutic, are simply ignored as expressions of human compassion, stewardship, or co-creatorship. The constructive and humane uses of laboratory and clinical research, medicines — to say nothing of food production — are not even mentioned. Now, these developments are not unambiguously good. Neither are they bad. The doctrines of grace and love as well as of sin and evil are inevitably and perplexingly mingled in respect to the doctrines of creation, history, and redemption. One can expound upon one or another with compelling illustrations and strong convictions, but the resulting picture of actual life in the world is then unbalanced and unrealistic. Indeed, the commanding themes of "justice, peace and the integrity of creation" in the Council's agenda require a more synoptic view of genetics than is defined by these recommendations, all eleven of which have their good claims to validity when considered separately.

2. National Council of the Churches of Christ in the U.S.A.

Three years earlier, in 1986, a policy statement was adopted by the Governing Board of the National Council of the Churches of Christ in the U.S.A. It was entitled "Genetic Science for Human Benefit."[2] The title did not convey an uncritical approbation of biotechnology; but in weighing the "promises and perils" of genetic engineering it expressed a preponderance of favorable judgment. Unlike many resolutions passed on contemporary social issues, which are intended to stimulate study and action by the Orthodox and Protestant member churches, the document on genetics was designated a *policy* statement. This gave it a normative standing in effect until the board should decide to amend it in light of rapidly changing states of the art. The statement was built upon the Council's studies during the six previous years.[3]

The theological guidelines are identified in the prefatory section as follows: God's purposeful creation; humankind's special place in creation; the sacred worth of human life attested by both creation in the image of God and the Incarnation; the reality of disease, sin, and

2. *Genetic Science for Human Benefit* (New York: National Council of Churches, 1986).

3. Frank Herron, ed., *Genetic Engineering: Social and Ethical Consequences* (New York: Pilgrim Press, 1984).

mortality; human care of creation as newly involved in evolution; the Church's role in human history and creation as witness of fairness, justice, and love; and (by implication) other theological themes.[4]

How should church groups address the genetic revolution? They "need to be informed and careful when pronouncing judgment on genetic science, especially due to their respect for the many scientists and others engaged in occupations touched by genetics who are deeply committed Christians. Reticence on the subject, however, is no sign of wisdom or virtue on the part of the churches."[5]

The spirit of moderation pervades the presentation of six areas of interest about human genetics and three about agriculture, ecology, and animals (or "other animals" as some prefer). Human gene therapy on somatic cells had not as yet been allowed in 1986, but was expected to be no more problematical than other treatments. Germ-line therapy, then as now because of its irrevocable consequences, was considered dangerous and to be approached with "extreme caution," though there was not total prohibition. Since Christians, like others, have been so divided in belief about abortion, the statement goes about the problem on tiptoe, but urges genetic counseling and pastoral care for those who agonize over decisions.

The always present ideology of eugenics, with its presumption to decide what sorts of humans are normally healthy and socially acceptable, is stoutly rejected as contrary to "Christian concern for personal integrity and value."[6] The cult of physical perfection is here challenged, whether in the neonatal ward or the gym.

Should Christians be concerned about scientific research as such? Yes, says the statement, as an expression of concern for human welfare, which, like human ills, is widely influenced by science. Microbiology has become an especially contentious field of research because of the potential financial rewards for those who make the first discoveries. Far more than in 1986, biotechnology has become big business, and it will continue to grow. The Council is not so naïve as to denounce commercial uses of genetic science; but it shows justifiable concern about

4. Conveying message to National Council of Churches of Christ General board, New Orleans, May, 1986 (unpublished).
5. *Genetic Science for Human Benefit*, 2.
6. *Ibid.*, 5.

secrecy and restrictions on information which ought to be publicly known through publications. And it supports the regulatory agencies of government, which presumably are or ought to be guided by the public interest in health and justice. These are the Food and Drug Administration for medicines, the Environmental Protection Agency, and the Recombinant DNA Advisory Committee of the NIH for human experimentation.

When weighed on "the scales of Christian faith," the Council set forth three standards of evaluation. These are: "(1) The worth of life and living, (2) the values of fairness, justice and love, and (3) responsibility to God through human activity in God's creation."[7]

The worth of life and living may seem self-evident on the plane of nature, but it is distinctly warranted by "the conviction that each and every human being belongs to God as Creator in a special way." For Christians, this is attested not only by the doctrine of *imago Dei* but also by the belief "that God's Eternal Word once became human in Jesus Christ, ministering, dying and rising for the salvation of all."[8] Such faith gives an extra emphasis when with all people of goodwill it is declared that "The worth of human life is not bounded by race, sex, nationality, culture, age or physical handicap. The ability to manipulate genes should not be used to reduce the rich diversity of humanity nor damage the integrity of the individual."[9]

A strong Christian concern is that all uses of genetic knowledge, medicine, and technology should be governed and judged by the ethical canons of fairness, justice, and love. Specifically this can apply powerfully, not sentimentally, to the general problem of accessibility to medical care. More and more, it is apparent that medical methods will involve genetic factors of diagnosis and therapy. They should not be available only to the prosperous, but to all. Therefore "monopolistic ownership of genetically modified organisms or substances which are known to be essential to human life for nourishment and health," which depend upon government patenting, should be stoutly opposed.[10]

Finally, the Council recognized the awesome possibilities opening

7. *Ibid.*, 12.
8. *Ibid.*
9. *Ibid.*, 13.
10. *Ibid.*, 14.

to the human race for joining in the evolutionary process, using still unsuspected ways of modifying physical and psychological properties over coming generations and centuries. These possibilities challenge the imaginations of seers and fiction writers, of course. But they also will keep posing problems about the limits of knowledge and limitations on research and production. Here, the Council's optimism toward genetics is tempered by its misgivings about human wisdom and ethical rectitude. "We cannot agree with those who assert that scientific inquiry and research should acknowledge no limits. All that can be known need not be known if in advance it clearly appears that the process for gaining such knowledge violates the sanctity of human life. Remembering its own history, the church should not oppose scientific advances, but it must speak out in judgment when the quest for new knowledge supersedes all ethical concerns."[11]

Having raised this standard, the Council urges church bodies and their members to become actively engaged in the genetic revolution. In fact, as the next section will show, such activity has been and remains disproportionately slow and inadequate: slow in comparison to the pace set by the scientists, and inadequate when viewed in relation to the need for ethical deliberation, theological reflection, and pastoral education.

B. Four Denominational Statements

Even one who is intimately acquainted with the distinctive teachings and traditions of various Protestant communions cannot predict accurately what an official denominational statement will say about genetics. Of course, the subject is new territory, so there are very few, if any, precedents to follow. Moreover, the contingencies of drafting and adoption are unforeseen, as is the outcome. Who authorized the process? Who are the participants? How rich is their knowledge and deep their experience? Are sufficient time and resources given to the team? How carefully and seriously does the church's governing body study and debate the drafts prior to adoption? And, once adopted, how widely and well is the report appropriated by the members? Furthermore, some

11. *Ibid.,* 15.

of the denominations are not accustomed to pronouncing their considered views on public issues, but leave it to individual leaders. So, sterotypes and generalizations are of limited validity.

Four communions have stamped approval on carefully prepared reports. They are the Church of the Brethren (CB; 1987), the United Church of Christ (UCC; 1989),[12] the United Methodist Church (UMC; 1992),[13] and the Episcopal Church (EC; 1991).[14] Others which have given much attention to genetics without having reached conclusions at this time are the Reformed Church in America, the Presbyterian Church (USA), the Evangelical Lutheran Church in America,[15] and the Lutheran Church–Missouri Synod. If there are others, they have gained little public notice as yet.

1. Church of the Brethren

Retaining their traditional name, but encouraging more prominent leadership of "sisters," the CB adopted a *Statement on Genetic Engineering* in 1987.[16] Although it has much in common with other church declarations of ecumenical and denominational provenance, it possesses a distinctive character as the product of an historic pacifist church. Four headings enclose numerous, short assertions and probing questions: Affirmations, Concerns, Recommendations, and Hopes.

The twelve affirmations constitute a confession of faith in biblical and doctrinal terms, as well as a manifesto of openness to new knowledge and perceived truth, even when it "may conflict with the majority opinion." (Majority of *whom?*) It affirms "its stance against the abuses of

12. *Church and Genetic Engineering,* Minutes of Seventeenth General Synod (New York: United Church of Christ, 1991), 41-45.

13. "New Developments in Genetic Science," *The Book of Resolutions of the United Methodist Church* (Nashville: United Methodist Publishing House, 1992), 325-40.

14. *Resolution on Guidelines in the Area of Genetic Engineering,* Seventieth General Convention of the Episcopal Church (New York, 1991).

15. *Questions about Life and Death,* ed. Edward D. Schneider (Minneapolis: Augsburg Publishing House, 1985), 71-119.

16. "Annual Conference Statement on Genetic Engineering," General Board of the Church of the Brethren (Elgin, Illinois, 1987).

knowledge," while positively restating the basics of a faith in creation, Incarnation, life in community, and the oneness of body, mind, and spirit.

Seven kinds of concerns are articulated in dozens of specific, unanswered questions. Among all these are, first, *theological* fears about "changing the genetic structures of life" and setting "moral limits" to "hazardous or sinful" procedures. The *ethical* concerns include ownership of "patents which come from products which result from government funded research," and misuse of "poor or uneducated" persons as subjects in research. The *social impact* of genetic engineering to enhance human strength and intelligence, whenever feasible, is unsettling. So are possible *long-term effects* on future generations of humans as well as on terrestrial ecology.

There is anxiety about the lack of proper *genetic counseling* and the church's ability to deal with "emotional, economic and moral issues" which are as important as the scientific information given. The unavoidable problem of abortion remains central here. Will *gene therapy* in the future modify only somatic cells, or also sex cells? The CB statement is also concerned about the influence of those who promote "genetic changes in order to produce a 'healthy' or 'perfect' human being." The peril of eugenic ideology is once again emphasized.

The seventh battery of disturbing questions includes concerns about new concepts and techniques in human reproduction. How threatening to accepted Christian standards of sexual and family mores are noncoital procreation, manipulation of gametes, frozen embryos, surrogacy, etc.?

After raising many thorny questions on every aspect of genetic science, the document outlines recommendations that are like an extended hand in a thick glove. There is commendable urging of members to affirm genetic research and become as knowledgeable as possible through education, both informal and academic. The training of genetic counselors and dialogue between nonscientists and scientists are encouraged. Also recommended is cooperation with such government agencies as the Recombinant DNA Advisory Committee. (This is both interesting and unsurprising, since the chairman of that important committee is LeRoy Walters, a prominent member of the Church of the Brethren!) Beyond these worthy but very general and noncritical recommendations, the statement can only express *hope* that genetic guidelines can be formulated which will be consonant with Christian ideas of personal "dignity, freedom, justice, love and respect."

2. *The Episcopal Church*

Episcopalians capped several years of exploring and evaluating the new genetics by passing four resolutions at the General Convention of 1991. The reasons for their positions, whether based on theology or social ethics, were evidently quite minimal. The EC found no cause for concern about genetically engineered medicines or human gene therapy, but drew no distinction between somatic and sex cells. There was general urging of equitable access to genetic medicine and disapproval of using genetic screening to discriminate in employment and insurance.

3. *United Methodist Church and United Church of Christ*

As we are looking to these few denominational documents in hopes of hearing "what the Spirit says to the churches," a comparison of the United Church of Christ statement with that of the United Methodist Church can be illuminating. What both declare in the indicative mood may be subsumed under the two headings of theology and policy. The statements were written independently, without the intention of being in ecumenical agreement. On some points they concur, while they also declare some points separately; but there are no real contradictions. They can thus be considered together.

In brief, there are six common theological affirmations and five given separately.

Statements in Common:

(a) The three Persons of the Triune God.
(b) Divine creation of all things, the creating process being a continuing action of God as Sustainer.
(c) Humanity's responsibility to God for stewardship of the earth, things both inanimate and living.
(d) The intimate relation of humanity to all organisms, sharing most of the genetic code and ecologically interdependent.
(e) Human compassion and service as manifestations of love, derived from God, particularly expressed in pastoral counseling.
(f) Hope for redemption of humankind and cosmos in the ultimate Reign of God.

There are also five separate emphases.

UCC only:

(g) The UCC stresses individual discipleship in terms of following Jesus' own example.

UMC only:

(h) Redemption in the UMC statement is healing, which is effected by the atoning work of Jesus Christ in life, death, and resurrection.
(i) The UMC speaks of the uniqueness of humans in creation as bearers of the image of God.
(j) The UMC also recognizes the limitations on humanity imposed by finitude and sin.
(k) The Church as community, agency, and corporate presence of Christ is important to the UMC.

These eleven theological concepts all have explicable bearing upon the way judgments may be made and attitudes shaped on the complex of questions provoked by new trends in genetic science. Just how they have bearing needs to be demonstrated. Additionally, however, there are ten matters of policy and practical reasoning which the UMC statement addresses. Seven of these are agreed, while three of them are not mentioned by the UCC. They are:

(l) Approval of somatic gene therapy;
(m) Provisional opposition to germ-line therapy;
(n) Approval of screening for disease carriers where discriminatory attitudes towards persons tested positive are unlikely to arise;
(o) Commendation of equitable access to genetic diagnosis, counseling, and clinical service;
(p) Rejection of gametic selection for eugenic reasons and cosmetic enhancement of traits by UMC (unmentioned by UCC);
(q) Approval of the Human Genome Project;
(r) Encouragement of governmental oversight and guidelines of human applications of genetic research;

(s) Opposition by UMC to patenting genes and genetically altered animals;

(t) Opposition by UMC to attempts to alter species of animals or combine humans with other species.

(u) Unanimous rejection of biological weapons.

All these twenty-one theses constitute the menu for a comprehensive elucidation, illustration, and justification in specific terms of theology and genetics (see Chapter Seven).

C. Analysis and Critique of Church Statements

Audrey R. Chapman

As part of the Washington, D.C., study group's preparation for the Houston Conference, a critique of church statements was written by Audrey Chapman, a staff member of the American Association for the Advancement of Science. Holding two degrees in theology in addition to a Ph.D., she is unusually well prepared to deal with religious matters within the scientific milieu.[17] The comments, somewhat abridged, which follow are hers only, and are clearly worthy of serious consideration. Dr. Chapman raises questions about methodology which constantly challenge persons concerned with theology and ethics. How should one arrive at concrete ethical positions or decisions in consonance with, or with the help of, theological formulations?

The documents in question do not engage in systematic and extended theological reflection as a basis for drawing ethical and policy guidelines. The absence of a consistent theological character derives in part from their policy focus and/or pastoral thrust. In developing these statements, the denominations were responding to policy issues raised by their

17. Audrey R. Chapman, "Theology and Public Policy: Closing the Gap," *Theology and Public Policy* 3 (Fall 1991), 39-46.

members, concerns about the potential impact of these new technologies, and requests for guidance in decision making.

These documents also reflect the problems mainline Protestant denominations have in relating theology to public policy.

Resolutions voted by judicatory bodies, like the action of the 1991 Episcopal General Convention, frequently lack any explicit biblical and theological content. Within the UCC polity, for example, pronouncements not only have more weight because they deal with broader issues, but also because they base their position on a more thorough theological grounding, but even so, the theological rationale tends to be relatively superficial. More technical and scientific issues pose even greater dilemmas for applied Christian ethics. While denominational study groups typically include ethicists and theologians, and the UMC is particularly impressive in this regard, theology tends to be compartmentalized in the statements they produce. It often appears in the section appropriately entitled theological rationale or grounding but is noticeably absent from the policy analysis and recommendations. Thus the Methodist section on theological grounding and the UCC articulation of the biblical, theological, and ethical rationale serve more as a statement of Christian conviction than as a systematic basis for drawing ethical and policy guidance.

It is also important to acknowledge that the issues which these documents address are very difficult and complex. As the UMC observes, "genetic science and technology force us to examine, as never before, the meaning of life, our understanding of ourselves as humans, and our proper role in God's creation." The very fact that four denominations have begun to deal with this subject matter is noteworthy. At the present time, however, they have gone much further in identifying issues and concerns than in developing ethical and theological guidelines.

(1) Theological Assumptions in the Documents

The most extended discussion of theological assumptions appears in the UMC report. It identifies five affirmations as providing the theological/doctrinal foundation of their work and recommendations.

  (a) All creation belongs to God the Creator;
  (b) Human beings are stewards of creation;

(c) Technology is to be used in service to humanity and God;
(d) Redemption and salvation become realities by divine grace;
(e) God's reign is for all creation.

In developing these affirmations, it underscores that, like everything in the creation, the goodness of our genetic diversity is grounded in our creation by God. Recognizing that God has given human beings the capacity for research and technological innovation, the Methodists realize that even careful uses of genetic technology for good ends may lead to unintended consequences.

The UCC focuses more on the themes of compassion and the potential of genetic engineering for healing and wholeness. Noting that Jesus fed the hungry and healed the sick, the UCC pronouncement dwells on the potential of genetic engineering to relieve suffering and increase food production. According to the pronouncement, genetic engineering opens new ways for people of compassion to help those in need. It calls on members of the church to follow the example of Jesus and to use our new abilities in genetic engineering to bring healing and sustenance to people everywhere. While the proposal for action accompanying the pronouncement identifies an additional assumption as central to both documents — that there exists an intricate interdependency among human, animal, and plant life as the natural order of God's creation — it does not either develop the theme or relate it to genetic engineering.

In terms of particular themes, the documents tend to acknowledge traditional theological formulations as the foundation for their work without clearly drawing out their implications for evaluating genetic research and application. They affirm God as Creator and sovereign over all of creation, God's creation as good, and redemption and salvation the purpose of the creation. To the limited extent that any of the documents characterize human beings, they describe humans as finite, contingent, interdependent, socially oriented creatures owing their existence to God. Created in the image of God, human beings have both power and responsibility. The pursuit of knowledge is a divine gift to be used in accordance with God's purposes. Although some of the documents refer to the reality of sin, they tend to have a positive view of the potential of using knowledge and technology in service to humanity and God.

Human dignity and equality emerge more as theological than bio-

185

logical constructs. The UMC emphasizes that God has claimed all persons as beloved sons and daughters with inherent worth and dignity irrespective of genetic qualities, personal attributes, or achievements. Its report affirms that all persons have unity by virtue of having been redeemed by Christ, a unity which respects and embraces genetic diversity.

Affirmations of a fundamental equality characterizing human beings with very different genetic endowments appear to be the basis of several policy concerns and recommendations. Several of the documents express apprehension that genetic screening may perpetuate discrimination and result in stigmatization. Others, for example the Episcopal resolution on genetic engineering, assert in very strong language that the use of results of genetic screening of adults, newborns, and the unborn for purposes of discrimination in employment and insurance is unacceptable. Conversely, several of the statements underscore that the benefits of genetic research and technology, like other components of medical care, should be available to all members of society. The UMC also stresses that such equal access includes genetic testing and genetic counseling by appropriately trained health care professionals. Building on these themes, the UMC urges that genes and genetically modified organisms (human, plant, animal) be held as common resources and not be exclusively controlled or patented. It also urges public funding of genetic research to assure greater public accountability and to provide funding for projects not likely to be funded by private grants.

In dealing with divine-human relationships, the documents implicitly or explicitly use a stewardship model. While recognizing the awesome power that genetic engineering confers, they do not link it with the concept of co-creation. UMC, for example, describes human beings as stewards accountable to the Creator. Because human beings are created in the image of God, they have both the power and the responsibility to use power as God does by love. Their discussion of stewardship emphasizes that humans are "to participate in, manage, nurture, justly distribute, employ, develop and enhance creation's resources in accordance with their finite discernment of God's purposes." They also link knowledge of genetics as a resource over which we are to exercise stewardship in accordance with God's purposes. It stresses accountability in the pursuit of knowledge in three directions: to God, the human community, and the sustainability of all creation.

(2) Defining Guidelines, Limits, and Restrictions

In its section on affirmations/recommendations/and conclusions, the UMC provides an admonition which in spirit reflects the views of the other documents as well. "We caution that the prevalent principle in research, that what can be done should be done, is insufficient rationale for genetic science. This principle should be subject to legal and ethical oversight in research design and should not be the prevalent principle guiding the development of new technologies." That said, the dilemma, of course, is defining these legal and ethical guidelines and identifying the appropriate role for the churches in the process.

Several of the documents mention criticisms articulated by others that genetic engineering confers too much power upon human beings and that in using this technology we are "playing God." While acknowledging that to probe the very structure of genetic life and develop means to alter the nature of life represents a new threshold, the statements do not address theologically the appropriate limits of human knowledge and power. Unable to provide answers as to where Christian theology or the church should draw lines, they opt for the need for further study. Some assign society the primary responsibility for decision making in this area, seemingly abdicating any role for the churches in providing society with ethical guidance.

While generally supporting somatic gene therapies, the documents that address the issue oppose germ-line therapy that can be passed on to offspring. According to the Episcopal resolution, for example, "There is no theological or ethical objection against gene therapy, if proved to be effective without undue risk to the patient and if aimed at preventing or alleviating serious suffering." Noting potential abuses, the UMC states its opposition to the use of recombinant DNA for eugenic purposes or genetic enhancements designed for cosmetic purposes or perceived economic, social, or sexual advantage.

The distinction made between the acceptability of somatic and germ-line therapies, however, seems more pragmatic than theological. Other than the UMC's acknowledging that such genetic therapy would have potential long-term effects on the human species, especially loss of genetic diversity, none of the documents specifically addresses the theological issues involved in undertaking germ-line therapies. In the case of the UMC, for instance, it seems more to be motivated by practical concerns with assuring safety, demonstrating the certainty of its effects, and documenting that risks to human life will be minimal. Once these concerns are addressed, they presumably would countenance germ-line therapies. Similarly, UCC cautions regarding germ-line therapy derive from their concerns with unforeseen effects, and the pronouncement acknowledges that future developments may resolve these anxieties. Implicitly accepting that such germ-line therapy will become a reality, the UCC urges extensive public discussion and, as appropriate, the development of federal guidelines.

Both the UMC and the UCC support the Human Genome Project. The UCC states the belief that there is potential benefit in mapping and sequencing the human genetic material but its priority should be evaluated in relation to other scientific and human needs. Of the documents, the UMC report most specifically identifies the ethical concerns that the enormously increased potential for screening and diagnosis raises. Among the issues they identify are the following:

(a) eugenic choices — the genetic treatment or reproductive decisions people might make based on perceived social, physical, sexual, cosmetic, and economic advantage;

(b) the morality of pregnancy termination for gender selection, minor genetic abnormalities, and in situations where there is a dispute about the "quality of life" of a fetus with a genetic disorder;

(c) confidentiality issues deriving from the conflict of interest between the need to protect an individual's privacy and the need to provide other family members with information that could affect their medical treatment and reproductive plans;

(d) the suffering and/or hardship that may result for persons with late-onset diseases or with a genetic predisposition to diseases because of employment or health care insurance discrimination;

(e) resource allocation decisions between the high cost of genetic technologies and other medical needs.

While a helpful starting point, this list parallels concerns articulated in secular resources. Moreover, the report does not offer guidelines to begin to deal with these issues nor suggest that the church has any particular role or competence in this area.

(3) The Role of the Church

In scoping out the potential role of the church, one shared priority is expanding education, resources, and dialogue around ethical issues associated with the development of genetic science and technology both in the church and the society. Another is training clergy in order that they be able to provide pastoral counseling for persons with genetic disorders and their families and those facing difficult choices as a result of genetic testing. A third is supporting persons who, because of the possibilities of severe genetic disorders, have to make difficult decisions regarding reproduction. There is also an expression of the need of the churches to monitor and participate in governmental, legislative, and public policy debates.

Thus ends Chapman's critique of the denominations' efforts to evaluate genetics in the light of Christian theology.

D. Prospects for a New Consensus?

A variety of Protestant churches in America have either promulgated policy statements on genetics or are in process of composing them. It is clearly the intention that these will be educationally useful for their memberships and also provide certain specific bases on which witness can be made to government agencies and the general public. It is intended, also, that professionals engaged in genetic research, clinical practice, counseling, and general medicine will take note. Where the statements have relevance to the biotechnology industry its leaders may also respond to the churches' concerns. This intention by no means implies that church voices can say in every case to all these others, "Thus saith the Lord about DNA." In some few cases, perhaps it can, especially where issues of life and death are at stake.

Can it be hoped, if not expected, that a truly representative voice of Christians can be heard with a high level of near consensus? Probably not. A voice of most Orthodox and Protestant Christians? That is what the NCCC and WCC intended; but those Councils never presume to speak for all, only for their governing bodies. Might there be a consensus expressed by many of the Protestant Churches, or at least of those still optimistically called "mainline?" This might be a realistic hope, and many would welcome such a statement. It would not have to be vulnerable to the charge of ecclesiocratic uniformity. And many in the fields of public policy, journalism, and science would welcome it, because these are the people who often ask, "What is the Christian (or Protestant) position" on certain questions of genetics? It seems, however, that there is little likelihood that a more authentically ecumenical position, formally backed by the denominations, will be forthcoming in the near future.

Dr. Chapman placed her finger on a most perplexing problem in the field of religious ethics: namely, how to derive ethical guidance from religious insights and theologies, and how to correlate these with empirically observed facts of any situation. She is probably correct in discerning no systematic answer in the denominational statements. The ecumenical declarations likewise exhibit no distinctive, systematic methodology. None of these reveals the consistency of Roman Catholic moral theology or the equally scholastic method of biblical literalists. Neither does any of the statements derive from what is known as "situation ethics," where the only standard is the subjective criterion of love without regard to moral law or justice. Another option might be the ethics of a variety of liberation theologies, which give priority to broad social goals such as egalitarianism, emancipation from the cycles of poverty, environmental protection, or justice and well-being for women. Yet the advocates of various types of Christian ethical persuasion are generally dissatisfied with a pragmatic utilitarianism ("the greatest good for the greatest number") or the philosophical triad of autonomy, beneficence, and justice. All cultures and religions have ways of teaching people to do what is right, and there are many similarities among them. Yet Christians are not content to make moral judgments and commitments which are not based upon, or consonant with, perceived directives of the will of God. Therefore, when they address problems, both old and new, which arise in the realm of genetics, they are still struggling to find the most fitting method.

A wise thinker of our century, who was constantly occupied with meaningful relations between religious faith and secular culture, was Paul Tillich. In addition to speaking on secular philosophy, politics, and the arts, he kept studying the practice and science of healing as areas with which personal faith and theology may be correlated. Indeed, "correlation" was for him the name of his method of overcoming the barrier separating the frontiers of modern science from biblical faith and philosophical theology. Whoever uses this method "tries to correlate the questions implied in the situation with the answers implied in the message."[18] The "situation" may mean virtually any event or process in human experience, and the "message" is the given core or marrow of the Christian faith and doctrine. Correlation is not a simple, one-way approach from questioning situation to answering message. Instead, in Tillich's words, there is reciprocity between "human existence and divine manifestations."

In particular, this means that each provides, in its own way, for reflection upon what the other provides. From the side of secular knowledge, scientific data, and reasoned theories, there are significant positions to be considered on many questions. These include data about laws of physics and chemistry; expanding knowledge of DNA, cells, tissues, organs, species; some theories and interpretations of the origins of all things; evolution of the human race; some concepts of the creative power which sustains physical existence; some views about the unique value of human life in both physiological and spiritual terms; some insights about the phenomenon of evil and the mystery of general mortality and personal death; some explanations for the reality of family intimacy, compassion, love, and caring; some understanding of why people show — or fail to show — respect for the created order of nature; why people have strong feeling, cultural habits, and civil laws about personal integrity, privacy, and justice; why people are motivated by prospects of discovery, and compelled by aspirations for a better future; and much more. In addition to secular knowledge, however, there are religious and theological insights, beliefs, and theories which likewise pertain to such issues. Between these bodies of knowledge there is the possibility of discussing at each point their correlation and dialectical interaction.

When the correlation of religious faith and scientific knowledge of genetics is thus itemized by persons who are knowledgeable and open-minded, there is profitable commerce across the frontiers. Specific

18. Paul Tillich, *Systematic Theology,* vol. 1 (Chicago: University of Chicago Press, 1951), 8.

articles of recommendation or disapproval in the statements of the churches are to be judged valid or faulty according to both their consonance with theological criteria and accuracy of scientific understanding. Considered theoretically, the method of correlation seems to be a promising way to understand what can happen along the lines where the frontiers of genetics and religion meet. In specific, practical terms this theory will be tested in the final chapter.

CHAPTER SEVEN

An Exercise in Correlation

THE twenty-one items chosen for emphasis in the UMC and UCC statements (a to u) do not exhaust the number of issues raised when genetics and religion meet (see pp. 179-80 above). They do indicate, however, the matters which the representatives of the two denominations regard as most important in this encounter. Other Christian bodies might not agree precisely on these priorities. And, surely, the professionals of genetic science would not all concur on this whole catalogue of concerns. Those who stand outside what Paul Tillich fittingly called "the circle of faith" would consider some of the doctrinal affirmations as wholly inappropriate to any discussion of genetics. Here the churches are addressing questions of religion and genetics that are important to believers, and thus they introduce the dialogue. It would be of much interest to know how the whole community of genetic scientists would choose to present *their* agenda for dialogue with religious ethicists and theologians. Given the variety of their attitudes toward religion, however, there is no likelihood that the scientists could agree on the questions.

The asymmetrical relation between genetics and religion, noted at the beginning of this book, is now reversed. In the history of genetic research and technology it was the theologians who had little to say, and that quite tardily. Now they have more points to discuss in the dialogue than scientists have. Those who speak for the churches want to say even more than the scientists do.

To speak of the dialogue leading to correlation and interaction between genetics and religion is really meaningless unless we can specify the categories of persons who participate. We can do this in an experimental way that still leaves out some persons who do not quite fit the three categories which are here proposed.

First are persons holding a view that can be variously identified as naturalistic, positivistic, or scientifically materialistic. They will be designated in the following chart as "scientific materialists." They are not all anti- or irreligious, of course, because some define religion in their own terms.

Second are those who regard themselves as enlightened religious believers, including Christians, who are open to any reasonable consideration of correlation, but who are not firmly committed to traditional doctrines of the church. Among these are many scientists as well as professional ministers and religious teachers. On the chart they are called, for lack of an exact term, "questioning believers."

Third are people of all professions and occupations who are convinced by faith of the truth of historic, theological doctrines, while keeping their minds open to scientific knowledge and to new data and theories. Without impugning the sincerity of faith held by those in the "questioning believers" class, we call the third group "confirmed believers."

Our project is intended, first, to show how the twenty-one beliefs, insights, and issues in the left column are variously regarded by persons of these three differing perspectives. The second purpose is to indicate how — or whether — there can be correlation of genetic and theological interests in respect to each item. Then we will discuss briefly the meaning of such interactions.

Note again that the first eleven are statements of faith made by the churches while the latter ten arise from the practice of genetic research, technology, and medicine.

Correlation of Genetic and Theological Knowledge Illustrated by Twenty-one Points of UMC/UCC.

	Scientific Materialist	Questioning Believer	Confirmed Believer
(a) The Triune God.	Doubtful, irrelevant.	Puzzling but symbolically important.	Attests God's transcendence and immanent activity.
(b) Divine Creation.	Doubtful, irrelevant.	Credible idea of the source of material world.	Basis for all thought about the world and existence.
(c) Stewardship.	Equivalent to a sense of responsible morality.	Reasonable expression of what God intends for humans and creation.	God's law to be obeyed because God wills it.
(d) Interrelation of all organisms: DNA.	Scientifically demonstrated.	Scientifically true.	Accepted as fact and understood as evidence of divine source and purpose of life.
(e) Compassion, love.	Recognized as natural phenomenon of altruism.	Appreciated as both natural and spiritual quality of life.	Divine love seen as the controlling principle of human life.
(f) Hope for personal and cosmic fulfillment.	Contingency, chance, and laws of nature prevail.	Religious faith supports idealism and hopefulness.	Hope is warranted according to God's covenant with humanity and God's faithfulness.

(g) Jesus' actual life and call to discipleship are our models.	Some admirable qualities of Jesus' life are recognized by some.	Jesus' example is compelling for moral and spiritual living in certain dimensions.	Jesus' life reveals God's purposes for humans, especially for mercy, healing, righteousness, and justice.
(h) Healing through atoning work of Jesus Christ.	Outside of scientific purview.	Exemplary commitment to healing, drawing on spiritual resources, is relevant to medical and genetic practice.	Faith in Jesus Christ's divine healing power and in reconciliation through suffering and death (the Cross) assists us in genetic medicine.
(i) Human uniqueness, "image of God" in human life.	*Homo sapiens sapiens* is unique as species but close to primates in sharing all DNA.	A unique human relation to God allows symbolic use of *imago Dei* as rationality and self-consciousness.	As body and soul are united in a human, it is believed that humanness bears the unique stamp of God's image, which determines the nature, value, and meaning of life.
(j) Human finitude and sin.	Human finitude is obvious, but scientific knowledge gives great power over nature. Excessive power can corrupt, but sin is literally and strictly a religious notion.	Finite and often evil? Yes. But humans are essentially well-meaning. Breaking biblical rules of morality is serious, especially when life and death are at stake.	Finitude, sin, and death are interrelated realities. Pride or miscalculation in biological manipulation is deceptively dangerous.

(k) The Church as community is essential and relevant to genetic concerns.	Religious societies such as churches can serve a nation's morality, and their input in public discussions of ELSI can be of value so long as it is in accord with science.	Religiously derived insights need to be heard in secular spheres on moral issues raised by science.	While acknowledging scientific disciplines and findings, Christian churches offer their meta-scientific insights about creation, human nature, ethics, and life's purpose.
(l) Somatic gene therapy.	Approved as are other therapies.	Likewise approved.	Approved by most churches.
(m) Germ-line modification.	Mainly a question of technical feasibility but debatable because of unknown risks and irreversibility of effects.	The same, but open to persuasion if the risk concern can be satisfied.	Cautious to negative position fortified by strong resistance to genetic manipulation for physical enhancement or eugenics.
(n) Genetic testing and public screening.	Acceptable so long as social discrimination avoided.	The same.	Generally approved as preventive health measure with strong objection to discrimination.
(o) Equitable access to services.	Approved.	Approved.	Approved.
(p) Eugenics and enhancement of traits.	Generally disapproved but subject to pragmatic judgment.	Generally disapproved, but open to marginal cases such as dwarfism.	Strong disapproval on grounds of a divinely conferred human dignity.
(q) Human Genome Project.	Approved by majority, challenged by minority.	Approved for anticipated benefits to humanity's health.	Approved for same reasons but also as indicator of stewardship and creativity.

(r) Governmental oversight.	Approved to greater or lesser degree according to political and economic factors.	The same.	Approved as just and equitable protection of public order but conditioned by concern for bureaucratic misuse.
(s) Patenting genes and transgenic animals.	Justified for commercial reasons by some but opposed by others on grounds of "human patrimony" and "species integrity."	The same, but probably greater opposition in line with churches' pronouncements.	Strong opposition on grounds of divine creation, justice, and human life's sanctity.
(t) Altering species, manipulation of human DNA.	Answers to questions depend upon freedom of research, economics, and public opinion.	Intuitive resistance in defense of human good as well as suspicion of abuses.	Strong opposition based upon doctrine of creation, protecting human dignity, and diversity of species.
(u) Biological weaponry.	Strongly rejected.	The same.	The same.

Correlation is realized only when the participants in dialogue can understand one another, communicate their own particular knowledge and interpretation, and show willingness to learn from one another. The chart indicates various matters on which correlation is either unlikely, possible, or very likely to be achieved.

Dialogue involves a witness, but it is not an evangelistic effort intended to convert the persons of opposing views and beliefs. With regard to the eleven Christian doctrinal affirmations (a-k) it is very unlikely that scientific materialists will be expected to accept and confess the same faith (at least, not in this context or in large numbers.) They may find themselves responding sympathetically, however, to the practical implications of certain theistic affirmations. For example, they might concur with the United Methodists' definition of stewardship (c), cited earlier — "Humans are to participate in, manage, nurture,

justly distribute, employ, develop and enhance creation's resources . . ."
— even though they may not share the Christians' belief that such
stewardship is "in accordance with their finite discernment of God's
purpose." The scientific materialists can share the ecological concern
about the use of human creativity and power in relation to nature. They
can also, as genetic scientists, help Christian theologians to understand
how the given environment is now seen to include our DNA, our genes,
which are rapidly coming under human control.

Christians and scientific materialists can usually agree that compassion and love (e) are important and indispensable qualities, even
though they have different explanations for them. Are these dispositions
derived from God, who *is* love (1 John 4:8), or from genetic compulsions of altruism to perpetuate the species? Here is strong disagreement.
And yet, in respect to persons needing access to genetic medical services
(o) the practical expressions of love, compassion, and altruism may be
indistinguishable.

Some scientists make seemingly exaggerated claims and predictions about human capacities for knowledge and power. Many others
concur with Christians who emphasize human finitude and warn
against any Promethean *hubris* or arrogance, whether or not this warning is engendered by a consciousness of sin (j). From the same consideration, both theological and secular, arise suspicions about errors
and abuses of genetic information which call for professional and
governmental guidelines and oversight (r).

The likelihood of positive and mutually supportive correlation
between the spheres of genetics and religion is also evident in respect
to eight of the items on the chart. These are: the recognition of a basic
homology of DNA in all organic life (d); rejection of genetically engineered biological weaponry (u); somatic and germ-line gene therapy
(l, m); approval of genetic testing of individuals and populations on
condition of assuring nondiscriminatory consequences (n); rejection of
deliberate eugenic programs (p); and endorsement of the HGP (q).
Useful interaction is also taking place concerning the patenting of genes
(s) and the limits to legitimate combining of human and nonhuman
genetic material (t).

The questioning believers in this exercise play a mediating role.
They may feel less compulsion than the confirmed believers in asserting
the relevance to genetics of such doctrines as those of the Triune God,

sin, and the healing atonement wrought by Jesus Christ. This is not a concession to disbelief or skepticism so much as a difference of theological interpretation and emphasis. Their very leniency, however, may facilitate the dialogue with scientific materialists. In fact, this has been demonstrated in recent years by their significant participation in conferences and studies.

There still remain formidable barriers to the interaction and correlation of genetics and religion. These are partly the blockages constituted of ignorance and dogmatism on both sides, partly the timidity and reluctance of people to engage in dialogue at a level of adequate information and seriousness, and partly the intractable nature of the substantive matters themselves. Easy harmonizations or agreements sought through intellectual struggle cannot be guaranteed by dialogue. Even so, the effort must be continued, for it is a quest of high and urgent importance for humanity itself. To refer once more to the popular idiom of Tillich, we are driven in our existence by questions of "ultimate concern." Genetic science and the basic beliefs of religion are differing ways of exploring the nature and meaning of the concern which all cherish as ultimate: human life in all its dimensions.

Recommended Reading

THE IMMENSE numbers of journal articles on genetics, religion, and ethics are not easily accessible to the general reader. Only book titles are included, therefore, in the following bibliography.

Abrecht, Paul, ed. *Faith and Science in an Unjust World.* Vol. 2. Philadelphia: Fortress Press.

Alliance of Genetic Support Groups. *Directory of National Genetic Voluntary Organizations.* Chevy Chase, 1992.

Annas, George, and Sherman Elias. *Gene Mapping: Using Law and Ethics as Guides.* New York: Oxford University Press, 1992.

Andrews, Lori. *Medical Genetics: A Legal Frontier.* Chicago: American Bar Association, 1987.

Atkinson, Gary M., and Albert S. Moraczewski. *Genetic Counseling, the Church and the Law.* St. Louis: Pope John XXIII Medical Center, 1980.

Barbour, Ian. *Religion in an Age of Science.* Vol. 1. San Francisco: Harper & Row, 1990.

Bartels, Dianne, et al., eds. *Prescribing Our Future Ethical Challenges in Genetic Counseling.* Hawthorne, N.Y.: Aldine de Gruyter, 1993.

Birch, Charles, and Paul Abrecht. *Genetics and the Quality of Life.* New York: Pergamon Press, 1975.

Bishop, Jerry, and Michael Waldholz. *Genome.* New York: Simon & Schuster, 1990.

Bouma, Hessel, et al. *Christian Faith, Health and Medical Practice.* Grand Rapids: William B. Eerdmans, 1989.

Cavalieri, Liebe F. *The Double-Edged Helix.* New York: Columbia University Press, 1981.

Cole-Turner, Ronald. *The New Genesis.* Louisville: Westminster/John Knox Press, 1993.

Cook-Deegan, Robert. *Gene-Quest: Science, Politics and the Human Genome Project.* New York: Norton, 1993.

Davis, Bernard, ed. *The Genetic Revolution.* Baltimore: The Johns Hopkins University Press, 1991.

Dobzhansky, Theodosius. *The Biology of Ultimate Concern.* New York: New American Library, 1967.

Duster, Troy. *Backdoor to Eugenics.* New York: Routledge, 1990.

Etzioni, Amitai. *Genetic Fix.* New York: Macmillan, 1973.

Fletcher, John C. *Coping with Genetic Diseases.* San Francisco: Harper & Row, 1982.

Fletcher, Joseph. *The Ethics of Genetic Control: Ending Genetic Roulette.* Buffalo: Prometheus Books, 1988.

Glover, Jonathan. *What Sort of People Should there Be?* Middlesex: Penguin Books, 1984.

Grisolia, Santiago, ed. *Human Genome Project: Ethics.* Bilbao, Spain: Fondacion BBV, 1993.

Haering, Bernard. *Ethics of Manipulation.* New York: Seabury Press, 1975.

Hamilton, Michael. *The New Genetics and the Future of Man.* Grand Rapids: William B. Eerdmans, 1972.

Hauerwas, Stanley. *Suffering Presence: Theological Reflections on Medicine, the Mentally Handicapped and the Church.* Notre Dame, Ind.: University of Notre Dame Press, 1986.

Herron, Frank, ed. *Genetic Engineering.* New York: Pilgrim Press, 1984.

Hilton, Bruce, and Daniel Callahan, eds. *Ethical Issues in Human Genetics: Genetic Counseling and the Uses of Genetic Knowledge.* New York: Plenum Press, 1973.

Holtzman, Neil A. *Proceed with Caution: Predicting Genetic Risks in the Recombinant DNA Era.* Baltimore: The Johns Hopkins University Press, 1989.

Jonsen, Albert. *The New Medicine and the Old Ethics.* Cambridge: Harvard University Press, 1990.

Judson, Horace Freeland. *The Eighth Day of Creation.* New York: Simon & Schuster, 1979.

Kass, Leon. *Toward a More Natural Science: Biology and Human Affairs.* New York: Free Press, 1985.

Kevles, Daniel J. *In the Name of Eugenics.* Berkeley and Los Angeles: University of California Press, 1985.

Kevles, Daniel J., and Leroy Hood. *The Code of Codes.* Cambridge: Harvard University Press, 1992.

Kogan, Barry, ed. *A Time to Be Born and a Time to Die: The Ethics of Choice.* Hawthorne: Aldine de Gruyter, 1991.

Krimsky, Sheldon. *Genetic Alchemy.* Cambridge: MIT Press, 1983.

Lammers, Stephen E., and Allen D. Verhey, eds. *On Moral Medicine: Theological Perspectives in Medical Ethics.* Grand Rapids: William B. Eerdmans, 1987.

Lappé, Marc. *Genetic Politics: The Limits of Biological Control.* New York: Simon & Schuster, 1979.

Lebacqz, Karen, ed. *Genetics, Ethics and Parenthood.* New York: Pilgrim Press, 1983.

Lee, Thomas F. *The Human Genome Project.* New York: Plenum Press, 1990.

———. *Gene Future.* New York: Plenum Press, 1994.

Levine, Joseph, and David Susuki. *The Secret of Life.* Boston: WGBH Educational Foundation, 1993.

Lewis, C. S. *The Abolition of Man.* New York: Macmillan, 1947.

Lewontin, Richard. *Biology as Ideology: The Doctrine of DNA.* New York: Harper/Perennial, 1991.

Macer, Darryl, and Norio Fujiki. *Human Genome Research and Society.* Tsukuba: Eubios Ethics Institute, 1992.

Milunsky, Aubrey, and George J. Annas. *Genetics and the Law, III.* New York: Plenum Press, 1985.

Milunsky, Aubrey. *Genetic Disorders and the Fetus: Diagnosis, Prevention and Treatment.* Baltimore: The Johns Hopkins University Press, 1992.

———. *Heredity and Your Family's Health.* Baltimore: The Johns Hopkins University Press, 1992.

Moraczewski, Albert S. *Genetic Medicine and Engineering: Ethical and Social Dimensions.* St. Louis: Catholic Health Association, 1983.

Murphy, Timothy, and Marc Lappé. *Justice and the Human Genome*

Project. Berkeley and Los Angeles: University of California Press, 1994.

Nelkin, Dorothy, and Laurence Tancredi. *Dangerous Diagnostics: The Social Power of Biological Information.* New York: Basic Books, 1989.

Nelson, J. Robert. *Human Life: A Biblical Basis for Bioethics.* Philadelphia: Fortress Press, 1984.

Nichols, Eva K. *Human Gene Therapy.* Cambridge: Harvard University Press, 1988.

O'Donovan, Oliver. *Begotten or Made?* Oxford: Clarendon Press, 1983.

O'Rourke, Kevin, and Benedict Ashley. *Health Care Ethics: A Theological Analysis.* 2d ed. St. Louis: Catholic Health Association, 1982.

Peacocke, Arthur R. *Creation and the World of Science.* Oxford: Clarendon Press, 1979.

————. *God and the New Biology.* San Francisco: Harper & Row, 1986.

Peters, Ted, ed. *Cosmos and Creation.* Nashville: Abingdon Press, 1989.

Pollack, Robert. *Signs of Life: The Language and Meaning of DNA.* Boston: Houghton Mifflin, 1994.

President's Commission for the Study of Ethical Problems in Medical and Biomedical and Behavioral Research. *Splicing Life.* Washington, D.C.: U.S. Government Printing Office, 1983.

————. *Screening and Counseling for Genetic Conditions.* Washington, D.C.: U.S. Government Printing Office, 1983.

Rahner, Karl. *Theological Investigations, IX.* New York: Herder & Herder, 1972.

Ramsey, Paul. *Fabricated Man: The Ethics of Genetic Control.* New Haven: Yale University Press, 1970.

Rosner, Fred, and David Bleich, eds. *Jewish Bioethics.* New York: Hebrew Publishing, 1979.

Rothstein, Mark A., ed. *Legal and Ethical Issues Raised by the Human Genome Project.* Houston: University of Houston Press, 1991.

Schneider, Edward D., ed. *Questions about Life and Death.* Minneapolis: Augsburg, 1985.

Schubert, Hartwig von. *Biotechnologie und evangelische Ethik.* Frankfurt/New York: Campus Verlag, 1992.

Shapiro, Larry J. *The Human Blueprint: The Race to Unlock the Secrets of Our Genetic Script.* New York: St. Martin's Press, 1991.

Shinn, Roger L. *Forced Options.* San Francisco: Harper & Row, 1982.

Simmons, Paul D. *Birth and Death: Bioethical Decision Making.* Philadelphia: Westminster Press, 1983.

Suzuki, David, and Peter Knudtson. *Genethics: The Clash between the New Genetics and Human Values.* Cambridge: Harvard University Press, 1989.

Watson, James D. *The Double Helix.* New York: Athenaeum Press, 1968.

Wertz, Dorothy, and John C. Fletcher. *Ethics and Human Genetics: A Cross-Cultural Perspective.* Heidelberg: Springer Verlag, 1989.

Index of Names

Index of Names

Servetus, Michael, 96
Seydel, Frank D., 54n.17
Shelley, Mary, 121
Shinn, Roger L., 21, 23
Siegel, Seymour, 23
Simmons, Paul D., 28, 58-59
Sudarshan, George E. C., 168-69

Teilhard de Chardin, Pierre, 17
Thomas Aquinas, 108
Thompson, Margaret W., 38n.1
Tillich, Paul, 190-91, 200

Vesalius, 99

Wallace, A. R., 98
Walters, LeRoy, 60
Watson, James D., 5, 11, 66, 68, 75, 104
Weismann, August, 3
Wertz, Dorothy C., 27, 86
Whitehead, Alfred North, 18
Wilkins, Maurice, 5
Wilson, Edward O., 105
Wright, Sewell, 3

Index of Subjects

Abortion (pregnancy termination), 32-33, 50, 84, 124, 149, 188
Adenosine deaminase (ADA) deficiency, 60, 61, 70
Adult polycystic kidney disease, 42, 78
Alcoholism, 104
American Association for the Advancement of Science, 39, 183
American Medical Association, 26
American Scientific Affiliation, 26
American Society of Human Genetics, 40
Americans with Disabilities Act (ADA), 82
Amniocentesis, 37, 85
Anderson, M. D., Cancer Center, 61
Anencephaly, 39
Artificial insemination, 85, 126, 134
Asilomar conference, 12

Baylor College of Medicine, 25
Behavior, 103-6
Bible, 13, 96-97, 152-54, 156

Cancer, 61-62, 75
Center for Ethics, Medicine and Public Issues, 26
Center for Theology and the Natural Sciences, 25

Chorionic villus sampling (CVS), 38, 85
Church of the Brethren, 179-80
Co-creator, humankind as, 30, 58, 110-14, 121
Correlation, 190-92, 193-200
Creator God, 97, 111-13, 120, 138, 181
Cyprus, 55
Cystic fibrosis (CF), 40, 56, 60, 62, 103

Department of Energy (DOE), 11, 25
Department of Health and Human Services (DHHS), 11
Determinism, genetic, 89, 104, 146-47, 159
Diagnosis, prenatal, 36-41, 89
Diamond v. *Chakravarty,* 8, 68
Discrimination, 69, 173
DNA, 5-10, 22, 43, 67, 90, 92-94, 98-100, 130-31
DNA "fingerprinting," 78-79
Down syndrome (trisomy 21), 39, 50
Duchenne muscular dystrophy (DMD), 42-43, 103

ELSI (Ethical, Legal, Social Implications), 12, 25

210